D1546427

UNCOVERING HISTORY

UNCOVERING HISTORY
Archaeological Investigations
at the Little Bighorn

DOUGLAS D. SCOTT

Foreword by Bob Reece

UNIVERSITY OF OKLAHOMA PRESS : NORMAN

This book is published with the generous assistance of the
Friends of the Little Bighorn Battlefield.

Library of Congress Cataloging-in-Publication Data

Scott, Douglas D.
  Uncovering history : archaeological investigations at the Little Bighorn /
Douglas D. Scott. — 1st ed.
    p. cm.
  Includes bibliographical references and index.
  ISBN 978-0-8061-4350-7 (hardcover : alk. paper)   1. Little Bighorn,
Battle of the, Mont., 1876.   2. Indians of North America—Montana—Little
Bighorn Battlefield National Monument—Antiquities.   3. Excavations
(Archaeology)—Montana—Little Bighorn Battlefield National Monument.
4. Little Bighorn Battlefield National Monument (Mont.)—Antiquities.
I. Title.
  E83.876.S29 2013
  973.8′2—dc23

                                                        2012028598

The paper in this book meets the guidelines for permanence and durability of
the Committee on Production Guidelines for Book Longevity of the Council
on Library Resources, Inc. ∞

    2   3   4   5   6   7   8   9   10

Contents

Figures

Foreword

Douglas Scott's *Uncovering History: Archaeological Investigations at the Little Bighorn* provides for the first time in one volume a complete history of all archaeological surveys—both professional and amateur—conducted on and off the Little Bighorn Battlefield National Monument.

Uncovering History began as an unpublished archaeological assessment report for the National Park Service; it was a top priority as part of the Monument's cultural resources program, which encompasses everything from history to cultural landscapes to archaeology. The assessment will be beneficial to all future administrations at the park when used to make sound decisions regarding any future archaeological surveys.

In August 2009, park superintendent Kate Hammond contacted me regarding a project idea for Friends of the Little Bighorn Battlefield, which is an official partner with the park. The Friends' purpose is to raise funds for projects that lack federal funding. Friends has successfully supported all project goals since the group's inception in 1998. Hammond explained that she had budgeted $10,000 for completion of the assessment but lacked the funding. She asked if perhaps the Friends could contribute a portion of the funds, with the remainder to come from grants.

I immediately understood the importance of this project. Besides the implications of a cultural resources program, the assessment would contribute to the interpretive activities at the Monument and ultimately provide one single volume that any visitor could take home in order to investigate the fabulous science of battlefield archaeology further. Knowing the value this volume could present, I suggested that the Friends support the project in full.

The Friends board unanimously approved the project and was able to promise a check within one week of Hammond's request. This enabled Scott to immediately begin his work on the assessment. In a statement to the Friends membership, Hammond said, "I wanted to pass on my sincere thanks to all Friends members for your support of this important project, which will give us tools that we need to more effectively and proactively manage archaeological research and archaeological resources at Little Bighorn Battlefield."

Within six months, Scott delivered his draft of the archaeological assessment to Superintendent Hammond and her staff for their comments. In turn, he incorporated those comments into the final draft, which he finished by the summer of 2010. So began the Friends' search for a prospective publisher of a re-edited version of the final archaeological assessment report.

While in the middle of reviewing bids for the publication of this volume, I attended the Fort Robinson History Conference at Fort Robinson, Nebraska, in April 2011. There, Scott suggested I speak with Bob Clark of the University of Oklahoma Press, who had showed interest in the project. While enjoying breakfast in the Fort Robinson Restaurant, Clark and I discussed the likelihood of the Press and Friends working together to publish Scott's work. We followed up this first meeting with a few phone calls, resulting in another Friends board vote that allowed Scott, the Press, and the Friends to sign a contract to publish this book. It is with great pleasure that Friends of the Little Bighorn Battlefield is able to partner with the University of Oklahoma Press to make *Uncovering History* available to the public. Thanks to Bob for his continual optimistic attitude in making all of this work.

Chief park historian John Doerner ensured that the original archaeological assessment project moved forward without interruption. He was the key to keeping me informed of the progress of the assessment all the way to completion. John has since retired from the Park Service and is now enjoying civilian life; he will certainly be missed at the battlefield.

I very much appreciate Superintendent Hammond asking the Friends to assist with this project and trusting us to make it properly available to the public. Since 1981, I have had the honor of working with—and getting to know—six superintendents at the Monument and two acting superintendents. Hammond empowers the Friends to take risks, knowing that great benefits for the organization, and therefore the park, will follow. Thank you, Kate.

On behalf of the Friends board and its members, I cannot thank Doug Scott enough for his unselfish years dedicated to leading many archaeological surveys at and around the Monument. His untiring work ethic for completing the original archaeological assessment, its re-edit into this book, along with building its index, are most appreciated. He will receive no royalties from this publication, but he worked quickly to completion and with seemingly effortless skill. It is good to know that even though he has retired from the Park Service, he is still very much involved with battlefield archaeology. Doug, I hope to see you leading more archaeological surveys at the Monument in the future.

Finally, to you the visitor at Little Bighorn Battlefield National Monument, and to the reader at home, your enthusiasm for battlefield archaeology, U.S. history, and our National Parks is very much appreciated. I invite you to learn more about how Friends of the Little Bighorn Battlefield helps the park protect its natural and cultural resources, as well as how to become a member, by visiting our website at www.FriendsLittleBighorn.com.

I'll see you on Last Stand Hill.

Bob Reece
President, Friends of the Little Bighorn Battlefield

Preface

Nothing as dynamic as the Little Bighorn story is ever static to the point that an overview is ever complete, but this work summarizes the archaeological investigations related to the Little Bighorn story through 2011. This work was originally produced for Little Bighorn Battlefield National Monument as a management tool—an archaeological overview and assessment. As such the product was published in a small print run as Technical Report 124 in 2010 by the National Park Service's Midwest Archeological Center in Lincoln, Nebraska. The report was distributed to the park, specific government repositories, and others as part of an effort to document the history of the archaeological investigations of the Little Bighorn Battlefield National Monument.

National Park Service guidelines define an archaeological overview and assessment as the fundamental component of a park's archaeological resources management program. It is intended to "describe and assess the known and potential archaeological resources in a park area" (National Park Service 1997:25). Therefore, the original document was an assessment of past archaeological excavations and investigations and was intended to be used to determine the needs and designs of future archaeological studies for research, interpretation, or park management purposes. The document serves as a source of information for General Management Plans, other related management documents such as the Cultural

Landscape Report and the Park Fire Management Plan, and as baseline data for an Archaeological Base Map of known resources, and it is intended as baseline data on park archaeological resources for use in creating or updating the Comprehensive Interpretive Plan as well as defining potential research needs relevant to the park's mission. Recommendations were made in Technical Report 124 for future archaeological studies that may aid the management and interpretation at Little Bighorn.

Widespread public interest in the archaeology of the Little Bighorn prompted revisions in Technical Report 124 so that it could be made available to the public. The changes between Technical Report 124 and this work are minimal but important. Some sections and information specific to management of the park and the archaeological resources have been eliminated or summarized, for they have limited appeal to the public at large. A description of one additional project conducted in July 2010 and two related projects in 2011 have been added to bring the project database up to date as of December 2011.

Acknowledgments

The development of this archaeological overview was made possible by a number of people. I thank the entire staff at Little Bighorn Battlefield National Monument for their assistance and patience through the years of our work at the site. I am particularly indebted to former chief park historians and superintendents Douglas McChristian and Neil Mangum and to retired chief park historian John Doerner for their aid and insight into the various projects. Each worked tirelessly to make sure the projects got off the ground, and each spent their time on the ground with the archaeological teams. I also thank curator Sharon Small and GIS specialist Melana Stichman for their assistance and comments. Without them and the work of former superintendents James Court, Dennis Ditmanson, Barbara Souteer, Gerard Baker, Darrell Cook, and Kate Hammond, none of these projects would have come to fruition.

Thomas Thiessen, formerly of the Midwest Archeological Center, Peter Bleed of the University of Nebraska, and historians Paul Hedren, Douglas McChristian, and Jerome Greene not only reviewed earlier drafts but provided advice and acted as sounding boards on many occasions, for which I express my deepest gratitude. Jim Bradford, archaeologist for the National Park Service Intermountain Region, was instrumental in seeing that the original overview and assessment effort for the park was funded, and his help is more than appreciated. Charles Haecker, of the Intermountain

Regional Office, Santa Fe, provided many useful comments on earlier drafts of the work. As always, his comments and observations are very much appreciated.

Bob Reece and the Friends of Little Bighorn provided a generous donation to the park to fund the completion of the overview begun in 2006, for which I am extremely grateful. Mark Lynott, manager, Midwest Archeological Center, National Park Service, Jill Lewis, and Alan Weber facilitated the completion of the original overview at the Center as Technical Report 124, and it could not have been done without their assistance. I especially thank Richard Fox, Jr., friend and colleague, for his review of the earlier draft of the original overview and assessment. Without his initial assessment of the battlefield after the 1983 fire, his constructive approach, and our work together during the mid-1980s fieldwork, the projects would not have had the detail or depth of interpretation that made the work so valuable for over twenty-five years. Melissa Connor, as always, provided a variety of support and encouragement during the work on this effort.

This overview draws heavily on previously published works and unpublished reports related to the archaeological investigations of the Little Bighorn Battlefield National Monument. Several of the previously published works summarized and interpreted specific elements of the story, but none have pulled together the full array of the archaeological investigations of the battlefield. This archaeological overview and assessment assembles the complete story as of December 2011. I thank the authors and coauthors of the earlier reports and publications who have contributed to the Little Bighorn archaeological story over the years and have allowed me to draw upon their combined work and knowledge to produce this comprehensive review.

UNCOVERING HISTORY

| # Little Bighorn Battlefield

Archaeological Beginnings

It might be argued that the Little Bighorn battlefield became an archaeological site the moment the battle ended, or perhaps when the burial parties left the field, leaving nature to take its course on the debris of war left behind from the fight. However, it seems unlikely that anyone in June 1876 or the remainder of the nineteenth century even remotely considered that possibility. That they were part of an event that had historical import was not lost on the participants, and some even used the distribution of the dead and clusters of fired cartridge cases to make deductions about what may have happened. Though the importance of physical evidence was not lost on these individuals, preservation of the debris of war and the context in which those artifacts were associated likely never entered their minds. It would take time and the evolution of the field of anthropological archaeology over the next hundred years before the necessary theoretical and methodological means were at hand to tease information from the context of the fight's debris to build an increased understanding of the multitude of individual actions that is the Battle of the Little Bighorn.

Interest in the physical evidence of the battle is not new. It began with the victorious warriors who took war trophies, with the soldiers who buried the dead and commandeered souvenirs, and with later visitors to the site who wished to have a tangible reminder of their sojourn on the hallowed ground. Souvenir collecting on battlefields has a long history, and the Little Bighorn battlefield is no exception to that story. Most early collection efforts are undocumented, and if an item surfaces today in private hands or at a public institution its association with the battle is often little better than hearsay. Those relics are of interest, but they are not the main concern of this archaeological overview. This work is intended to pull together the story of how the battle's physical evidence came to be regarded not as mere relics or souvenirs but as artifacts and data that can aid our understanding of the events of the past in greater and more precise detail.

That insight did not begin with the first professional archaeological studies in the late 1950s conducted by Robert Bray, or with the opportunity presented by the range fire in August 1983; it began with researchers of the 1930s, like Lt. Col. Elwood Nye, Joseph Blummer, R. G. Cartwright, and Edward S. Luce. Their efforts to find, document, and interpret relics of the fight were incipient archaeological investigations, although not performed by trained archaeologists. At the time, Monument superintendent Edward Luce was well aware he needed professional archaeological assistance to aid his endeavors. He requested it as early as 1943, but it was not forthcoming until 1958. Even then the work of Don Rickey and archaeologist Robert Bray did not engender a wellspring of interest beyond Little Bighorn enthusiasts. It took the range fire of 1983 and project funding by private donations to conduct the first comprehensive professional archaeological investigation of the Little Bighorn Battlefield National Monument (then Custer Battlefield National Monument). The professional archaeological work that began with Richard Fox in August 1983 continued on a sporadic but annual basis until 2005. Additional projects continue to be undertaken, with the latest in 2011.

The number of words and reams of paper resulting from these investigations is impressive, but they do not begin to convey the whole story of what was found or how profoundly traditional interpretations of the battle were affected and revised as a result of the discovery and careful recordation of thousands of pieces of physical evidence of the fight between Lakotas, Cheyennes, Arapahos, and the Seventh U.S. Cavalry on June 25 and 26, 1876. The archaeological projects have varied from broad-level inventory to some that have focused on specific questions. In terms of the battle sequence, the projects were not undertaken in any particular sequence. Rather, each was done as park needs or funding permitted. This has resulted in a large number of reports and documents, some published and others with only limited distribution. Putting it all together, however, yields a substantial body of new information about the battle and its aftermath. In the course of the archaeological projects there has been the opportunity to study the Custer fight, the Reno-Benteen defense, movements to and from Weir Point, the fight in Medicine Tail Coulee, the actual remains of some of the soldiers who fought the battle, and one of the Seventh's pre-battle camps.

On another level, the archaeological investigations and broad public interest in the work became a signal event in the history of American archaeology. The project results were quickly published and widely disseminated, and in a short time they had worldwide influence. The Little Bighorn archaeological work became the focal point of the rise of a new field of archaeological investigation—battlefield archaeology—now more appropriately referred to as conflict archaeology. In what is now a well-established discipline, battlefields around the world are being archaeologically investigated, with new insights to the past being revealed almost daily. The field and analytical methods, as well as the theoretical underpinnings of battlefield archaeology, were pioneered at the Little Bighorn. Today conflict archaeologists investigate sites of prehistoric conflict, classical conflicts like the destruction of three Roman legions by the Germans in A.D. 9; historic conflict and war, such as Coronado's entrada into the American Southwest, the 1745 crushing of the Jacobites at Culloden Scotland, the 1861 Battle of Manassas or Bull Run, the World War I battlefields of the Somme and Flanders, and the Ardennes sites of World War II; as well as recent conflicts like human rights and war crimes investigations in El Salvador, Rwanda, Croatia, Bosnia, and Iraq. They employ or have adapted to their specific site or situation the basic theoretical and methodological constructs developed at the Little Bighorn. It all began with a grass fire in August 1983.

The earliest documented items collected from the Battle of the Little Bighorn are those made by an army medical doctor, assistant surgeon Robert W. Shufeldt, who visited the battlefield in late June, or possibly early July, 1877. At that time he collected a human skull, not as a souvenir but as a medical specimen. Surgeon Shufeldt was with a party of Sioux scouts under the command of Capt. Calbraith

Rodgers of the Fifth Cavalry, who were conducting cavalry patrols in the area in June and July of that year (Hardorff 1984:57–58; Hedren 2011:154–55). Within a few days of Shufeldt's visit, the second documented collector, Philetus W. Norris, arrived on the field, on a personal mission to recover the skeletal remains of his friend Charley Reynolds for reburial in the East. Norris's party met Rodgers's Fifth Cavalry scout as he returned to Post No. 2, soon to become Fort Custer, on July 6 (Norris 1884).

Norris, a colorful individual who had traveled widely through the American West, first visited Last Stand Hill, where he picked up army carbine cartridge cases, a fired Henry .44-caliber cartridge case, a fired lead ball, and a tack-decorated stock and breech of a Sharps carbine. Later that day he found the bones of his friend Charley Reynolds and removed them from his burial site in the Reno valley fight area. Norris's checkerboard career included experience as a businessman, soldier, legislator, writer, poet, explorer, second superintendent of Yellowstone National Park, traveler, and field archaeologist for the Smithsonian Institution (Binkowski 1995; Chittenden 1900:303–305; Scott et al. 2006). Shufeldt and Norris may not have been the first persons to take away relics from the Little Bighorn battlefield, but they appear to be the first to have documented their collection efforts.

Throughout the ensuing years scores, if not hundreds, of people scavenged the field of battle for souvenirs of the famed 1876 fight, some picking up a single cartridge case or some other relic of the event, others undoubtedly taking many more. Until the beginning of the twentieth century, relic collecting was legal and even encouraged by the site caretakers. Even so, there were voices that decried the loss of this heritage and tried to bring these activities to the conscience of the American public (*New York Times*, February 16, 1908). Such concerns were the nascent voice of early preservationists, and one of the first to be able to do something about both natural and cultural resource preservation was President Theodore Roosevelt. He advocated laws to protect important historic and archaeological sites, and in 1906 Congress passed and Roosevelt signed the Antiquities Act, which protected any archaeological resource over one hundred years of age (Lee 1970; Waldbauer and Hutt 2006).

The Little Bighorn was then but a thirty-year-old memory, and its resources did not yet fall under the Antiquities Act. Nothing further was done until late in the second quarter of the twentieth century, when a different perspective to the site's use arose—one of interpretation, preservation, and protection—beginning with the site's administration by the National Park Service (NPS). The first NPS park superintendent, Edward S. Luce, began a long tradition of compiling and documenting battle relic find locations and seeking additional evidence of the battle not recorded in the historical documentary record (Greene 2008). Although many of Luce's and his fellow researchers' finds made their way into the park collections, many others were kept by individual discoverers with Luce's blessing. Soon, though, he among others realized that indiscriminate relic collection would soon destroy the very physical evidence he wished to find, document, and interpret. Luce was the first superintendent to halt collection on the park property and to seek professional archaeological assistance. He and other early researchers learned to appreciate that physical evidence of the battle was important and deserved preservation, and they did their best to document their field efforts. Unfortunately, others did not share their attitude, and over the years many persons, some under cover of night, illegally took America's shared heritage from the park and Crow tribal lands.

NPS archaeologist Robert Bray's 1958 work at the Reno-Benteen defense site began an era of professional archaeological research at the Little Bighorn Battlefield that now has a history of over fifty years of professional investigations. However, it was the wildland grass fire of 1983 that spurred the most intense archaeological studies of the park and its surrounding lands. Since Richard Fox, Jr., first walked the burned ridges and swales of the Little Bighorn Battlefield National Monument conducting the initial post-burn archaeological assessment, there have been four major inventories, two major excavation projects, and over a dozen cultural resource management and small research projects completed in the park and on the lands surrounding the monument.

The goal of this overview is to document the history of the archaeological investigations of the Little Bighorn Battlefield National Monument. This effort describes and assesses the previous archaeological excavations and investigations conducted at monument. Where records or documentation exist, it also describes and assesses the work of relic collectors relative to the professionally conducted archaeological investigations. The professional archaeological work is well documented in the form of trip, project, training, and technical reports as well as published monographs and books. In this book, discussions of these investigations are presented chronologically by project date and year and in narrative format that describe the investigations and results by subject and spatial area.

A variety of records were consulted to assess the archaeological resources at Little Bighorn Battlefield. These consist of field notes and completion reports collected from 1958 to the present that are currently housed at the park and the Midwest Archeological Center (MWAC). Other relevant information consulted includes project-specific memoranda contained in the park museum collections and in the administrative files under file headings H-22, cultural resource studies and research, and H-24, archaeological and historical data recovery programs. A file search was also conducted with the Montana State Historic Preservation Office to ensure that no other archaeological resources are recorded in their system that are not known to the park.

There are ten archaeological resources recorded in the park. One is the battlefield itself, designated 24BH2175 in the Montana trinomial system, which is listed on the National Register of Historic Places. The National Register of Historic Places form lists one of the contributing factors to the battlefield's significance as its potential to yield information employing archaeological techniques. The national significance of Little Bighorn Battlefield National Monument has long been established under Criteria A, B, and C, which are associated with important places, people, and events in American history. The results of the archaeological investigations (Fox 1983; Scott and Connor 1986; Scott and Fox 1987; Scott et al. 1989) of the battlefield documented an added dimension of the site's national significance and supported its inclusion on the National Register under Criterion D, which is an open-ended criterion that uses the phrase "potential to yield important information." This criterion is used for archaeological sites if they meet a variety of legal assessments of their potential to yield important information that cannot be acquired from other sources, such as historical documents. With the Little Bighorn the archaeological record clearly has yielded new information on the battle that is not recorded in the historical documents or the oral history of American Indians, making the battlefield eligible for listing on the National Register of Historic Places under all four criteria.

The other nine archaeological sites found within the park boundary are prehistoric sites or isolated finds, which are discussed in the chapter 2. Copies of the archaeological project records are found in MWAC museum property accessions 207, 319, 541, 552, 565, 870, 871, 1071, and 1077. All original project records and artifacts are now in the park collections. Copies of all project reports are in the MWAC library and files and the park library and files.

In summary, this work assesses, lists, and describes previous archaeological investigations that have occurred in and around the park. In part, the archaeological overview should be viewed as a companion volume to the park's administrative history (Greene 2008).

| # Environmental Background and Regional Archaeological Context

Little Bighorn Battlefield National Monument is located in Big Horn County, southeast Montana, on the right bank (east side) of the Little Bighorn River, about fifteen miles east of Hardin. It comprises 765.34 acres. The acreage is divided into two separate parcels of land: Custer Battlefield, designated Custer Battlefield Historic District 1, includes Last Stand Hill, the Indian Memorial, the visitor center/museum, Custer National Cemetery, the Stone House/White Swan Library, and the NPS Mission 66 buildings and housing area; Historic District 2 encompasses the 162-acre Reno-Benteen defense site located about five miles south. The land between the two battlefields is under private ownership. A right-of-way for the battlefield tour road, also known as Route 10, connects the two battlefields. On June 28, 1938, the respective landowners granted the right-of-way for public purposes to the War Department, which maintained jurisdiction of the site from 1877 to 1940. The entire monument lies within the Crow Indian Reservation, one of seven American Indian reservations in Montana.

Environment

The Little Bighorn battlefield lies within the Central Grasslands vegetative zone (Payne 1973) and in the geological formations of late Cretaceous sandstone and shale (Alt and Hyndman 1986). The soils range from sandy and gravelly along streams and rivers to heavy alluvial clays with a grayish brown topsoil on the upland areas. The monument has two distinct ecological and topographic zones, the dry uplands and the Little Bighorn River floodplain, with an elevation range of 3,000–3,400 feet. The uplands are formed from the Bearpaw and Judith River formations. The floodplain is a Quaternary alluvium.

Climatically, the park is characterized by a dry continental type of extreme fluctuations in temperature and moisture. The battlefield consists of natural hills and hogback ridges cut by ravines and coulees that lead to natural fords of the Little Bighorn River. Outside of these natural fords, the river on the east (battlefield) side is lined with steep bluffs. The vegetation is mainly native grasses, sagebrush, yucca, and prickly pear cactus, with western snowberry, chokecherry, and wild rose commonly found in better moisture conditions such as coulee bottoms. Common grasses and shrubs are Sandberg bluegrass, green needlegrass, bluebunch wheatgrass, northern reedgrass, prairie junegrass, mountain muhly, prickly pear cactus, fringed sagewort, and rabbit grass (figure 1).

Animal species were once quite diverse, before the Euro-American ranching era. Today horses and domestic cattle dominate the grazing species. At one time the area supported bison, bear, elk, deer, rabbit, fox, coyote, badgers, pronghorn antelope, and the ubiquitous prairie dog, among other species. Small mammals are regularly seen in the park, as are deer, the northern grasshopper mouse, thirteen-lined ground squirrel, and northern pocket gopher. A variety of birds are regularly seen in and around the park, including the western kingbird, American goldfinch, western meadowlark, and golden and bald eagles. The park forms a small wildlife refuge in the midst of the intensely grazed Crow Reservation.

Although technically outside the purview of an archaeological overview, it should be noted that the park has yielded a significant paleontological resource. In November 1977 park maintenance staff were excavating a grave in the National Cemetery when backhoe operator Clifford Arbogast partially disturbed a fossilized bone deposit. Robert Stops and William Hartung notified superintendent Richard Hart, who in turn contacted Alan Tabrum of the University of Montana's Department of Geology. Tabrum (1978) excavated

Figure 1. General view of the rolling hills and northern plains grassland vegetation that predominates at the Little Bighorn Battlefield National Monument.

the remains and determined them to be a relatively complete example of a short-neck plesiosaur (*Dolichorhynchops osborni* Williston), a Mesozoic reptile and perhaps the first one found in Montana. The fossil was later transferred to the Smithsonian Institution, National Museum of Natural History, where it was on display during the 1980s. It is currently in the collections as USNM Specimen 419645.

Regional Archaeological Context

Little Bighorn Battlefield National Monument is located in the prehistoric cultural subarea known as the Northwestern Plains.

The immediate area surrounding the park has not been the subject of extensive investigation. Only two sites, both historic bridges (24BH2427 and 24BH2247), are recorded in the vicinity of the park, although the park has nine sites recorded within its boundaries.

Walker-Kuntz and Walker-Kuntz (1999:4.1–4.8) presented a review of the regional archaeological data associated with the park. This regional cultural summary draws heavily on their work. The Northwestern Plains range from central Alberta, Canada, to southern Wyoming and from western North Dakota to western Montana. For at least the past 12,000 years American Indians occupied the area and practiced a seminomadic hunting and gathering economy. Initially their livelihood focused largely on now extinct Pleistocene fauna. Around 10,000 years ago modern bison replaced the megafauna as the main prey species. Although a single economic adaptation persists throughout prehistory, slightly different environmental adaptations and different tool types do serve to differentiate cultural period and phases. The prehistory of the region is divided into four major traditions: Early, Middle, and Late Prehistoric periods and the Protohistoric period. The Historic period begins with the introduction of early Euro-American explorers and written documentation in the area.

EARLY PREHISTORIC

Early Prehistoric groups, commonly identified as Paleoindian, are documented as living in the region in postglacial periods that are usually characterized as cool, moist, and conducive to expansion of forests (Bryson et al. 1970). Pollen profiles from Paleoindian sites, such as Mill Iron in southeastern Montana, indicate the presence of a cool but dry sagebrush steppe environment (L. Scott 1987) in contrast to the forested view. In general, the forests probably extended lower into the foothills and farther upstream into tributary valleys than they do today, and it appears that upland locations consisted primarily of grasslands or more arid sagebrush steppes.

Most Paleoindian sites in Montana are located in foothill settings, and none have been identified in the immediate area around the park. Paleoindian sites are reported in the southern flanks of the Bears Paw Mountains (Davis 1976), the foothills of the Limestone Hills (Davis et al. 1980), the Pryor Mountains (Loendorf 1969), and on old terraces of the Missouri River, particularly in the area south of Great Falls (Shumate 1965).

MIDDLE PREHISTORIC OR PLAINS ARCHAIC PERIOD

The early part of the Middle Prehistoric period occurred during a relatively dry climatic episode (Atlantic, Hypsithermal, or Altithermal) roughly 8,500 years ago. Archaeological evidence of human occupations suggests that people generally concentrated in protected and humid locations such as mountains, foothills, and major river valleys during this episode (Husted 1969). The Middle Prehistoric is defined by a noticeable change in subsistence economies as the emphasis on big-game hunting gave way to a more diversified plant and animal usage. Hunter-gatherers appear to have relied on a wide range of small animals and birds, but with little use of the bison herds (Beckes and Keyser 1983; Lahren 1976).

Projectile points of this age include the Bitterroot/Mummy Cave complex of large side-notched points. Local lithic materials were emphasized, with evidence of more recycling and conservation than during the Early Prehistoric (Reeves 1990).

During the middle part of the Middle Prehistoric, groups began to adopt increasingly specialized subsistence and settlement strategies. The McKean complex (4500–3100 B.P.) roughly corresponds with a cool and moist climatic episode, basically reflecting modern conditions. These climatic conditions likely led to increased resource availability, which in turn probably led to two distinguishing—McKean complex characteristics, population growth as reflected in a dramatic increase in the number of sites (Deaver and Deaver 1988; Frison 1991; Gregg 1985) in the region, and a wider geographic distribution of sites. McKean materials are found throughout Montana, Wyoming, the Dakotas, northern Colorado, western Nebraska, Alberta, Saskatchewan, and Manitoba (Gregg 1985). Topographically, these sites are found in foothill-mountain areas, river valleys (Davis 1976), intermontane basins, and open plains/prairies (Deaver and Aaberg 1977). Artifacts of this age—Oxbow, McKean, and Duncan/Hanna points—have been recovered in greater numbers than Early or early Middle Prehistoric types (Deaver and Deaver 1988).

The settlement pattern for southern Montana McKean sites appears to have been based on a broad-spectrum subsistence economy that exploited seasonally available resources. Loendorf (1973) posits that this lifestyle was practiced in the Pryor Mountains from approximately 7000 B.P. until several hundred years ago.

The middle of the Middle Prehistoric period is defined by the archaeologically recognized evidence of stone boiling and bone grease extraction techniques in the Northwestern Plains. This activity is represented by pit features filled with rock and bone, fire-cracked rock, and large quantities of singed or burned bone and piles of bone. The end result of bone grease extraction was the production of pemmican, a new meat preparation and storage technology that permitted an increased surplus of stored food. Greater attention was devoted to bison hunting, resulting in increasingly regular movement across open prairie settings.

The final part of the Middle Prehistoric is marked by further adaptations toward upland living and the exploitation of open prairie resources. Groups continued to occupy river valley and foothill settings while devoting greater time and attention to the prairies. This change is archaeologically interpreted as the adoption of cooperative hunting techniques and the development of the tipi, a specialized structure suited for open plains habitation. Complexes identified include Pelican Lake and Sandy Creek.

LATE PREHISTORIC OR PLAINS HUNTERS

The Late Prehistoric period is seen as an increasing specialization toward upland living and the utilization of open prairie resources, the most important being bison. The vast majority of Late Prehistoric sites are in open prairies. The major complexes associated with the Late Prehistoric are Besant, Avonlea, and Old Women's.

According to Frison et al. (1996:25), "Besant peoples were without question the most sophisticated pedestrian bison hunters to occupy the North-western Plains." Besant sites are common across the Northern Plains. The Besant complex is the earliest known archaeological unit within the Northern Plains region where ceramics have been found.

During the Avonlea period, the use of the bow and arrow

became widespread, as did an increased use of bison as a primary resource (Reeves 1990). The Avonlea projectile point is characterized by thinness, extreme symmetry, and excellent manufacture.

The final complex associated with the Late Prehistoric is Old Women's. Most sites investigated from this complex reflect bison procurement or processing activities. The jump-and-pound or corral was employed through most of this complex. The diagnostic projectile points of this phase, which are the predominant artifact type found at these sites, are the Prairie Side-Notched and Plains Side-Notched points (Kehoe 1973; MacNeish 1958). Many styles of ceramics are found in association with Old Women's occupations. They are commonly dark gray to brown, with cord-roughened and smoothed, fingernail- or fabric-impressed, grooved-paddle-stamped, or other simply decorated exteriors (Forbis 1962; Roll and Deaver 1980).

PROTOHISTORIC OR PLAINS EQUESTRIAN TRADITION

The Protohistoric—the transition between the Prehistoric and Historic periods—is marked by the introduction of Euro-American trade goods (Deaver and Deaver 1988; Duke 1991) with specific adaptations within Native American groups to accommodate the expansion of trade networks. Of all trade items, the introduction of the horse had the greatest impact on native cultures. With the introduction of the horse, new methods of bison procurement developed— especially the horse-mounted chase. Bison could be followed more efficiently and quickly. The horse could also be used as a pack animal for the transportation of shelter materials and food (Ewers 1980). The horse, in combination with the bow and arrow, resulted in an increased efficiency in bison killing previously unseen on the Plains. By 1800 even marginal hunter-gatherers had become specialized bison hunters (Ruebelmann 1983).

The horse offered an increased mobility that no longer relegated Plains groups to upland living for their primary subsistence focus. Larger winter villages in lowland areas were a direct result of this mobility. Larger groups were able to congregate, but ability to pursue bison via horseback resulted in a decline in communal bison drives, which had characterized earlier Prehistoric populations. The horse also allowed the location of herds to be reported more quickly, with the result of a quicker response time by hunters.

The appearance of guns on the Northwestern Plains occurred by the early 1700s (Ewers 1958). During this time, projectile points made from stone were slowly replaced by metal points.

Protohistoric sites are not common or at least not easily recognized archaeologically on the Northwestern Plains.

HISTORIC PERIOD

The history of the region can be divided into three general periods. The exploration era includes the period between the first documented case of Euro-American exploration and the final government-funded river surveying expedition. The military era encompasses the activities surrounding the military presence in the area, including the Battle of the Little Bighorn and the establishment of Fort Custer. The final era concerns farming, ranching, and modern transportation.

Exploration

The explorers credited with the most important explorations of the lands around the Big Horn and Little Bighorn rivers are Francois Laroque and John Colter. Between 1807 and 1808 these two men traveled widely in the area and came into contact with several Crow bands (Brown 1961). Colter and George Droulliard, veterans of Lewis and Clark's expedition, worked with Manuel Lisa, who brought a keelboat of supplies up the Missouri from St. Louis. The party followed the Yellowstone to the mouth of the Bighorn River and established the first permanent structure built by Euro-Americans in Montana, Fort Manuel Lisa, also known as Fort Raymond (Malone et al. 1991). George Droulliard is also credited with an 1808 exploration of the Little Bighorn River (Brown 1961).

Little other officially sponsored survey or exploration was attempted in the ensuing years. In 1856 a government-authorized survey was undertaken by Lt. Gouverneur K. Warren. Three years later an expedition led by Capt. W. F. Reynolds mapped the Yellowstone and Bighorn rivers (Brown 1961). Reynolds's survey effectively ended government-funded exploration of the Bighorn River.

Military

Civilian travel to and from the American West did not cease with the beginning of the Civil War, but the federal government withdrew its regular troops from the frontier for service in the eastern theaters of the war. Volunteer troops, most from the West, soon replaced the veteran frontier regulars at western posts. Although there were small raids and conflicts throughout the Civil War period in Montana and Wyoming, they did not become prominent until 1865. Events that led to out-and-out conflict are myriad and include the Dakota War, or Minnesota Uprising, in 1862, during which many Santees fled the state and moved into the Dakotas and Northern Plains. Subsequent punitive expeditions led by Gen. Alfred Sully, Col. Henry Sibley, and Brig. Gen. Patrick Connor made no distinctions between Sioux divisions, causing native tensions with the military to rise. A significant factor was the late November 1864 Sand Creek massacre in Colorado, which inflamed an already volatile situation; Cheyennes and Lakotas struck back at homesteaders, ranchers, telegraph stations, and even military posts all along the overland trails in Colorado, Wyoming, and Nebraska. McDermott (2003) framed the widespread conflict—now termed the Indian War of 1865—as an area embroiled in a "circle of fire." Several military expeditions attempted to bring the conflict under control, but none were particularly successful in part because of the War Department's focus on the Civil War (McChristian 2009). This legacy of unresolved conflict between Cheyennes, Lakota Sioux, and Arapahoes and the U.S. government carried over into the postwar years and on the Northern Plains culminated in the Great Sioux War of 1876.

After the Civil War, the United States increased its military presence in Montana Territory as a direct result of the development of the Bozeman Trail. Fort C. F. Smith was established on the Bighorn River, and Fort Phil Kearny near Sheridan, Wyoming. Army occupation and trail traffic increased an adversarial relationship with the Lakota tribes and resulted in open warfare that was not settled until 1877 in the region. A variety of treaties aimed at halting raiding and open warfare did little to resolve the situation. The Fort Laramie Treaty of 1868 created a reserve for the Sioux that included the Black Hills (Malone et al. 1991). The same treaty effectively reduced Crow lands from 38.5 million acres to 8 million.

Although a few groups of Sioux, including Sitting Bull's band, refused to be forced onto the reservation, the Fort Laramie Treaty of 1868 was partially successful, with many bands agreeing to stay on their reservation in present-day South Dakota. However, Lt. Col. George A. Custer and the Seventh Cavalry led a survey expedition into the Black Hills in 1874. One result was the report of the presence of gold. The 1868 treaty was ignored and prospectors poured into the area despite army attempts to halt them. The government changed its mind and ordered the Black Hills opened to mining and homesteading, exacerbating an already tense situation between the Lakotas and white settlers. The Lakotas, both individuals and band units, who had agreed to stay on the reservation left to join the defiant bands in the Bighorn and Powder River country. In December 1875 and January 1876, the federal government issued orders to all bands to return to the reservations and declared those who refused "hostiles" (Malone et al. 1991). In the spring of 1876 three columns of U.S. military, more than two thousand men, moved into the region, led by Brig. Gen. George Crook, Col. John Gibbon, and Brig. Gen. Alfred H. Terry. Terry's column included the seven-hundred-man Seventh U.S. Cavalry, commanded by Custer. That spring the three units advanced into Montana Territory, reaching closer to the Bighorn River. On June 25, 1876, the Seventh Cavalry engaged the Sioux and their allies on the Little Bighorn River. The cavalry suffered a decisive defeat.

Less than three weeks after the Little Bighorn battle, plans began for a memorial to commemorate Custer's fallen soldiers (Greene 2008; Rickey 1967). On January 29, 1879, the secretary of war authorized the creation of Custer National Cemetery. The cemetery was initially administered by the War Department. Administration was provided by the commanding officer of Fort Custer. Later, resident superintendents administered the grounds. In 1940 the National Cemetery administration was transferred to the Department of the Interior under the auspices of the NPS.

Public outcry over the defeat at the Little Bighorn led to the nearly immediate establishment of Fort Custer at the confluence of the Bighorn and Little Bighorn rivers in 1877 (Hedren 2011:159–60). In 1884 the U.S. government renegotiated the terms of the 1868 treaty with the Crow tribe. The land containing the original Crow agencies near Livingston and Absorakee became ceded lands open to settlement by nonnatives. The current Crow Agency was built at this time and became the focus of tribal administration.

Today the Little Bighorn area overlaps a portion of the Crow Reservation. From an ethnographic perspective, the Battle of the Little Bighorn is a significant symbolic event for two major cultural groups seeking to maintain their respective values and life ways in the face of cross-cultural contact and conflict. These diverse groups each visit Little Bighorn and reflect upon the battle fought here in their own unique way. American Indian visitors remember this battle as their greatest victory over the U.S. Army (west of the Mississippi River) and the high point of their traditional way of life, while also remembering the sacrifices and losses resulting from the battle.

Farming, Ranching, and the Modern Era

While Fort Custer was in operation, the major nonmilitary economy in the area was supported by travel and freight hauled by riverboat, train, and stage. The Chicago, Burlington and Quincy Railroad line was opened on the reservation in 1893. Cattle ranching developed in the region, first as support for Fort Custer, but by the time the railroad was built the beef industry was flourishing.

A homesteading boom in southeastern Montana began in 1909 (Malone et al. 1991). The various homesteading acts (Carstensen 1968:481)—including the original act of 1862, the Desert Land Entry Act of 1877, the 1904 Kincade Homestead Act, the Enlarged Homestead Act of 1909, and the 1916 Stockraising Homestead Act—as well as advertising by railroads and land speculators made dryland farming attractive. This was especially true after the beginning of the twentieth century, when new homesteading laws increased acreages up to a square mile of land that could be patented.

The marginal agricultural environment was always a challenge for the late nineteenth- and early twentieth-century settlers. By 1917 economic hard times befell the farmers and ranchers in Montana, and this was followed by the Great Depression of the 1930s in which economics and the environment exacerbated each other. Eastern Montana saw a population decline, but federally funded work projects aided the economic recovery of the area. Changes in farming and ranching practices after World War II as well as the expanding national economy allowed a generally settled agrarian lifestyle to become well established for the region.

Prehistoric Sites at Little Bighorn Battlefield

The archaeological sites currently recorded within Little Bighorn National Monument are representative of the human activities that have taken place there for the past ten thousand years. Those who visited the area followed a hunting and gathering subsistence that resulted in primarily low-visibility sites—that is, small scatters of discarded tools and the remains of limited maintenance activities.

The 1984 and 1985 archaeological inventory projects not only recovered 1876 battle-related artifacts but identified several prehistoric sites and some isolated projectile points. These were documented by Scott (1987a) in an inventory report. Two lithic scatters and seven isolated finds were found on the Custer battlefield. No prehistoric resources were found at the Reno-Benteen defense site.

The prehistoric sites are both small lithic scatters composed of secondary lithic debitage. Diagnostic materials were recovered from one site. Site 24BH2466 is several hundred meters east of Deep Ravine. Four secondary flakes of basalt, agate, and porcellanite were seen and collected in a 20 by 20 m area. The site appears to be a small, sparse, surface scatter. It may have been a tool maintenance location.

Site 24BH2467 is a sparse lithic scatter west of Calhoun Hill. The site covers an area of 100 by 20 m. It produced nine secondary flakes of chert and quartzite. Two corner-notched projectile points (one each of quartzite and porcellanite) were also recovered. The site may have been truncated by road construction, and it may have been impacted by the 1876 battle and, later, visitation. The site appears to be surface and may date to the Middle to Late Archaic period of the Middle Prehistoric period.

Others sites are simply isolated finds:

24BH2465: secondary porcellanite flake
24BH2468: utilized secondary flake of porcellanite
24BH2469: tip of translucent agate projectile point

24BH2470: large corner notched biface of red porcellanite

24BH2471, Location 28: corner notched projectile point of Knife River flint, Late Middle Prehistoric (Archaic) to early Late Prehistoric in style

24BH2472: corner- and basally notched quartzite projectile point, Early to Middle Archaic in style

24BH2473: tip of chert projectile point

The two prehistoric sites were evaluated by testing in 1989 and found to be not eligible for the National Register (Scott 1989a). None of the isolated find locales are eligible for the National Register, and since the isolated finds were collected and documented the locations of the finds have no significance or other value.

| # Brief Historical Overview of the Battle

The history of the Battle of the Little Bighorn is well documented in a hundreds of books, monographs, articles, and a variety of other publications (e.g., Graham 1953; Gray 1976, 1991; Kuhlman 1951; Utley 1988). None needs to be repeated here except to provide the historical context for discussing the battle's archaeological resources.

In the spring of 1876, a three-pronged campaign was launched to shepherd the Sioux and Cheyenne back to their agencies on the reservation (figure 2). One column, under Col. John Gibbon, marched east from Fort Ellis (near present-day Bozeman, Montana). A second column, led by Gen. Alfred Terry (and including Custer), headed west from Fort Abraham Lincoln near Bismarck, North Dakota. The third column consisted of Gen. George Crook's men moving north from Fort Fetterman, Wyoming (near modern Douglas) into Montana.

Unknown to Terry and Gibbon, Crook encountered the tribes near Rosebud Creek in southern Montana and was defeated by them about a week before Custer's battle (Vaughn 1956, Mangum 1987a). After this, his force withdrew to Wyoming, breaking one side of the triangle. Meanwhile, Terry was moving west up the Yellowstone River to the Bighorn. The Seventh Cavalry, under Custer, was to scout ahead and departed Terry's command on June 22. On the morning of the 25th, the Seventh Cavalry was at the divide between

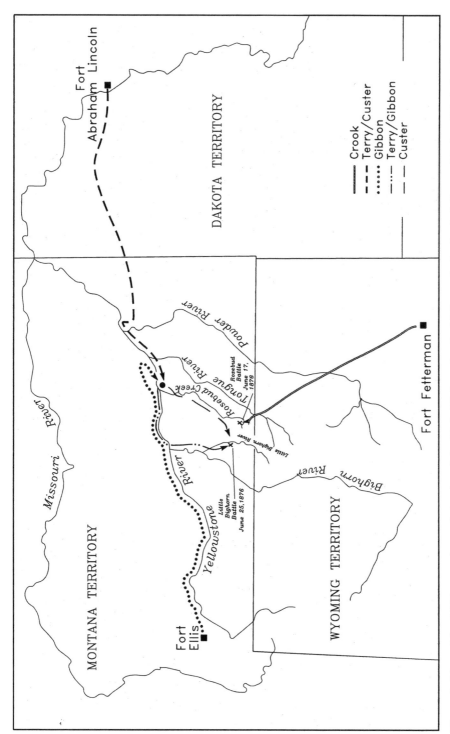

Figure 2. Map of the 1876 campaign and the site of the Little Bighorn battle. Midwest Archeological Center, National Park Service.

the Rosebud and Little Bighorn rivers. From a spot known as the Crow's Nest, army scouts observed a large American Indian village (figure 3).

Worried they might escape, Custer decided to attack and descended into the valley of the Little Bighorn. Capt. Frederick Benteen was ordered to scout southwest with three companies to block a possible southern escape route. A few miles from the Little Bighorn, Custer again divided his command, ordering Maj. Marcus Reno to advance with three companies along the river bottom and attack the village on its southern end. The remaining five companies would follow Custer in support of Reno.

Custer took the remaining five companies along the east side of the river to an ephemeral tributary of the Little Bighorn. He must have finally realized the gravity of the situation as the north end of the village came into view. From here, he sent a message back to Benteen: "Benteen, Come on. Big village, be quick, bring packs. P.S. Bring pacs. W. W. Cooke." The messenger, trumpeter John Martin, was the last soldier to see Custer and his command alive.

Custer and five companies rode to their fate. Custer apparently further divided his command in the lower reaches of Medicine Tail Coulee, sending one wing of two companies to the ford at the mouth of the coulee where it debouches into the Little Bighorn River. Custer and the other three companies held higher ground to the east, now known as Nye-Cartwright Ridge. Whether because of increasing warrior pressure on the wing at the mouth of Medicine Tail Coulee or pressure on his wing, Custer apparently ordered a withdrawal from the coulee, with the five companies rejoining at the southern end of what is now called Custer Ridge or Battle Ridge and Calhoun Hill. There Custer evidently deployed Lts. James Calhoun and John J. Crittenden with two companies of soldiers to hold the position while he rode to the north with the remaining three companies.

Custer's goal may have been to move farther north and cross the river with the intent of attacking the village from the north and relieve the pressure on Reno's command. He likely deployed Capt. Myles Keogh about 300 yards in the rear of Calhoun and Crittenden's position while he moved on to the north with two companies, E and F. Some of Custer's command seemingly did move to the northwest along a spur of land or extension of Custer Ridge, now

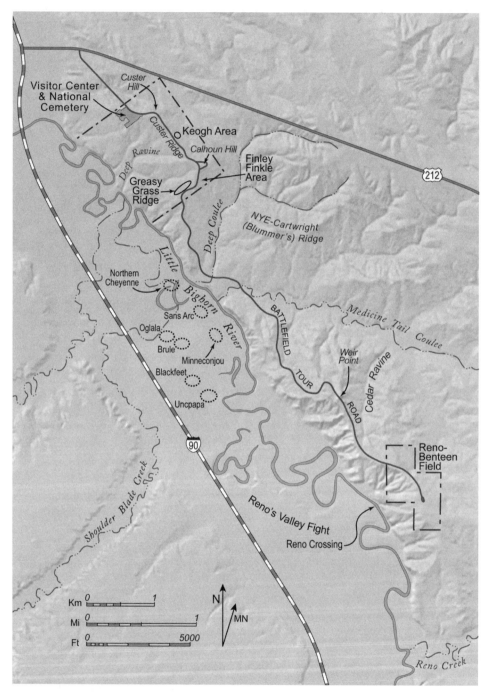

Figure 3. Little Bighorn field of battle with prominent natural and battle features noted.
Map by Tom Jonas. Copyright © 2013 by the University of Oklahoma Press.

just outside the park boundary, but at some point was forced back to take positions at Last Stand Hill. The command was under attack by increasing numbers of Cheyenne and Lakota warriors, who soon outnumbered, outgunned, and outfought Custer and his men, destroying the command to a man by late that Sunday afternoon.

In the meantime, warriors had forced Reno and his men to retreat across the river and up the bluffs to a defensible position. On the hilltop, the soldiers were joined by Benteen's forces and the pack train, both following along Custer's line of march in order to bring up the ammunition packs. The warriors pinned down all until June 27, when their village broke up into small groups that withdrew as Terry's and Gibbon's combined column arrived. For that day and a half, Reno, Benteen, and the men fought to keep their defensive position and wondered when Custer would relieve them. Reno sent two men to meet the advancing column, and they found Terry and Gibbon near the abandoned village. Here, a scout brought the news. Custer and his men lay dead on a ridge above the Little Bighorn.

CHAPTER 4

From Souvenirs to Data

The Evolution of Archaeological Research
at Little Bighorn Battlefield

Data collection at the Little Bighorn began in one form the day
of the battle. Trophies and souvenirs were taken by the victorious
warriors and those who buried the dead. Informal and formal collection efforts continued for many years afterward. Here those documented efforts are discussed and placed in context of the evolution
of the historic preservation movement in the United States. Historic
preservation encompasses not only the details of archaeological discovery but the larger scope of how and why archaeological work is
done. At the Little Bighorn Battlefield, it also involved addressing
legal issues surrounding the archaeological investigations, applying
new methods of finding and recording the physical evidence, and
handling massive public interest in the investigations.

The Era of Souvenirs and Trophies, 1876–1940

Relics of the Little Bighorn battle have been of interest to the general public almost since the day after the battle. Cartridge cases,
arrows, and other items were collected immediately after the battle
(du Mont 1974; Hutchins 1976). One of the most colorful figures
and earliest visitors to collect on the Little Bighorn battlefield was
Philetus W. Norris. Born in the state of New York in 1821, Norris
acquired a large tract of land near Detroit, Michigan, after the Civil

War. There he established the town of Norris, where he published a newspaper, the *Norris Suburban*. Norris is perhaps best known to history as the second superintendent of Yellowstone National Park (1877–82) and as the recoverer of the remains of the famous scout "Lonesome Charley" Reynolds from the Little Bighorn battlefield (Gray 1963).

Norris traveled widely through the West (Binkowski 1995), making observations on natural history and even archaeological resources he encountered. In the early 1880s and nearly to the time of his death in 1885 he was employed as a field archaeologist by the Smithsonian Institution, investigating a variety of prehistoric sites in the upper Midwest and Southeast.

Through a *Suburban* column titled "The Great West" and a book, *The Calumet of the Coteau, and Other Poetical Legends of the Border* (published in 1884, less than a year before his death), Norris published a great deal of information about his travels. However, his romantic disposition typically infused both his prose and poetry to the extent that even contemporary Victorian-era critics regarded his writing style as florid and tortuous at best. An anonymous editorial about his book concluded that "no publisher in his sober senses would undertake the bringing out of such a collection" of writings (*The Word Carrier*, November/December 1886, 3).

Although they are not as factual as might be desired, it is fortunate that many of Norris's writings appear to have survived. The *Norris Suburban* was in existence for only three years (1876–78; see Binkowski 1995:9n8). Clippings from his "Great West" column have also been preserved in a notebook at the Huntington Library at San Marino, California. These clippings are published versions of letters written by Norris during his travels. He arranged and annotated them in the notebook, evidently in anticipation of publication in book form, but died in 1885 before this could be accomplished.

One of the more extensive notations is a lengthy note that starts: "The following is the heretofore unpublished portion of the above letter to the New York Herald which was lost." This handwritten section describes Norris's visit to the Little Bighorn battlefield while on his way to assume the duties of Yellowstone National Park superintendent. His intent to visit the battlefield was to recover the bones of his friend Charley Reynolds for eventual reburial back East. He arrived at Fort Custer after Michael Sheridan's expedition to recover the officers' bodies had completed its work and returned to what soon became Fort Custer. Norris was denied official permission to visit the field, but enlisting the aid of Collins J. Baronett, George Herendeen, possibly former 1876 Sioux War scouts Curly and Half Yellowface, and perhaps in the company of the battlefield's first photographer, John Fouch, they traveled seemingly clandestinely to the battlefield. There Norris reported in his annotation that he traveled

> thence to the north abrupt terminus of the Coteau where Custer fell and the bones of many whom he led there still remain. There was little evidence of a prolonged struggle but an exploded Henry cartridge shell, a battered old style round bullet, and the broken britch of a Sharps rifle with brass nail marks of Indian ornaments which I found within twenty yards of where Custer fell proved the Indians had a diversity of arms and used at least some of them in close conflict. I brought away the broken britch, bullet, and fully one hundred carbine cartridge shells. . . .
>
> I found the scout Gerard ['s] sketch of the field mainly correct and from it found where the famous friendly Indian Bloody Knife the half breed Cherokee [sic] Lt. McIntosh and my bosom friend Charley Reynolds Chief of scouts fell.
>
> Bloody Knife went down as he fought in a willow thicket on the right flank in advance the others and many more in the smooth open valley during the retreat. Although there was far less grass than in the lower part of the village still it so delayed our search that it was nearly sunset before I had with throbbing heart and vengeance aroused to rather court than shun a fight that the remnant of his [Reynolds] bones and well known auburn hair were found and strapped to my saddle and we retraced the wagon trail down the valley.

A further account of the recovery of Reynolds's remains is found in the *New York Herald,* July 15, 1877:

> Barronette and the writer went in search of the remains of the gallant scout Charley Reynolds. . . . We were aided by a rough but accurate map made by Major Reno's scout, Gerard, who saw Charley fall. All that we could find were a few small bones, which were but partially covered with

earth, the bones of his horse, fragments of his hat and clothing, a few tufts of his well known auburn hair which clung to
the earth after wolf or ghoul had removed the skull.

The hair, small bones and fragments of clothing were
gathered in a large handkerchief the only mortal relics of
the once most accomplished scout and finest shot on the
plains, were brought carefully away for decent burial in a
Christian land. . . . after Colonel Sheridan and the train
had left the field part of the company and scouts remained
hunting up and covering the scattered bones and gathering
relics, especially carbine cartridges in the lofty basin where
Calhoun fell.

By rough map of the scout Gerard who saw him fall, I
found where my gallant comrade of the preceding season—
Charley Reynolds—fell, and brought away all that wolf and
ghoul had spared of his mortal remains for decent burial in
a Christian land.

A thorough view and map there drawn, of the fields,
and ruins of the old Indian village with accurate notes of all
saw and heard, from many both white and Indian participants in these various events are retained for use at a proper
occasion.

A handwritten note following the column adds: "As the letter
and map sent the New York Herald, is supposed to have been captured by the Indians, and the copy of the map loaned General Gibbons, was lost in his fight with them, I supposed all trace of both
were lost until I recently found rolled around some specimens the
first pencil sketch of both, and commenced publication." This map
is undoubtedly the map published by Norris in 1884 in his *Calumet
of the Coteau* and discussed by Donahue (2008:250–53). It appears
to be a revision of the Maguire map and may be a reasonably accurate map of the battlefield, although the meanders of the Little Bighorn River appear to be copied from the Maguire map (figure 4).

Norris's exaggerated and florid writing style as well as his tendency to diverge into romantic descriptions of places and events
tend to make analysis of his work difficult at best. Exacerbating the
problem, he appears to have written in a stream-of-consciousness
manner as well. Nevertheless, careful parsing and vetting of his work

Figure 4. Norris's 1884 map of the battlefield overlaid on a modern aerial
photograph. Note the significant changes in the river meanders.

yield some gems of historical import. Norris noted that Sheridan's
recovery group collected cartridge cases and other relics from the
Calhoun Hill area, and that he collected the Sharps rifle or carbine
action, probably a lead ball, and more than one hundred army carbine cartridge cases on or near Last Stand Hill. This is the earliest
reliable record of a collection of relics other than human bone on
the battlefield. The recovery of Reynolds's bones is interesting and

important, but the collection and removal of numerous firearms-related artifacts from the vicinity of Last Stand Hill and an undetermined number from Calhoun Hill are an invaluable bit of history overlooked by researchers over the ensuing years.

Norris did not specifically state what he did the with relics collected from the Little Bighorn, but he did record in an earlier column (*Norris Suburban,* February 18, 1876) that he secured specimens for the "present and future interest and value to myself, my friends, and the Scientific Association of Detroit." On the chance that Norris donated some of his Little Bighorn relics to the Scientific Association of Detroit, which morphed in the late nineteenth century into the Detroit Arts Institute, the curator of collections there was contacted, but no objects related to Norris or Little Bighorn repose in those collections.

As with the Norris collections, with one or two exceptions, the earliest battlefield recoveries have disappeared into the mists of time. At least two reasonably documented early Little Bighorn relics are part of Smithsonian Institution's Museum of American History collection. One is a human cervical vertebra transfixed by an iron arrowhead (figure 5), collected by 2nd Lt. George S. Young, Seventh Infantry, during a trip to the battlefield in 1878 or 1879. He picked up a .45–55 cartridge case, an iron arrowhead, and the vertebra. The items were retained by Young's family for many years and were donated to the Smithsonian Institution in 1967 (correspondence relating to accession 275426, Smithsonian Institution). A second relic in the Museum of American History was collected by Dr. A. M. Hawes. It is an army McClellan saddle (figure 6) that has been modified, presumably by American Indians and was collected from them around 1882. Some of the saddle straps and the stirrups have been modified from army configuration. The saddle leather is stamped "M7C," presumed to mean Company M, Seventh Cavalry. The assumption is that this saddle was captured at the battle (files and correspondence related to catalog number 59741, accession 11523).

The largest artifact collected from the field of battle was the horse Comanche. His story of survival and the pampered life he led as the Seventh Cavalry mascot is well chronicled (Brown 1973; Dary 1976; Lawrence 1989; Luce 1939; Mengel 1969). Comanche died on November 7, 1891, at Fort Riley. Prof. Lewis Lindsay Dyche

Figure 5. Iron arrowhead transfixed in a human cervical vertebra, found by Lt. George Young about 1878 or 1879 at the Little Bighorn battlefield and now in the Smithsonian Institution collections. Courtesy Museum of American History, Smithsonian Institution.

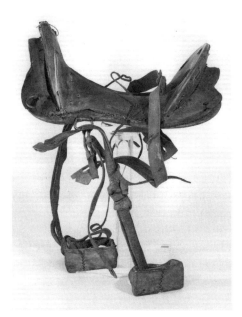

Figure 6. McClellan saddle possibly associated with the Little Bighorn collected from American Indians in 1882 by Dr. A. M. Hawes and now in the Smithsonian Institution collections. Courtesy Museum of American History, Smithsonian Institution.

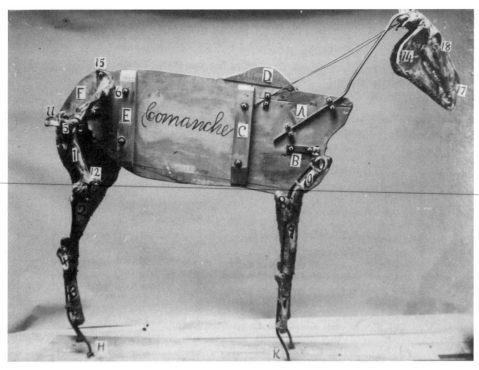

Figure 7. Skeletal elements of the horse Comanche as used in the mounted display at the University of Kansas Museum of Natural History. Little Bighorn Battlefield National Monument.

from the University of Kansas Museum of Natural History traveled to Fort Riley, where he skinned the horse and collected the skull, forelegs and scapulae, pelvis, and hind legs for use in mounting the old war horse for display (Dary 1976:10–12). Those bones are the first large artifacts from the Little Bighorn battle to be collected and preserved as part of a museum collection (figure 7). Comanche's mounted remains, recently conserved, remain on display at the museum to this day.

Early Efforts to Document Physical Evidence, 1940–1970

Although there was no lack of interest in the Little Bighorn story during the army's administration of the battlefield, it was not until the

NPS assumed control of the site that any attempt at a coordinated research agenda was even considered (Greene 2008:75–80). The first park superintendent, Edward S. Luce, was appointed in 1940. He had a long and serious interest in the story and was himself an ex-cavalryman, a published author (Luce 1939), and an acknowledged authority on the battle. Luce was acquainted with many of the battle participants and researchers of the day, and he had walked much of the battlefield with other researchers long before his appointment to the NPS.

Luce almost literally served as a rallying point and sometimes lightening rod for research on the field. He, along with several active Little Bighorn researchers including Elwood Nye, Ralph G. Cart-wright, and local rancher Joseph Blummer, began an intense, if sporadic, study of the ground beyond the Custer field (a designation of the area where Custer and the men who accompanied him were killed) in an attempt to find the route Custer's command followed in approaching the battlefield. Luce's shortcoming in his research was that he tended to focus almost exclusively on the Seventh Cavalry, their route and positions, to the exclusion of Lakota and Cheyenne combat positions or movements. Regardless, Luce and other researchers of the era were interested in the physical evidence as a means to refine the battle story and place events more precisely on the landscape. They used the finds as a means to support their theories of movements and refine their understanding of the history. Although this "handmaiden to history" approach is now passé in anthropological archaeology (Fox 1996c:87–88), it was very much the standard at the time Luce began his data collection efforts.

As early as the 1920s, Blummer (ms dated 1959, A-123 C5188x, Little Bighorn Battlefield National Monument files [hereafter LBNM files]) discovered cartridge cases on a ridgetop about one mile southeast of the battlefield (Greene 2008:194–95). Luce learned of Blummer's finds, and he and his researcher friends realized that physical evidence could aid them in sorting out Custer's route and other issues related to the battle.

Cartwright compiled notes on his finds on the Custer battle-field, Custer's route to the battlefield, the Reno-Benteen defense, and the valley fight in 1941 (ms titled "Custer's Advance toward the Battlefield, Little Bighorn National Monument," Accession 278, Field Research Notes [hereafter Acc. 278, Field Notes]). Cartwright included a description of his finds keyed to a map with letters indicating where he found or observed items. He noted finding human remains near the Custer field as well as in the Reno valley fight area, and he recalled finding in 1938 well over one hundred cartridge cases grouped in threes along a ridge south of Custer field. A few cartridge cases Cartwright collected remain in the Adams House Museum collection in Deadwood, South Dakota. With additional cartridge case finds and other battle-related items made by Luce and his fellow researchers in 1943 (Memorandum from Superintendent, Custer Battlefield to Superintendent, Yellowstone NP, dated September 6, 1943, Acc. 278, Field Notes), the locale took on the name of Nye-Cartwright Ridge (Greene 2008:195). Luce was perceptive enough to engage experts in other fields, such as Col. Calvin Goddard of the U.S. Army Ordnance Department, to identify Custer-era cartridge cases and bullets that he and his colleagues recovered from their battlefield searches (Luce to Goddard, letter dated September 6, 1943, Acc. 278, Field Notes). The artifact finds compelled Luce to write his supervisor at Yellowstone National Park and ask for the aid of an archaeologist to conduct a study of the battlefield (Luce to Coordinating Superintendent, Yellowstone NP, Sept. 28, 1943, Acc. 278, Field Notes; and Sept. 30, 1943; RG 79 National Park Service, Central Classified file, 1933–1949 National Monuments, Custer Battlefield—120, Box 2129, File 2, NARA). Luce's appeal for archaeological aid went unheeded until 1958.

Luce's interest in the physical evidence was not limited to finding relics of the battlefield; he always wanted to record them. He was the first person to attempt to consolidate the relic finds of various researchers onto a map. He prepared an enlarged map of the battlefield, based on the 1891 USGS topographic map, first published in 1908 (figure 8). From the boundary of the park he created a grid across the area encompassing Deep Coulee, Medicine Tail Coulee, and Weir Point. The grids were numbered west to east 1 through 28 and lettered north to south A through X. At the enlarged map scale, the grids were approximately 375 feet on a side. Luce then roughly plotted the finds made up to that point, denoting them as a series of *x*'s.

Luce distributed the map as part of a mimeographed item he titled "Bulletin No. 1, Enlarged Map of Custer Battlefield National Cemetery Area and Surrounding Country." The bulletin was sent to

Figure 8. Superintendent Edward Luce was the first person to attempt to document find locations when he and other early researchers walked the area in search of Custer's route to the final battlefield. Here Luce's map, based on the 1908 USGS topographic map, is shown overlaid on a modern aerial photograph.

fellow researchers along with some text attributing the finds by grid to individuals. He attributed finds in Grids 5F, 6E, 7E, 8E, 11E, 12E, 13E, 14C, and 14D to Elwood Nye and R. G. Cartwright. Fred Johnson, assistant superintendent of Yellowstone National Park, is credited with a September 16, 1943, find in Grid 13D. Luce himself had finds in Grids 5F, 6E, 7E, 8E, 11E, 12E, 13D, 14C, 14D, 15D, 13G, 13D, and 7E. Local residents George Oston, Verne Johnson, and Charles Gatchell found items on December 19, 1943, in Grids 6E, 7E, and 8E. 1st Lt. Gerald Nelson found items in Grid 4H. The bulletin further identifies several numbers on the maps. The numbers generally correlate with the find location but appear to provide some explanation or interpretation of the "X marks the spot" approach. According to the bulletin, No. 1 indicates empty cartridge cases found at intervals about nine feet apart; No. 2 signifies about 150 cartridge cases found in small groups and in a linear pattern, suggesting to Luce that perhaps forty men had fought a dismounted action at that location; No. 3 was a cavalry spur and buckle found by Fred Johnson; No. 4 signified empty cartridge cases found nine to ten feet apart, suggesting to Luce a mounted action; No. 5 was a McKeever style cartridge box and part of a cartridge belt; No. 6 indicted the area of fighting around Weir Point; No. 7 was a group of seventeen cartridge cases, to Luce's thinking likely representing a vidette location; No. 8 was an incomplete horse skeleton, some leather fragments, and three brass saddle rings; and No. 9 was a Henry rifle found in 1936 by Lieutenant Nelson.

Luce also noted that the find locations were marked by wooden stakes driven into the ground. Some of these find areas appear to have been formally surveyed on November 24, 1943, by Philip Hohlbrandt (field survey notes for November 23 and 24, 1943, LBNM files). Using the northeast corner of the park fence, Hohlbrandt plotted four separate locations of cartridge case finds and the location of a cavalry spur. His notes mention that he plotted the sites of 135 cartridge cases and the spur. These surveyed locales are likely some of the same locations mentioned in Luce's Bulletin No. 1. Some of those stakes survived until the 1990s before disappearing through the ravages of time and range fires (Donahue 2008:340).

Luce's stated plan was to update the map as new finds were made and to distribute those updates to interested researchers. No subsequent bulletins have come to light, however. Regardless, the Luce map, as Donahue (2008:337–40) aptly notes, was the first effort to document findings of physical evidence by mapping the find locations. The map has limited research value today since the find descriptions cannot be linked to specific artifacts in personal or park collections; thus, modern identification methods and current analytical techniques cannot be applied to test Luce's assumptions regarding their origin. Nevertheless the map and descriptions are an important, if rudimentary, legacy in the attempt to document artifact distributions that aid interpretation of the Little Bighorn battle events.

World War II and NPS funding reductions certainly contributed to the lack of response for professional archaeological assistance, but there were other larger issues at work as well. American archaeology was almost entirely the purview of academics at the time, and their interest focused on the prehistoric past. The field of historic archaeology was in its nascent beginnings in the late 1930s and early 1940s (Orser 2004:28–55), largely spearheaded by park service archaeologists J. C. "Pinky" Harrington and John Cotter. Even so, their efforts were centered on colonial American sites like Jamestown and Washington's Fort Necessity. Not until the postwar era, and the 1950s in particular, was there a change not only in park management attitude but in the archaeological profession as well, setting the stage for cooperation between historians and archaeologists on an unprecedented scale.

Luce was also innovative in his thinking about the use of metal detectors to find artifacts associated with the Little Bighorn battle. He first mentioned the idea of metal detector use, which he referred to as a "radio metal finding machine," in 1943 (Luce to Elwood Nye, October 11, 1943, Acc. 278, Field Notes), but World War II continued to disrupt his plans. Luce did not lose interest in finding further physical evidence, and encouraged by the continuing development of the mine detector during World War II he experimented with one in 1947 (Rickey 1967:126) to find relics of the battle. The effort was a failure, but perhaps only because he believed the machine capable of finding only iron objects. The system tested by Luce may have been of limited capability, but it is also conceivable that this early equipment was either improperly tuned or most likely not sensitive enough to find small items like cartridge cases or bullets. It would be another decade before metal detectors were found to be useful at Little Bighorn.

Don G. Rickey, one of the doyens of Indian Wars history, became the park historian in July 1955 (Greene 2008:92). Probably spurred by Superintendent Luce, but propelled by his own long-seated interest in the physical evidence of history, Rickey soon began a formal collaboration with Jesse W. Vaughn, an attorney and avocational historian and archaeologist from Windsor, Colorado. Vaughn (1966:145–66) was aware of the advances in metal detector technology and had been using one on his research at other sites with some success. Rickey and Vaughn began an attempt to scan the battlefield systematically in 1956 (Greene 1986:23). They worked various areas between 1956 and 1959 (Jesse W. Vaughn Research Notes, Acc. 278, Field Notes; Rickey and Vaughn n.d.). Their first effort was a metal detector survey of the Reno-Benteen defense site in 1956. They found and marked with wooden stakes a variety of artifacts, mostly army carbine cartridge cases found in linear arrangements along the presumed army perimeter. Rickey and Vaughn also located nails and what they believed were pieces of human bone.

The two men continued their collaborative effort that year by extending their metal detector search to the ridgetops south and east of the Reno-Benteen defense site. There they discovered a variety of cartridge cases indicating combat positions used by the warriors during the battle, totaling eight separate fighting areas, and they collected nearly six hundred cartridge cases from these positions (Rickey 1956). In reporting the finds, Rickey (1956) called for a park boundary expansion to include these previously unknown fighting positions. He also noted that the find locations were mapped and that a copy of the map was attached. Unfortunately, such a map has not been relocated, and carbon file copies of the report do not include the map. There is, however, a hand-annotated copy of the 1954 aerial photograph (figure 9) of the Reno-Benteen area in the park files that does appear generally to denote the find areas mentioned by Rickey. It also generally locates two new warrior positions, 9–9 and 10–10, discovered in 1969 by park historian B. William Henry, Jr. Although the map is not attributed, it appears that the locations were plotted by Henry.

Rickey and Vaughn continued their metal detector efforts in 1957, 1958, and 1959, confirming the work of Luce on Nye-

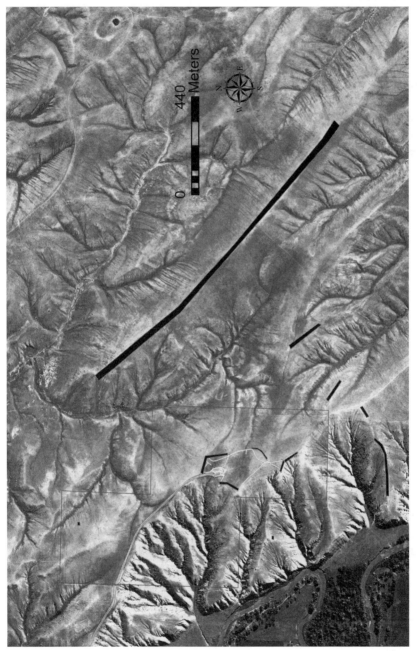

Figure 9. J. W. Vaughn and Don Rickey's soldier and warrior positions taken from a 1954 aerial photograph and replotted on a modern aerial photograph. These same areas have yielded large numbers of cartridge cases, bullets, and other items to other collectors and professional archaeological investigations.

Cartwright Ridge and finding a previously unknown fighting area near the mouth of Medicine Tail Coulee (Jesse W. Vaughn Research Notes, Acc. 278, Field Notes; Rickey and Vaughn n.d.; Green 1986:21–25). Rickey and Vaughn made what they thought was an exciting find during their 1957 metal detector work. One of the cartridge cases recovered contained paper inside. Hoping this might be a note related to one of the burial spots of Custer's men, they sent the cartridge case sent to an NPS museum preservation specialist (Rickey to Director, NPS, Sept. 17, 1957, Acc. 278, Field Notes). A response was quickly received (Preservation Specialist Nitkiewicz to Superintendent LIBI, Nov. 13, 1957, Acc 279, Field Notes) identifying the paper as a cardboard roll. Although not realized by the museum personnel, the paper was a cardboard tube used by the Frankford Arsenal as liner to reduce the diameter and powder capacity of the cartridge case for cavalry carbine rounds, which used fifty-five grains of black powder instead of the seventy grains for infantry rounds. The two types of rounds used the same size cartridge case.

Vaughn (1966:145–66) continued his metal detector use in his research efforts after Rickey left the park in 1960, and in 1964 he walked over and metal-detected the presumed area of Major Reno's first skirmish lines in the Little Bighorn River valley. Jerome A. Greene (1986) later scoured the park files and interviewed Rickey and recorded his recollections of his finds.

Rickey did not just find artifacts and have them mapped; he revised the interpretation of the Reno-Benteen defense site based on the artifact finds. He went on to use the information in placing wayside exhibits more accurately on the defense perimeter, determining the route of the new interpretive walking trail, incorporating three newly restored rifle pits as part of the walking trail, and locating and marking the site of Dr. Henry R. Porter's field hospital. He also employed the find information to create a Reno-Benteen defense site brochure and experimental self-guiding trail guide; although subsequently revised several times, it is still used on site today. Rickey's contribution to the early and effective use of archaeological data has been somewhat underappreciated. His artifact collections appear to be present in the park collections, but they were unfortunately later lumped for cataloging purposes and proveniences were lost or not recorded during the cataloging process, thus further obscuring the real value of his and Vaughn's documentation efforts.

The first professional archaeological investigation to take place in the park was in response to a cultural resource management issue, the construction of a visitor footpath at the Reno-Benteen defense site, essentially today's walking tour route. Initially the work was to be funded by NPS, but priorities shifted and the funds were reallocated to another park in the region. At the last minute the Custer Battlefield Historical and Museum Association came to the rescue and donated funds to secure the work (Rickey 1996:58–59), beginning a long tradition of support of archaeological research and investigation in the park.

Archaeologist Robert Bray (1958), then associated with the NPS Midwest Regional Office in Omaha, Nebraska, mapped many of Rickey's finds at the Reno-Benteen defense site, and with Rickey and locally hired day laborers he excavated several features that were determined to be soldiers' rifle pits. Bray also excavated several test trenches through the presumed hospital area. Rickey's earlier human bone finds led Bray to recover three incomplete soldier burials. These were not formally examined at the time but simply reinterred in the National Cemetery in August 1958. They were exhumed in 1986 (Connor 1986) in preparation for reburial of additional soldier remains that had been discovered since that time (Pieters and Barnard 1986).

Bray was one of the few archaeologists of his era to advocate the use of metal detectors in studying historic sites. He was exposed to the value of metal detecting in archaeology in 1958 during his Little Bighorn work with Rickey and Vaughn (Bray 1958; Connor and Scott 1998). His experience with Rickey and the near ideal detecting conditions present at the Little Bighorn, including good soil conditions, shallowly buried artifacts, and little modern trash, led Bray to employ metal detectors at many other historic sites during his years with the University of Missouri, especially at Wilsons Creek National Battlefield (Bray 1967:10–11). Unfortunately, his recovery rate was generally poor. Developed in World War II as a device for finding buried land mines and booby traps, by the 1960s metal detectors were not much more than sophisticated electronic tools meant to be used to find large buried iron pieces or utility and sewer lines. Their application to relic collecting was new, and manufacturers were only beginning to recognize the need to refine their sensitivity to find smaller and more discrete targets. Bray's advocacy of the use of metal detectors makes him a leader in the area of their archaeological use, but he was ahead of his time given the limitations of the technology.

Bray's map of the Rickey and Vaughn finds within the Reno-Benteen defense perimeter exists in several files as blueprint copies. The map was made using a plane table and alidade, a common archaeological mapping technique of the era, with the excavation trench locations denoted along with rifle pits, human remains burial sites, and other features. Bray also mapped the earlier cartridge case find locations that had been marked with wooden stakes (a few of those stakes were relocated and mapped during the 1985 archaeological project, but these were subsequently lost to the 1991 range fire). Normally it would be a simple matter, using Bray's control datum, to transfer his information to modern aerial and topographic maps along with 1985 and later archaeological data. Unfortunately, there is a cumulative error in Bray's map that makes it difficult to more than approximate his plotted finds on a modern map (figure 10). The source of the error has not yet been ascertained.

Park staff, led by seasonal park technician Frank Norris, attempted to restake the Rickey find locations in the summer of 1981 (Norris 1981) for interpretive purposes. They employed the compass-and-tape method but found significant errors between the few remaining original stakes and the locations derived from measured angles and distances taken from the Bray map. Norris was unaware of the cumulative error on the Bray map and was unable to reconcile the differences between his effort and that of Bray. The Bray 1958 map was scanned for this effort and a layer created in the GIS to overlay the modern aerial photography and topographic maps. The Bray map was georeferenced and rectified to modern map scales. The results show the unresolved error with the map. Bray's 1958 archaeological map should be used as representational only, and not for precise or detailed measurements.

Bray's notes were left with the park, where they reside today. His notes and plan drawings of the rifle pit excavations and some of his trenching efforts contain information that was not included in his report. The plan view of the two rifle pit excavations and his notes indicate that there were at least six cartridge cases in the fill of the

Figure 10. Approximate locations of the Don Rickey find spots and Robert Bray 1958 excavations. There is an unidentified error in the Bray map, and it cannot be accurately correlated to modern maps, but a reasonable approximation is possible using modern GIS georeferencing techniques.

46

pit and along the western berm or parapet of the western rifle pit
(Trench A, as he designated it). Also found in the fill were horse bones
(locations not specifically recorded), metal fragments probably from
tin cans, and at least seven glass bottle fragments. The glass was not
saved, according to his notes, so it not now possible to determine
the container type or even if these were 1876-era bottle fragments.
Bray believed they were fragments of liquor or wine bottles. The
eastern rifle pit, Trench B, contained a similar artifact assemblage,
with similar numbers represented. Bray recovered at least six cartridges and cases (three unfired, two fired .45-caliber, and one fired
.50-caliber), four pieces of clear glass, nine fragments of blue glass,
five fragments of amber glass, part of a tin can, a canteen cork, and
fragments of a piece of blue cloth. In each excavation artifactual
material was found near the surface to a depth of 20 inches, which
he considered the bottom of the original pit. Such depths are consistent with what the army called hasty entrenchments or rifle pits
during the nineteenth century (Mahan 1861).

Bray's barricade area trenching effort located the upper torso
and skull of a human skeleton, with army buttons still in place running the length of the torso. Horse bones were found in the trenches,
as was an isolated human humerus. Another excavation site, rifle pit
No. 1 (Rickey map point 8), located northeast of the current parking lot, yielded little evidence, and the trenching effort could not
clearly refine the size or edges of the pit, if indeed it was one. Rifle
pit No. 2 (Rickey map point 9) was also tested, with similar results,
although two fired army cartridges cases were found in the fill about
12 inches below the surrounding ground surface.

Bray continued his excavations by trenching in the presumed
hospital area. The work there was extensive and yielded a tin can,
pistol cartridge case, "hostile bullet" otherwise unidentified, animal
vertebra, and some unidentified bone fragments. The final Bray
excavation area was Rickey's map point 25, the so-called L-shaped
entrenchment. Bray recovered at least thirteen army blouse and iron
trouser buttons in the excavation as well as small cut nails, evidence
of a fire at the northeast end of the rifle pit, a cartridge, and the disarticulated remains of a partial human skeleton. Bray was unsure if
the L shape was a real cultural feature. He was sure that a packing
crate or similar box had been burned at the site, and the location

served as a resting place for one of the soldiers killed during the Reno-Benteen defense.

Rickey was transferred in 1969. In 1970 park historian B. William Henry conducted several metal detecting surveys of warrior positions on private lands around the Reno-Benteen defense site. He metal-detected Rickey and Vaughn's previously located warrior positions 4–4 and 7–7 and discovered two new positions, which he designated 9–9 and 10–10. Henry recovered 496 cartridge cases in many different calibers and four bullets (B. William Henry research notes dated Oct. 5, Nov. 8, 1969, and June 1970, Acc. 278, Field Notes).

Historian Jerome Greene (1986) was the first professional researcher after Henry to take a serious interest in plotting and analyzing the distribution pattern of many of these relic finds. He interviewed many collectors and local ranchers and combed the park files and archives for notes, letters, and memoranda related to finds by many of the early Little Bighorn researchers; he first published his research in 1973, with subsequent editions in 1978, 1979, and 1986. His work used relic finds coupled with documentary evidence and American Indian testimony to reevaluate the traditional view of the battle. Greene's analysis of the relic finds was insightful, and he developed probable routes for Reno's advance in the valley and subsequent retreat to the bluffs. Likewise, he built on Luce's work, using information from collectors and other sources to refine the Custer column movements to Medicine Tail Coulee and along Nye-Cartwright Ridge, thence to the main battlefield.

Greene (1986:47–51) was the first person to offer a critique of some of the early Little Bighorn researchers, like Kuhlman and Graham, who had nearly ignored tribe members' testimony regarding the battle. Greene noted that these early researchers often lacked a sense of the terrain on which the fights took place, and they did not understand cross-cultural approaches to analyzing testimony. Greene's argument for appropriate analysis and use of oral history went largely unheeded until Fox's (1988, 1993) anthropological approach to Lakota and Cheyenne testimony, rigorously tested against the archaeological data, brought the value of such testimony to the center of Little Bighorn research. Thus, the work of Greene, Rickey, and Bray built important foundations for developing research designs for the archaeological investigations that began in 1983.

One other avocational collector has published interpretations of the battle based on his relic finds. Henry Weibert (Weibert 1989; Weibert and Weibert 1985) began researching the battle in the 1940s, although he and his father had discovered the bones of a soldier while doing culvert work in 1925 or 1926. Weibert began collecting relics from Little Bighorn, Fort Custer, and other frontier sites in the late 1950s. He was a local rancher, had a solid knowledge of the land around the battlefield, and became acquainted with many of the researchers of the middle to late twentieth century. He began his serious collecting efforts about the time Vaughn and Rickey began their metal detecting efforts. Weibert worked the same area as Vaughn and Rickey, but he expanded the search to most lands surrounding the Reno-Benteen defense site, Weir Point, Nye-Cartwright Ridge, and the ridges around the Custer battlefield. As a rancher and lessee, he had access to more land than NPS employees, and he used his contacts to enable him to search far and wide for battle evidence. He worked with friends and family members for many years and repeatedly scoured lands outside the park for decades, but he does not appear to have been spurred to document his findings until the success of the mid-1980s professional archaeological investigations. Since much of the documentation was done from memory, the precise locations and types of finds in the many areas he collected must be carefully vetted.

The Advent of Battlefield Archaeology, 1977–2005

Robert Bray's 1958 archaeological work was the first professional archaeological investigation within the park, and it was not until 1977 that another professional archaeological survey was undertaken at Little Bighorn. Connie Bennett (1977) from MWAC conducted a visual survey of a waterline alignment at that time but found nothing. No further archaeological investigations were done at the site until a range fire in August 1983 burned the vegetation of Custer battlefield. Richard Fox, Jr., was contacted by park superintendent James Court to conduct a field reconnaissance to determine if relics and features related to the battle were visible. Fox (1983) did find artifacts and several features, and he recommended that a full-scale inventory project be implemented. Without Court's strong support for Fox and his findings it is unlikely further action would have been taken by regional park personnel.

Such a project was commenced in 1984 under the codirection of Douglas Scott from MWAC and Fox, then a Ph.D. graduate student at the University of Calgary. The project, and much of the subsequent work at the battlefield, was funded by the Custer Battlefield Historical and Museum Association. The 1984 project included a metal detecting inventory of the Custer battlefield and selected testing at several marble markers under the direction of Connor (Scott and Fox 1987). The marker testing yielded several human remains assemblages that all proved to be soldier related. Following in the footsteps of the 1984 investigations, the project was expanded in 1985 to inventory the Reno-Benteen defense site and conduct a stratified random sample excavation at 15 percent of the markers to determine which were incorrectly placed. The results of that work and a reassessment of the 1984 work were later published (Scott et al. 1989). Subsequent to the 1984 and 1985 projects, a variety of other research and cultural resource management investigations have taken place in and around the park (figure 11). The entire range of projects is discussed in chapter 5.

The archaeological projects were supported by donated funds from 1983 through 1994. The Custer Battlefield Historical and Museum Association, the Southwestern Parks and Monuments Association, and the Friends of the Little Bighorn donated over $110,000 to support archaeological work over the years. NPS funds and Federal Lands Highway Improvement Funds between 1994 and 2010 totaled over $85,000 specifically used to conduct cultural resource management projects to comply with the National Historic Preservation Act, as amended, within the park. The total expended on Little Bighorn archaeological work is about $195,000 in public and private funds as of 2010. The funding covered travel costs and some staff time to clean and analyze the artifacts. The project director's salary was paid from MWAC base funds through 1996, then as part of project costs thereafter. The projects were extensively supported, almost literally, by an army of volunteers (Barnard 1985). Without their help the work could not have been as well or productively accomplished. From 1984 through 2010 there were 271 different volunteers who contributed 12,840 hours to the various projects (figures 12, 13). Using the standard 2005 NPS volunteer

Figure 11. Areas inventoried by metal detector between 1984 and 2004. The line is the area inventoried in 2004 on either side of the tour road.

hourly rate equivalent of $17.55 per hour, this amounts to a contribution of over $221,000 in time and expertise, more than doubling the actual donated amounts.

The volume of paper generated to document that work is significant, including two master's theses, one Ph.D. dissertation, four books, three monographs, twenty-five published articles or book chapters, and thirty-seven short park service internal reports. One result of the archaeological work was the development and

Figure 12. One of the first groups of volunteers to assist on the Little Bighorn project. Back row: Murray Kloberdanz, Mike Parks; Middle row: Al Herem, Jess Schwidde, Ed Smyth, John Craig; Front row: Jim Lafollette, Richard A. Fox, Jr., Stanley Hart, Marlin Howe, Bob Johnson, Douglas D. Scott. Little Bighorn Battlefield National Monument.

Figure 13. The 2004 tour road archaeological team. Left to right, Thomas Sweeney, Dick Harmon, Chris Adams, Douglas Scott (in rear), Larry Ludwig, Carl Carlson-Drexler (in rear), Charles Haecker, Brooks Bond (in rear), Derek Batten, Conrand Angone (in rear), Dave Thorn, Dennis Gahagen (in rear), Larry Gibson, Phil Whitlow, Dave Powell, Tom Frew (in rear), Mike Clark, Harold Roeker (in rear), Anne Bond, Douglas McChristian. Midwest Archeological Center, National Park Service.

Figure 14. Excavations at the marble markers not only found human remains but captivated the public's imagination. Midwest Archeological Center, National Park Service.

publication of an archaeological model of battlefield behavior (Fox and Scott 1991) based on the Little Bighorn investigations, which became an internationally recognized standard of methodology and theory of the emerging field of battlefield and conflict archaeology.

Also springing from the Little Bighorn archaeological investigations were two more in-depth studies of specific issues. First, the analysis of the human remains caught the public attention (figure 14). Two sets of remains were identified (Scott 2004a; Scott and Connor 1986; Scott et al. 1989), and as a result of that attention additional remains, collected from the field in the nineteenth century, were found in the Smithsonian Institution and Armed Forces Institute of Pathology collections. These were analyzed and reported (Scott and Owsley 1991). The interest that effort generated led to a proposal to exhume seven graves in the National Cemetery that contained purported soldier remains found on the battlefield between 1903 and the 1940s (Scott 1992a).

The other research spinoff was identification of actual firearms used at the battle. Firearms identification procedures were applied to the study of weapons in public and private collections that had a reliable chain of evidence to suggest that they could have been used in the battle. Several firearms were positively identified (Scott and Harmon 1988a, 1988b, 2004). Some of this spinoff research was funded by the Winchester Gun Museum of Cody, Wyoming, through several Kinnican Arms Chair grants.

Compliance with Law

The National Historic Preservation Act of 1966 (NHPA) is the basic cultural resource legislation that the NPS and other public entities are guided by when dealing with archaeological or historic properties. Fox's (1983) initial post-fire assessment was initiated by the park as an emergency response to determine the effect of the fire on archaeological materials, but it was done without the park filing any compliance documents or research designs with either the Rocky Mountain Regional Office or the Montana State Historic Preservation Officer, which under the circumstances was understandably overlooked. The archaeological research design for the 1984 inventory work, developed by MWAC (Scott 1984a) for the park and regional office, took into account that the NHPA and NPS cultural resource guidance (then NPS 28 and now designated DO 28) noted that archaeological inventories of historic properties required an approved research design to comply with Section 110 of the act. Section 110 advocates the full archaeological and historical inventory of properties. The 1984 investigations were undertaken with this philosophy in mind.

Almost at once some NPS officials as well as other interested parties became concerned that the archaeological investigations, specifically the use of metal detectors, were in violation of Section 106 of the NHPA. Section 106 requires that any federal undertaking be reviewed by the State Historic Preservation Officer and potentially the staff of the Advisory Council on Historic Preservation to ensure that there are no significant impacts to a National Register property or that those impacts are properly mitigated. A brief meeting was held with NPS Washington office Cultural Resource Program leader Jerry Rogers in late May 1984 to provide information on the ongoing field operations and to suggest that Section 106 did not apply to the situation, and that the work should fall under Section 110 as a park-wide inventory effort. This approach was accepted.

The 1985 efforts built upon the success of the 1984 fieldwork followed the same approach, in that the investigations were to concentrate on the Reno-Benteen defense area to complete the archaeological inventory of the park, test some burial marker locations, and test Deep Ravine. Once again the research design, reviewed by park and regional office staff, took the approach that the work fell under Section 110, which allowed not only inventory but limited archaeological testing of properties. Renowned and retired NPS historian Robert Utley (1986, 2004) added fuel to the fire by disagreeing with the value of the 1984 investigations. Utley, coming from a strict constructionist view of historic preservation, voiced his concern that the battlefield, like all national parks, is a preserve of archaeological data and should never be used for research. He further espoused the view that only sites that were threatened in some manner should be archaeologically studied or mitigated. Utley's eminence in the field of historic preservation had a profound effect on the 1985 fieldwork. The work started in early May, but the Montana State Historic Preservation Officer and the Advisory Council staff in Denver became concerned that the project did not comply with Section 106 review requirements. They rejected the idea that the project was a Section 110 undertaking that did not require as stringent a review process. Their concerns shut the project fieldwork down for several days until a compromise could be worked out. NPS agreed to revise and resubmit the review documents under Section 106, primarily because the use of metal detectors to find and recover artifacts was such a new and, in state's and council's view, unproven technique. With the passage of time and the extensive use and proven value of metal detectors as an inventory tool on battlefields as well as other sites, the technique is now routinely accepted as part of standard survey methods. The metal detector is now a recognized and standard tool of historic archaeologists.

Informing the Public

The public has been especially captivated by the archaeological investigations at Little Bighorn, and this widespread interest led to the development of an archaeology public relations campaign. Fox's initial work generated a great deal of interest, and it was recognized during the formulation of the research designs during the winter of 1984 that the media and public interest would continue. From its inception, the project research plan included a specific element that addressed the need to deal effectively with the public's unflagging interest in the Little Bighorn story.

The original plan called for a spokesperson to coordinate activities (Scott 1987b). Also acting as press contact, this individual would handle telephone inquiries and meet with and brief the press on the project's status. When field operations actually began in 1984, the park superintendent assumed the duties of coordinator. In response to overwhelming public interest, a literal media blitz descended on the park. Because nearly 40 percent of the superintendent's time was devoted to this special project—time taken away from his normal press of business—a professor of journalism and project volunteer, Warren "Sandy" Barnard, took over as full-time coordinator during the 1985 fieldwork (Barnard 1985; Mangum 1987b).

Daily early morning briefings were proposed and proved to be very valuable. Each evening, archaeologists reviewed the results of the day's findings, planned the next day's assignments and work areas, and determined what interpretations would be given to the coordinator the next morning. The coordinator thus received the latest details on important discoveries, current project status, and the location of fieldwork. The coordinator, in turn, prepared press releases, posted information at the entrance of the visitor center, and furnished the park's interpreters and staff with copies of all information for public use. This kept the information fresh and uniform and helped avoid the dangers of off-the-cuff comments and interpretations.

Questions from the public directed to park interpreters and accessible field archaeologists set the tone for the interpretation (figure 15). The public was most interested in what types of artifacts were being found and how—not if, but how—the archaeological study was changing history. In response to the public's demands, the team implemented several approaches to what was termed "field interpretation." First and foremost was the daily briefing posted at the visitor center entrance and distributed to the interpreters. The briefing statements contained information on the types and quanti-

Figure 15. Dr. P. Willey, a project volunteer from the University of California–Chico, is being interviewed by a reporter during the 1989 project. Media interest was intense during the 1984 and 1985 field seasons and continued for all of the fieldwork efforts, although it was generally limited to local media in subsequent years. Midwest Archeological Center, National Park Service.

ties of artifacts found. The briefing also attempted to ensure that any informational statements placed the finds in context. If the archaeological work was focusing on the so-called Last Stand Hill, then the briefing included the historical information relevant to that element of the battle. If the archaeological data appeared at odds with the traditional interpretation, this was pointed out. No conclusions were made, but the briefings stressed that future planned, detailed analysis of all the project data would help resolve discrepancies.

A temporary display was also established in the visitor center. The display contained a few traditional archaeology tools, a variety of artifacts found during the investigations, a few photographs of fieldwork in progress, and text to explain the process briefly. This display drew a significant amount of attention and generated numerous questions. The staff interpreters used the display as a means to not only tell the archaeological story but discuss the varying historical theories on the battle. They could then point out how archaeology could help confirm or reject one or more of those opinions.

A third level of interpretation scheduled during the project was small group tours for in-field interpretation by the archaeologists. At the location, usually the site of an excavation for human remains, the archaeologist would present an overview of the project and a summary of findings. The primary focus of the 15- to 20-minute presentation was the work actually being conducted before the visitors. Every effort was made to stress the roles of both historic archaeology and analytical laboratory techniques in the study of historic sites. In essence, the presentation was an attempt to inform the public about the processes of archaeology.

When the archaeologists were working in accessible areas, visitors tended to congregate to watch them. An archaeologist was assigned to provide impromptu interpretations about the locations and answer the torrents of questions. In numerous cases, the interest was so great that a single interpretive event often ran to nearly an hour.

The staff interpreters were well versed in the battle's history, and most had some interest in the material culture of the era. Thus, a natural feedback system developed between the archaeologists and park interpreters, which kept the information flowing in a positive, two-way loop. Archaeological interpretations of specific elements of the battle were literally changing daily, and the interpreters were able to share these changes with the public within 24 hours.

Early in the project a means was devised to help the public understand the archaeological process. The approach, which met with great success, involved comparing the archaeological investigation to a crime scene investigation. Most people could easily relate to the analogy of historians as detectives interviewing victims, suspects, and witnesses and archaeologists as forensic personnel gathering the physical evidence for a more detailed analysis. Visitors readily accepted the concept that oral accounts could be suspect—for example, someone did not remember correctly, did not see part of the action, or was opinionated. Archaeological data, or the forensic analyses, provided a more complete picture of the situation than oral accounts could alone. As physical evidence, artifacts do not have opinions, and they are the actual remnants of the battle, although their position and context (provenience) has to be interpreted. It was stressed that the archaeological artifacts, as they were found, were deposited as a result of decisions made in the past. Perhaps neither those decisions nor the processes of making them could be reconstructed from the artifacts and their provenience, but the results of such decisions could be interpreted.

From the archaeologist's point of view, the opportunity to conduct public interpretation was invaluable. On the one hand, it was enlightening to witness firsthand the public's perception of what archaeology is and how it contributes to understanding the past. On the other hand, it gave archaeologists the opportunity to explain field and laboratory techniques to the visitors. Most archaeologist-to-visitor interpretation took place at one of the many marker sites that dot the field and purport to identify where soldiers died in battle. The visitors' fascination with the recovery of human remains at these excavations provided an ideal opportunity to explain why the study of the bones is important and what a variety of detailed scientific examinations can tell the archaeologist about the people who died in the battle. In no case did a visitor voice an opinion that the excavation of marker sites was improper. In fact, descendants of the soldiers killed at the battle visited the excavations and expressed their approval of the investigations.

There were pitfalls to the interpretive effort, as is the case with any project. First, the amount of time project archaeologists devoted to interpretation was not adequately planned for in the project schedule. Field adjustments had to be made, and a great deal of planning went into maximizing the archaeologists' exposure to the public without jeopardizing the project mission. Second, the public demanded that immediate conclusions be made in the field. It took a great deal of thought and constraint to answer questions when the data required detailed analysis before conclusions could be drawn. It was also recognized that not all the public's questions were possible to answer. It was important to help the public realize that much more behind-the-scenes work was required to formulate conclusions.

Just as there were pitfalls, there were benefits. The positive personal interactions between the archaeological team, the staff interpreters, and the visitors, as well as the project's public visibility, are credited with a 20 percent increase in park visitation. A bonus of the increased visitation and project publicity was a 150 percent increase in sales at the Museum Association bookstore. Association membership also tripled in the same time period. Since the Association funded the majority of the archaeological investigations, the archaeology was, in a sense, paying for itself. The Custer Battlefield Historical and Museum Association ceased to be an NPS cooperating association in 1993. The new cooperating association, Southwest Parks and Monuments, continued the tradition of support for park archaeological investigations with the study of adjacent private lands in 1994 (Scott and Bleed 1997), and that organization continues to offer the various archaeological publications in its on-site sales outlet.

Archaeology of the Little Bighorn has continued to engender public interest, and during the 1980s and early 1990s the park developed an archaeological slide show and short documentary film—"Brushing Away Time: The Story of Archeology at the Little Bighorn Battlefield"—which was shown in the visitor center on a regular schedule. During the 1980s and 1990s the results of the archaeological work were included in personal interpretive programs, park literature, and temporary and later permanent museum exhibits. In 2003 two wayside exhibits were created that are oriented to the archaeological discoveries. One is located on Last Stand Hill and interprets the Seventh Cavalry horse grave discovered there in 2000; it is now commemorated by a white stone marker similar in design to the soldier's markers. The second wayside exhibit is located just off the walkway to Last Stand Hill, and it focuses on archaeology in the park. In addition, other interpretive wayside exhibits were installed at various points along the park tour road at the same time. Those interpretive panels, though not mentioning the archaeological finds specifically, incorporated the latest historical discoveries and archaeological findings to provide an integrated interpretation for the visiting public of the battle sequence and events.

Another public legacy of the archaeological investigations is the number of television and other documentaries made between 1985 and 2010 that featured the archaeological work in some form or another. At least fourteen made-for-television documentaries were filmed that focused on the archaeological work or used the archaeological information as part of the program (figure 16). The documentaries were shown on U.S. Public Television, The History Channel,

Figure 16. Douglas Scott being interviewed by the Australian Broadcasting Company for a documentary on the archaeology of the battle. At least fourteen such documentaries have been made and aired worldwide since 1985. Midwest Archeological Center, National Park Service.

Arts and Entertainment Network, Discovery Channel, Archaeology Channel, Smithsonian segments, ZDF (German) television, Italian television, Granada (English) Television, BBC (English) Television, and Australian Broadcast Company television, among others. Such global exposure of the archaeological work is nearly unprecedented in North American archaeology.

Archaeological Methods at the Site

Since 1984 all archaeological inventory projects conducted in and around the park by the NPS and MWAC have followed the same general methodology (figures 17, 18). Each project applied the methods with some modification of mapping technology or other methodological adaptations, but each modification was predicated on advances in method and theory that enabled better data collection and analysis.

Figure 17. Typical metal detecting transect line at work during the 2004 tour road inventory project. Little Bighorn Battlefield National Monument.

Figure 18. Former park historian Douglas McChristian and volunteer Conrad Angone excavate a target during the 2004 tour road project. The individuals in the background are discussing a recent find. Midwest Archeological Center, National Park Service.

The Little Bighorn Battlefield National Monument data were initially recorded using optical transits, then with electronic distant meters (EDM), then with total station transit technology, and beginning in 2004 using GPS. Initially, in 1984, a grid system divided into 100 m by 100 m units was established by a professional contract land surveyor, on the Custer field, to facilitate the recording of artifacts (Scott and Fox 1987). The grid was established so that its arbitrary origin (0,0) was near the nearby Garryowen post office, and the grid was oriented with the fenceline of Custer battlefield, about 39 degrees west of true north. The grid numbers were higher moving north and east. The southeast fence corner on Custer battlefield was established as North 6400 m and East 3000 m (N64E30).

When the same surveyor set the grid for the Reno-Benteen defense site in 1985, he inadvertently numbered the east-to-west line the reverse of the 1984 scheme. The grid numbers are higher as one moves west, or opposite the Custer numbering system. During the 1985 fieldwork that numbering system was not corrected. The 1989 (Scott 1991a, 1991b) field investigations required establishing of a series of 1 m square units within the larger 100 m square units. The excavation units were established at the Reno-Benteen defense site and were numbered in the correct order—grid numbers increasing west to east. With the advent of GPS technology, the project used GPS units to record field data (figure 19).

The 1984 through 2003 investigations relied on computer-aided design technology to produce project maps acquired from the transit field data. Initially Fastdraft (figure 20) was used, then Auto-CAD in its various permutations allowed detailed and accurate data plotting and analysis. Sokkia Map was used as the initial field data processing software from 1989 through 2003. In 2003 ArcView's geographic information system was employed, and in 2005 all earlier CAD data were transferred to GIS format. The first attempt to transfer the earlier CAD data was made by Maj. Christopher Benson and a class in GIS at the U.S. Air Force Academy (Benson 2005). The effort also included at attempt at employing the Track Analyst function to see if new insights into the battle could be obtained. Subsequently Michael Athanson, a Ph.D. student at Oxford University, used the distribution of fired bullets to test the validity of some of the interpretations of troop movement. He employed external ballistic simulation coupled with target visibility obtained using GIS

Figure 19. Former MWAC employees Harold Roeker and Carl Carlson-Drexler display the GPS unit used in mapping features and artifact finds during the 2004 tour road project. Midwest Archeological Center, National Park Service.

view shed analysis (Athanson 2006:1–7). His results correlated well with the postulated soldier and warrior positions and the original data analysis (Scott et al. 1989). The archaeological GIS data set was edited and updated to meet current park service metadata standards in 2009 and 2010 (figures 21, 22).

Essentially each investigation followed a set of general field investigation methods. Fieldwork consisted of metal detecting and visual inventory using the transect method. Transect widths, and thus sampling intensity, were determined by each project's requirements. Much of the work was done using a sampling level or detector spacing of about 3–5 m to achieve an approximately 35 percent sampling of the park and surrounding areas. Detailed or more intense detecting work, such as was done prior to construction of the Indian Memorial, used metal detector spacing of 2 m with transects run across the project area in one direction and another set perpendicular to the first to ensure as full an artifact recovery as possible.

Standard archaeological data recording methods were used in each phase of the operations. Individual artifacts, spatially discrete clusters of identical specimens, and associated dissimilar specimens

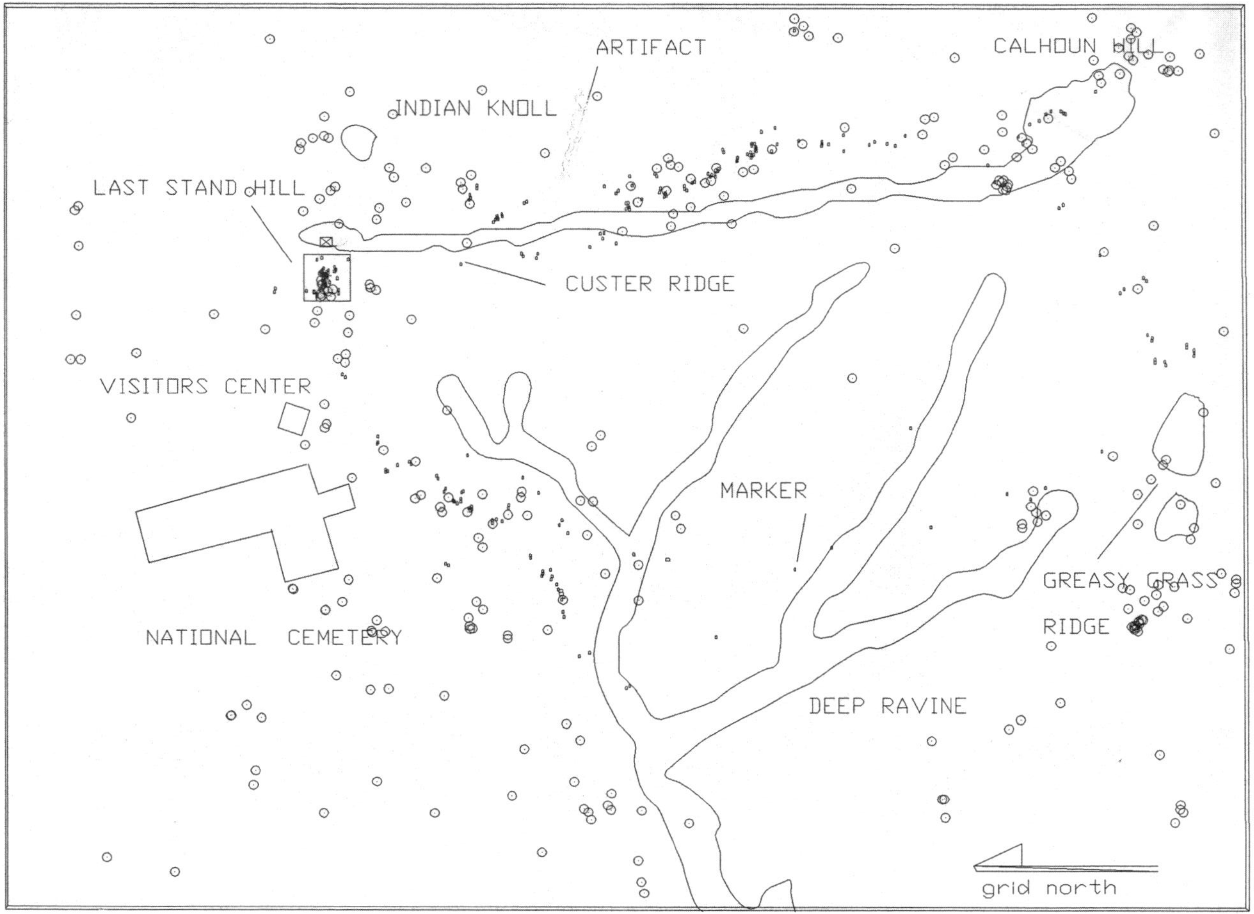

Figure 20. The first artifact distribution maps used Fastdraft and early versions of AutoCAD to create figures for the reports. Here distributions of army-related cartridge cases are shown. Midwest Archeological Center, National Park Service.

65

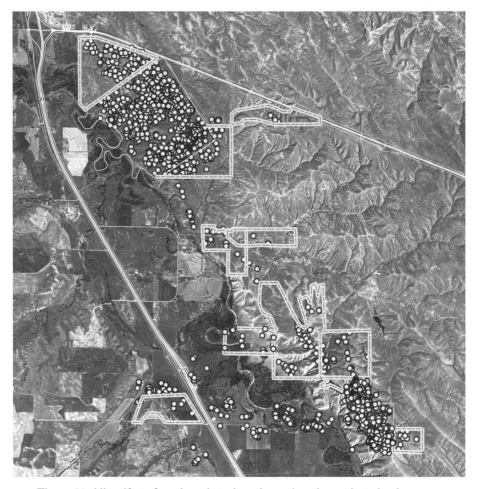

Figure 21. All artifacts found or plotted on the park and on private lands and the areas formally inventoried between 1984 and 2004, with all data transferred to GIS. Midwest Archeological Center, National Park Service.

received unique field specimen (FS) numbers. Field notes and standardized MWAC forms were used to record field data. Selected in-place artifact specimens and topography were photographed and recorded in black-and-white film, color slides, and later digital format.

Inventory work included three sequential operations: survey, recovery, and recording. During survey the crew located and marked artifact finds. The recovery crew followed and carefully uncovered subsurface finds, leaving them in place. The recording team plotted individual artifact locations using an optical transit, an EDM transit, a Sokkia Total Station transit, or a Trimble Pro XL global positioning system, depending on the technology available at the time of the field investigations. The recovery recording team assigned field specimen numbers and collected the specimens.

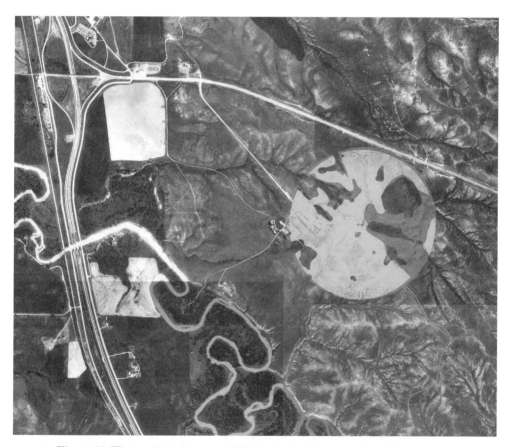

Figure 22. The analytical power of GIS is shown here: a weapons fan or viewshed analysis of what the soldiers on Last Stand Hill could see is shown as gray areas, and what they could not see up to 600 m (circle), the effective carbine range. This analysis clearly shows blind spots, mostly low areas that the warriors could and did exploit to get within effective firearm range to destroy the surviving men of the Seventh Cavalry.

Metal detecting operations were designed to locate subsurface metallic items. Visual inspection of the surface was carried out concurrently with the metal detector survey. Various brands of metal detectors were employed during the fieldwork. The standardization of machines (i.e., all one brand), though perhaps methodologically desirable, was highly impractical during the 1980s. Like models operated on the same frequency, causing interference at close intervals. Thus the metal detecting teams alternated different brands of machines on the line to ensure adequate survey coverage and minimize electronic interference.

Once the collected materials were returned to MWAC they were cleaned, sorted, and analyzed. The methods employed in cleaning the artifacts were MWAC standards. Essentially they consisted of washing the accumulated dirt and mud from each artifact and then determining the condition of the artifact to see whether it required further cleaning or conservation. For analysis and identification purposes some metallic items required a treatment with E-Z-Est (a commercial coin cleaner found to be very effective in removing verdigris and not harmful to the underlying metal) to remove oxides that built up on them during their years in the ground. Other objects were subjected to electrolytic reduction preservation methods, and dilute glycolic acid was used to clean cartridge cases and bullets during the first two years of the project. After cleaning and stabilization, each artifact was rebagged in a self-sealing clear plastic bag with its appropriate FS number and other relevant information on the bag. The artifacts were then identified, sorted, and analyzed.

The identification, sorting, and analysis consisted of dividing the artifacts into classes of like objects and then subsorting them into further identifiable discrete types. Sorting and identification of the artifacts were undertaken by personnel experienced with artifacts of this period, who compared the artifacts with type collections and with standard reference materials. Firearms identification procedures followed established analytical standards (Harris 1980; Hatcher et al. 1977; Scott and Fox 1987; Scott et al. 1989).

Excavation methods employed during the testing of the selected marble markers and at the prehistoric sites followed standard MWAC procedures. Individual units were usually 2 by 2 m (see figure 14) and were excavated with shovels, trowels, and smaller hand tools as required. All excavated material was screened through 0.25-inch wire mesh screens. Artifacts were mapped using standard practices and bagged according to provenience. Post-excavation processing followed the same basic procedure as the metal-detected materials. All excavations were backfilled by hand after documentation and recording of the unit. No soil samples were collected. Natural plant succession was maintained after backfilling operations.

Evaluation of Inventory Methods

In 1985, Richard Fox (Scott et al. 1989) designed and implemented an evaluation phase to test the validity of the metal detecting procedure used throughout the project. The evaluation was a simple one. Seven previously inventoried 100 m by 100 m units were selected and reinventoried with a more detailed procedure. The selected units represented areas on the Custer field that had yielded a large quantity of artifacts (N6500 E3000), a moderate quantity (N7100 E2700 and N7500 E2400), a small quantity (N6600 E2200 and N7300 E2000), and two areas at Reno-Benteen defense site, one (N2400 E2400) representing a warrior position and the other (N2000 E2300) an army position. The relative quantity of artifacts was a subjective judgment of the archaeologists. The reinventory procedure divided the units into a series of transects 2 m wide. The metal detecting staff members were lined up and each walked the area very slowly, sweeping it with the detector in an arc four to six feet wide. When one transect was completed, the crew supervisor pivoted the group to the next set of transects and a new sweep began. The project procedures for pin flagging and artifact recording were used.

Each reinventoried 100 m square yielded about twice the number of artifacts recovered during the initial detector sweeps. Statistically, this is a 30–35 percent sample of all the artifacts. From a statistical point of view this sample size is well above a minimum necessary to assess and interpret patterns and spatial distributions. The artifacts were cross-tabulated by the number of artifact classes and types of artifacts initially recovered against those found in the evaluation phase. In evaluating the data, it was determined that the artifacts were truly representative of the metal-detected artifact population and that a valid sample for interpreting the patterns of artifact distribution had been recovered using the project methodology.

Subsequent mitigation work on the Indian Memorial site and along the tour road (Scott 1998a, 2006) used detailed metal detecting with transect spacing of 2 m or less and additional transects run perpendicular to the first set. Both mitigation project results reinforced the validity of the original sampling design and artifact recovery. The number of artifacts in the various classes and types are also representative of all the artifacts on the battlefield and are also a valid sample of the metal in the ground.

One additional test of metal detector efficiency was undertaken in July 2010 to evaluate the effectiveness of newer very low frequency (VLF) metal detectors relative to a newly marketed pulse induction (PI) metal detector on two previously inventoried areas. Two areas were chosen for the test, an identified warrior position on Greasy Grass Ridge and a soldier position, known as the Finley-Finckle or Company C position, which includes the locations of five marble markers. Both areas were metal-detected with VLF machines in 1984 during the initial park-wide inventory. That search employed a 3 m spacing that was designed to achieve an approximately 35 percent statistically valid sample of the park (Scott and Fox 1987). Each area was also subsequently metal-detected again at 2 m intervals during the Tour Road mitigation project (Scott 2006) using later-model VLF machines.

Each area yielded additional artifacts. Fifty-seven percent were not battle related, 43 percent were battle related, 90 percent were found by the VLF machines, and 10 percent were found by the PI metal detector alone. The test indicated that the 1984 sample strategy was sound in that it did recover a representative sample of the range of artifact types present. The PI metal detector did find about 10 percent more than the VLF machines. Most of those items were either deeper than the capability of the VLF machines or were very small. The test grids indicated that the PI metal detector has the potential to increase artifact recovery in areas where materials may include very small or deeply buried artifacts.

An aside on the inventory work is in order. During the 1984 fieldwork about eight individuals approached the park offering to find the human remains in Deep Ravine and elsewhere on the battlefield by dowsing for bone. Each individual was allowed to walk over portions of Deep Ravine that were under investigation and areas along the Deep Ravine Trail. Each dowser used some form of wire rod that either crossed or separated when they believed they found buried bone. One individual had small alligator clips soldered to his rods to which he clipped bone that he brought with him, for he believed the rods were then sensitized to the type of item he was trying to find. The archaeological team later validated a sample of the locations. In each case the dowsers were found to be 100 percent in error. No human remains or other archaeological materials were discovered at any location identified by any dowser.

| # Battlefield Archaeological Investigations

Chronology and Findings

Since 1984 more than 1,900 acres of land in and around Little Big-horn Battlefield National Monument have be surveyed and inventoried. The park itself consists of 765 acres, all inventoried in 1984 and 1985. In subsequent years more than 1,200 acres outside the park boundary—including private and Crow tribal property—have been inventoried (see figure 11). In the process, more than five thousand battle-related artifacts have been collected, analyzed, reported, and cataloged.

This chapter provides a chronological listing, narrative summaries of archaeological investigations undertaken in or around the park by professional archaeologists, and discussions of what the recovered artifacts can tell us about the battle, the combatants, and the nature of battlefield archaeology.

Chronology of Archaeological Investigations

1956–59: Robert Bray, Don Rickey. The first formal investigations conducted at the battlefield. Metal detecting and excavations were confined to the Reno-Benteen entrenchment area. Artifacts and three human burials were recovered (Bray 1958).

1977: Connie Bennett. A preconstruction inventory of the battlefield. No resources were identified (Bennett 1977).

1983: Richard Fox. A reconnaissance survey of the battlefield conducted after the 1983 range fire. Some artifacts
were found and some possible cultural features identified (Fox 1983).

1984: Douglas Scott and Richard Fox. Metal detector survey of the Custer battlefield and testing of several marble marker locations. Fox's possible features were tested
and found to be natural features (Bozell 1985; Scott
1984a, 1984b; Scott and Fox 1987).

1985: Douglas Scott and Richard Fox. Continuation of the
1984 investigations of the battlefield. A metal detector
inventory was completed at the Reno-Benteen defense
site. Stratified sampling of the marble markers was
undertaken and an inventory of prehistoric resources
completed (Bozell 1989; Fox 1983; Haynes 1989; Heinz
1989; Phillips 1989; Scott 1987a, 1987b, 1987c, 1987d,
1990, 2002a, 2002b; Scott and Connor 1986; Scott et
al. 1989; Scott and Harmon 1988a, 1988b; Snow and
Fitzpatrick 1989). A coincidental study of cremated
remains was also undertaken (Scott 1987a).

1986: Melissa Connor. Exhumation of a grave in the
National Cemetery containing battlefield remains in
preparation for the reburial of all human remains (Connor 1986; Pieters and Barnard 1986; Scott and Connor
1988; Scott et al. 1988).

1989: Douglas Scott. Evaluative testing of two prehistoric
sites, with negative results (Scott 1989a).

1989: Douglas Scott. Investigation of a find of human
remains near the Reno Retreat Crossing (Scott and
Snow 1991b).

1989: Douglas Scott. Mitigation of the Reno-Benteen equipment disposal site (Connor 1991; Haynes 1991; Heinz
1990; Scott 1991a, 1991b). Mitigation of a marker on
Custer battlefield (Scott and Snow 1991a).

1992: Douglas Scott. Exhumation of seven graves in the
National Cemetery. At least ten individuals thought to
be Seventh Cavalry soldiers were exhumed from the
seven graves (Scott 1992a, 1992b, 1992d, 1992e; Scott
and Owsley 1991; Scott et al. 1998; Willey 1993). A

small reinventory of the site of the Deep Ravine overlook was also conducted (Scott 1992c).

1993: Douglas Scott. Mapping of the Reno attack and retreat lines. General artifact find locations on private property in the Little Bighorn River valley were recorded to help refine the actual lines (Scott 1993a). A visual inventory was also conducted of the Reno-Benteen walkway removal prior to laying a new concrete walking trail. No archaeological features or artifacts were noted (Scott 1993c).

1993: Melissa Connor. Exhumation of a disturbed burial site on the Pitsch property (Connor 1994).

1994: Douglas Scott, Peter Bleed. Metal detecting inventory of 1,000 acres of private land adjacent to the battlefield (Scott and Bleed 1997).

1994: Douglas Scott. Walkover of burned area. A grass fire in August burned about 200 acres. No artifacts were exposed or effected. No damage to the markers was observed (Scott 1994).

1995: Douglas Scott. Remote sensing test and inventory of soil percolation test area for new sewage system (Scott 1995).

1995: Idaho National Engineering Lab. Testing of a rapid geophysical surveyor in Deep Ravine, at Reno-Benteen, at selected markers, and in Cemetery Ravine (Josten and Carpenter 1995).

1996: Douglas Scott. Metal detecting of portions of the Farron Iron property located in Cedar Coulee and Sharpshooter Hill near the Reno-Benteen defense site. Artifacts confirming the line of movement to Weir Point were recovered (Scott 1996b).

1996: Coleman Research. Geophysical remote sensing studies in Deep Ravine, Cemetery Ravine, and Reno-Benteen in an attempt to locate buried features (Applied Ground Imaging (1996; Coleman Research 1996). An anomaly was identified in Deep Ravine that is consistent with historical accounts and geomorphology, suggesting a site for the burial of the purported twenty-eight missing men.

1998: Douglas Scott. Detailed visual and metal detector inventory of the proposed Indian Memorial site. Battle-related artifacts were located (Scott 1998a). Additional inventory was undertaken on the Iron property and the Stops property in the Little Bighorn valley, with the recovery of a few additional artifacts (Scott 1998b).

1999: Douglas Scott. Inventory of the site of a new water gauging station on the Little Bighorn River below the park housing area, with negative results (Scott 1999b). Selected areas adjacent to the Reno-Benteen defense site and private lands in the river valley were inventoried and a variety of artifacts collected (Scott 2000a). The site of Custer's June 23 campsite on Rosebud River was inventoried, with positive results (Scott 2000b).

1999: Patrick Walker-Kuntz, Sunday Walker-Kuntz. Visual inventory along the park boundary where it joins Highway 212 as part of a Montana Highway project, with negative results (Walker-Kuntz and Walker-Kuntz 1999).

2002: Douglas Scott. Geophysical investigations to locate the horse burial pit from 1881 (De Vore 2002a, 2002b; Nickel 2002). Mitigation excavations of the horse pit were undertaken to document the site during construction of a walkway to the new Indian Memorial (Scott 2002c).

2002: Steven De Vore. Investigation of human remains discovered during reconstruction of the parking lot at Last Stand Hill (De Vore 2002c). De Vore determined that they were bones overlooked during exhumation of the Fort Phil Kearny cemetery for relocation to Custer National Cemetery.

2004: Douglas Scott. Detailed metal detecting of the tour road to mitigate potential effects of road rehabilitation. The entire road from Last Stand Hill including the Reno-Benteen parking lot and 20 m either side of the road were inventoried, as was the Calhoun Hill loop. More than three hundred artifacts were found (Scott 2006). The visitor center grounds were also inventoried in anticipation of planning activities that might call for the expansion of the center. The area is highly disturbed, and no battle era materials were found (Scott 2005a).

2005: Steven De Vore. Geophysical investigations of the Reno-Benteen parking lot area and adjacent land to determine if buried rifle pits might be impacted by the tour road rehabilitation. Two anomalies, consistent in size with rifle pits but outside the area of impact, were recorded (De Vore 2005).

2010: Douglas Scott. Metal detecting inventory of the Little Bighorn River oxbows, with negative findings. Two types of metal detectors were tested in area previously inventoried, and changes in the oxbow configuration through time were investigated (Scott 2010a).

2011: Chris Finley. Visual inventory of flood impacted areas of Deep Ravine Trail and Little Bighorn River. No artifacts or sites were found to be affected (Chris Finley, personal communication, September 15, 2011).

2011: Chris Finley. Visual inventory and metal detecting of possible new visitor center site adjacent to Highway 212 and park entrance road. There were no battle-related finds (Chris Finley, personal communication, September 15, 2011).

Events of the Battle: The Archaeological Evidence

The chronological listing above is a simple laundry list of investigation efforts and results; it does not convey a full sense of how much of the battlefield has been investigated, or of the specific elements of the story it tells. The narrative descriptions of these investigations in this section, organized by battle event and locale, take detail the material evidence recovered in these investigations.

CUSTER TRAIL

Richard Fox, in association with the National Forest Service, began a project in 1992, deemed the Custer Trail Project, to inventory and document various military routes through the Little Missouri Badlands and sites associated with the 1876 expedition. Field investigations took place in 1992, 1993, 1994, 1999, and 2011. The project sought to documented trails, road cuts or areas of leveling, possible bridge locations, as well as campsites. The areas investigated had been traversed by several different military expeditions including Sully's expedition against the Minnesota Sioux, David Stanley's 1872 and 1873 Northern Pacific Railroad surveys, Terry's route during the 1876 Sioux campaign, as well as Crook's expedition after the Little Bighorn battle. Several military-related campsites have been documented, but none can be definitively associated with the 1876 campaign or Custer and the Seventh Cavalry (Fox draft report, n.d., and personal communication, September 27, 2011).

CUSTER'S JUNE 23 CAMP

Frank Anders (1983) and Laudie Chorne (1997) charted the Seventh Cavalry route from Fort Abraham Lincoln through the camp of June 22, 1876, when Custer left the Yellowstone River valley and began his fateful march into history. The only Custer column campsite to be archaeologically investigated to date was done in fall 1999 (Scott 2000b), when initial archaeological reconnaissance was conducted at the site of Custer's June 23 camp on Rosebud Creek (figure 23). Landowner Jack Bailey allowed access to about 50 acres of land north of Lame Deer. Only a handful of artifacts (figure 24) were recovered, a .45–55 cartridge case, the back of a general service button, a trouser button, a broken mess spoon, a crushed camp boiler, a badly rusted one-gallon can that may have held roasted coffee beans, a Burden horseshoe, and the tips of several horseshoe nails found near a firepit. Taken together, these artifacts are the lost bits of the Seventh's camp equipage from a thirteen-hour overnight stay by more than six hundred men. The fired cartridge case suggests that the no-firing orders were not rigorously enforced in some element of the command, and the firepit and clipped horseshoe nail tips suggest that some farrier probably reshoed at least one horse before turning in for the evening. The findings, though limited in number, are consistent with relic finds recovered from Seventh Cavalry campsites associated with the 1874 Black Hills expedition and documented by Horsted et al. (2009).

Located near the June 23 campsite is the site of the Lakota Sundance where Sitting Bull had a vision of the upcoming victory by

Figure 23. Monument and area of Custer's command's June 23, 1876, evening layover or campsite. The area was tested by archaeological metal detecting in 1999. Midwest Archeological Center, National Park Service.

seeing soldiers falling upside down into the camp. Also nearby is Deer Medicine Rocks (figure 25), an important prehistoric and historic sandstone feature that has rock art from many different ages carved and pecked into its surface. Deer Medicine Rocks is not only highly significant to the Sioux War era but has been and continues to be an American Indian sacred site. It was recently listed as a National Historic Landmark.

RENO'S VALLEY FIGHT

This physical evidence relates to Maj. Marcus Reno's deployment and attack on the American Indian village. Jason Pitsch metal-

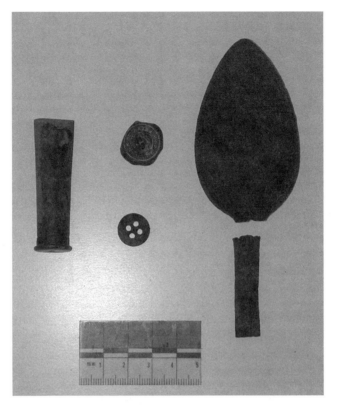

Figure 24. A .45-55 fired cartridge case, general service
button back, trouser button, and spoon recovered at
the Seventh Cavalry June 23, 1876, campsite. Midwest
Archeological Center, National Park Service.

detected his family's land and some adjacent landowners' property for several years seeking to clarify the site of Reno's attack on
the southern end of the village (figure 26) and developed a private
museum—the Reno Battlefield Museum—near Interstate 95 where
it intersects Reno's first skirmish line. Pitsch plotted his finds on
maps and aerial photographs and kept his artifacts organized by
find area. In 1993, Scott (1993a) mapped the location of many of
Pitsch's finds, including evidence of Reno's skirmish lines in the valley, elements of the timber fight, and the retreat to the river.

Perhaps more exciting, in some ways, was the opportunity to
see and map Pitsch's finds in Sitting Bull's Hunkpapa camp circle,

Figure 25. Deer Medicine Rocks is a prominent landmark and sacred site and was so in 1876. Custer's command camped near the rocks on June 23, 1876, and passed by it on June 24. Midwest Archeological Center, National Park Service.

located just north of the Garryowen store, and a recently discovered Sioux camp on the east side of the river. These were the southern-most camps in the large village that lay scattered down the Little Bighorn valley for over a mile. The Cheyenne camps were at the northern end of the village, with different Lakota bands between them and Sitting Bull's camp. Pitsch found the Sioux campsite east of the river and extensive evidence of warriors firing at the bluffs and Weir Point before the story of Spotted Tail's disaffected warriors became generally known to present-day researchers. Lt. Oscar Long (Brust 1995) learned of the story from a group of young disaffected warriors of Spotted Tail's band and reported it to his superiors. The Brulé warriors set up an essentially all-male camp on the east side of

Figure 26. Finds made by Jason Pitsch and mapped in 1993, plotted on a modern aerial photograph.

the Little Bighorn just north of Weir Point and across the river from the other Lakota camp circles. When Reno's attack began, these young men joined the fray by rushing up the ravines that led to Weir Point and along the east side of the river, where they fired on the soldiers. That story and a map of the events were unknown to most Little Bighorn researchers until it was published in the 1995 issue of *Greasy Grass*. The map shows the camp to be on the east side of the river in a location consistent with that found by Pitsch.

Artifacts recovered in the camp areas are highly diverse. Because the sites had been plowed and one area leveled for irrigation, the identified perimeters were mapped as concentrations rather than individual find sites. The artifacts from the campsites are typical of camp debris. They include cooking vessel fragments, beads, firearms parts, individual decorative items, and other basic camp furniture. The village sites yielded large quantities of trade goods to Pitsch's metal detector. The debris was scattered over a broad area.

Pitsch also found numerous warrior-associated fired cartridge cases on a bench just east of the east bank campsite. The presence of those cartridge cases as well as a few army bullets suggest this was the site of a group of warriors who fired on soldiers at Wier Point.

Pitsch found eleven .45–55 cartridge cases in the fields west of the Garryowen post office. These cases were in a roughly linear alignment from northwest to southeast. Presumably they identify Reno's first skirmish line. The angled alignment is more in keeping with an attack on the village site at Garryowen than an east-west alignment as postulated by Vaughn (1966). A due east-west alignment would cause the soldiers to face obliquely away from the now-identified campsites. The archaeological data suggest that the village was near the river. The river flows to the northwest, and the various camp circles would follow along its contour. Logic dictates that the attack lines would be angled to meet the enemy. The skirmish line cases were found in a field that is subject to cultivation, so some of the cases may be out of context. The fact that such a linear alignment is present strongly suggests that pattern disruption by agricultural practices is minimal.

Supporting the supposition that the linear case alignment represents Reno's skirmish line was the presence of .44-caliber Henry, .50-caliber Spencer, and .50–70-caliber cartridge cases on a bench to the west of the line. These cases, about twenty-five in number, indicate firing positions occupied by warriors. The location is consistent with the fact that Reno's line was outflanked and forced to fall back. Nine additional cases were also recovered at the west edge of the fields several hundred meters to the south, essentially below an old gravel quarry.

In addition to the .45–55-caliber cartridge cases on the presumed skirmish line, Pitsch recovered seven cartridge cases on a terrace above the Hunkpapa village site. These cases were intermixed with seven .44 Henry cases, five .50–70 cases, a Spencer case, and a round ball. The mixing may be indicative of several episodes of use by both combatant groups. The .45–55 cases may represent soldiers or Arikara army scouts gaining the ground and firing into the village, as is reported in Libby (1920). The .50–70 cases may also be associated with this incident. Conversely, all cases may represent Sioux warrior positions and a mixed variety of weapons. In any event, the cases were not aligned, and all were clustered on the terrace. Such a disposition pattern is consistent with the American Indian fighting pattern. The bench also yielded glass trade beads (seed beads), bovid bone, and charcoal stains identified as possible fire hearths.

Other .45–55 cases were recovered in the areas Vaughn identifies as Reno's second skirmish line, the timber area, and a large number were found on the land circumscribed by the abandoned river meander. At least seventeen cartridge cases were recovered there. They were clustered, suggesting a tactical disintegration, which is consistent with Reno's disorganized retreat from the timber. However, the possibility of warrior use of captured army guns is also feasible.

The artifacts found in the vicinity of the second skirmish line and in the presumed timber area were also clustered. One location of numerous cartridge cases and other artifacts found by Pitsch was along a slough disturbed by heavy equipment in recent years. The perimeter of this area was mapped, but not individual artifact locations. If this is the timber fight area, and if Vaughn and others are correct that the so-called Garryowen bend was an active channel during the battle, then Reno's timber fight area was protected by the river on two sides. This may shed some light on comments by witnesses at the Reno court of inquiry (Nichols 1992) that the timber area was defensible, suggesting that a skirmish line could have been extended from river bank to river bank. The court witnesses and the archaeological evidence suggest that no such skirmish line was deployed, thus requiring the retreat to the ford.

The warrior-related .44 Henry cases, .50–70 cases, Spencer cases, and other miscellaneous cartridge cases were clustered in several areas. Several, at least six, were found in the field areas where the Reynolds, McIntosh, and Dorman markers were located. Few army cases or other artifacts have been recovered in that area. These cases also tended to group on and around the meander. Some were intermixed with the .45–55 cases, although most were spatially separate. A significant cluster of warrior cases of all calibers was recovered in the field adjacent to the Preservation Committee holdings that contain the retreat ford site. Again some army cases were found in this general vicinity, but the large number of warrior cases, at least thirty, indicates that Reno's retreat was under pressure. These data very accurately confirm the historical accounts.

Not surprisingly, the bullets recovered by Pitsch tended to be found in association with the cases. Also of no surprise is the tendency for bullets from warrior weapons to be found among the .45–55 cases and army bullets among the warrior-associated cases. Again these data confirm the impression of combat positions and movement and correlate well with the historical record. The same can be said for warrior-associated arrowheads. They were found primarily among the assumed army positions.

The miscellaneous artifacts, such as tin cans, percussion caps, cap tins, horse tack and equipment, as well as personal items, are associated with the appropriate class of combat material. Items usually associated with army personnel, including saddle parts, other tack, eye glasses, and parts of equipment, were clearly intermingled with the army cartridge cases and the warrior bullets.

A significant departure from the expected patterning is that of the firearms parts. About thirty items were mapped, of which all but four were found in and around a slough or abandoned river meander. This slough is situated on the north edge of Reno's retreat line and about midway between the Hunkpapa village site and the retreat crossing. The clustering was made up of a variety of firearm parts, including many Colt and Springfield army weapon parts. Also intermingled in significant quantities were older gun parts as well as others that suggest a Sioux association. Although the deposit may reflect an immediate post-battle cleanup and firearm destruction effort, it is equally possible that the deposit postdates the battle by a year or more. In any case, such a disparate deposit of dissimilar gun parts suggests intentional disassembly of the weapons. This most likely occurred when press of battle was not imminent.

It is possible that Pitsch's linear alignment of finds is merely the result of where he looked. However, the lack of finds by other collectors (e.g., J. W. Vaughn) beyond the area in which Pitsch made his finds makes it unlikely that the pattern is completely fortuitous. Assuming that the pattern represents a near approximation of the retreat route, the correlation with the historical record is excellent and generally follows that postulated by Greene (1986) during his earlier relic find assessment efforts, and it is in concert with interpretation of the Reno valley fight offered by Moore (2011) and by Swanson (2011) on the Pitsch relic evidence.

While cleaning an irrigation ditch in spring 1993, Pitsch spotted a large crumpled sheet of brass. It was roughly rolled and covered with heavy green patina, but he collected it and noted its location, which was in the location traditionally identified as the site of the Sioux camp circle occupied by Sitting Bull's band of Hunkpapas. Returning to his ranch house, Jason gently washed the dirt from the brass artifact. As he turned the item, it caught the sun's rays in such a way as to expose some incised lines. Intrigued, he carefully unfolded the crumpled sheet to find that the lines became a series of figures scratched into one face of a brass plate.

The figures (Scott et al. 1997) depict a scene of warriors pursuing and shooting at a group of fleeing soldiers. All available evidence supports the conclusion that the brass plate is an authentic American Indian representation of a specific confrontation between warriors and U. S. Army soldiers. The discovery context at the site of the Sioux camp at the Little Bighorn battlefield is certainly significant and suggests that it was deposited no later than June 27, 1876. The plate's condition is entirely consistent with that interpretation. All of the elements portrayed on the plate—the horses, human figures, and American Indian equipment—also fit conventions of the second and third quarters of the nineteenth century. The depictions of the soldiers' carbines are accurate enough to identify them as Springfield carbines, which date the inscribed image to sometime after 1874. As a unique artifact presenting a powerful image offered from the Sioux perspective, this brass plate constitutes a truly important contribution to American frontier history (Logan and Schmittou 2007, 2008), but the item was sold at auction to a private bidder when the Reno Battlefield Museum collections were sold to recover loan losses by the Small Business Administration.

Two other valley finds are of interest. Both are human skeletal assemblages. One was found in 1994 on Pitsch land and excavated by Melissa Connor and Dick Harmon with assistance from Jason Pitsch (Connor 1994). They proved to be the partial remains of more than one individual. In fact there were parts of two people (Scott et al. 1998). Those few bone fragments matched two partial sets of remains that had been recently removed from the Custer National Cemetery for possible identification. As it turned out, Willey was able to determine that one set of remains were those exhumed in 1928 by a National Cemetery superintendent. One partial set did indeed belong to a soldier, as yet unidentified. The other set were those of an elderly American Indian woman, probably buried many years after the battle. Those remains were repatriated to the Crow tribe (see chapter 6 for a more complete description of the remains and recovery).

It is possible that these remains are the same ones originally found by local rancher Joseph Blummer in about 1928. Blummer was guided to the site by Frank Bethune, and while they were digging up the remains Smokey Other Medicine is reported to have arrived on the site and stated that a woman and child were buried there, not soldiers (Joseph Blummer ms, LBNM files; R. G. Cartwright complied notes 1941, Acc. 278, Field Notes). National Cemetery superintendent Eugene Wessinger later removed all the remains for reburial in the National Cemetery assuming they were soldiers, a fact only partially borne out by the archaeological and osteological investigations.

Another partial skeleton was found eroding from the Reno retreat crossing in 1989 by the Kloberdanz brothers (Scott and Snow 1991a; Scott et al. 1998). Clyde Snow was able to determine an age and height for the individual that compared favorably with four soldiers killed with Reno. With a bit of luck and some quick insight from Sandy Barnard, a photograph of Sgt. Edward Botzer, one of the likely candidates, came to light (Barnard 1995). A photographic superimposition of the skull and photograph shows that the remains are most likely those of Botzer. His remains are buried in the Custer National Cemetery, as are all the soldiers' physical remains found on the battlefield during the archaeological work.

Unfortunately, now that the Pitsch valley artifact collection has been broken up and sold to private collectors, it is nearly impossible to analyze Pitsch's data set for details beyond the gross distribution pattern. The Pitsch mapped data suggest some interesting details regarding the location, duration, and intensity of the fight on the skirmish lines, the fight in the timber, and Reno's retreat, but these are now lost to posterity. Likewise, material recovered in the Sitting Bull campsite could have elucidated more about life in the camp and possibly something of the haste in abandoning the camp when the bands became aware of the Terry and Gibbons column's approach on June 26. Their loss to researchers is inestimable and only makes the Little Bighorn National Battlefield archaeological collections even more important to our collective knowledge of the past. Fortunately, much of the Pitsch land and other properties important to the Little Bighorn story, including Weir Point and parts of Medicine Tail Coulee, have been acquired by the Custer Battlefield Land Preservation Committee. The Committee is protecting and preserving these lands with the hope of someday transferring title to them to a public entity for long-term preservation.

RENO'S RETREAT TO THE BLUFFS

When Major Reno's command made its unorganized movement from the timber in the valley to the bluffs, the first area it traversed after crossing the river was steep slopes and ravines of the river's east side. Reno's men were under fire during their movement up the slopes, and some were killed or wounded in the attempt to reach the heights (Stewart 1955). The available historical documentation notes that the movement was somewhat random and perhaps on a broad front (Nichols 1992). The command may not have used any one locale or trail to climb to the bluff tops. The men appear to have scrambled up the slopes wherever they could. Dr. James M. DeWolf and his orderly went up a slope that angles to the east-northeast and away from the defense site. They were warned by some members of the command that they were about to run into warriors above them. Before they could retrace their trail, both were killed by fire from above. White marble markers have since been placed on a bench of the slope where they were believed killed.

Archaeologists have not formally investigated the Reno retreat crossing, although Retreat Ravine above the crossing, at least that portion within the park fence surrounding the Reno-Benteen defense site, was inventoried in 1985. Various relic collectors are known to have metal-detected the retreat crossing and the route up to the park fence. Only Henry Weibert (Weibert and Weibert 1985) made any effort to document his finds.

Evidence for Reno's chaotic retreat up to the defense site is abundantly clear in the archaeological record. Bullets and cartridge cases (figures 27–32) from both combatant groups were found along the route, as was lost equipment and personal items. The lack of distinct patterning in the artifact distribution in the retreat ravine is consistent with the historical accounts of the disorganized endeavor. However, a group of army .45–55-caliber cartridge cases found at the head of the ravine and just below the park tour road (Scott 2006)

Figure 27. Metal-detected .45-55 cartridges and cartridge cases found at the Reno-Benteen defense site.

Figure 28.
Distribution of
.44-caliber cartridge
cases and bullets
fired by warriors at
the Reno–Benteen
defense site.

89

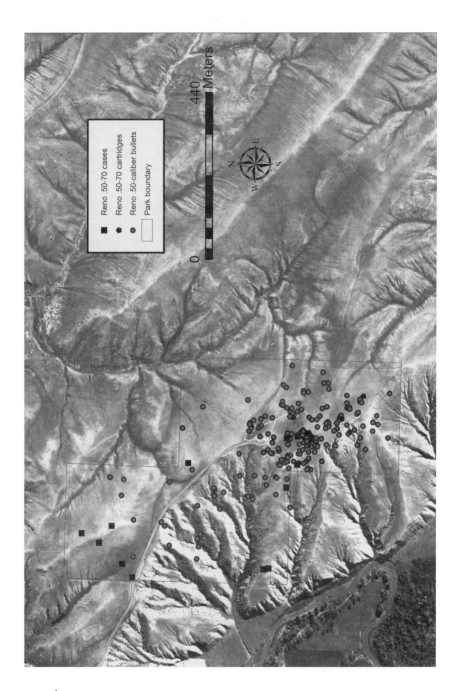

Figure 29.
Distribution
of .50-caliber
cartridge
cases and
bullets fired
by warriors
at the Reno–
Benteen
defense site.

90

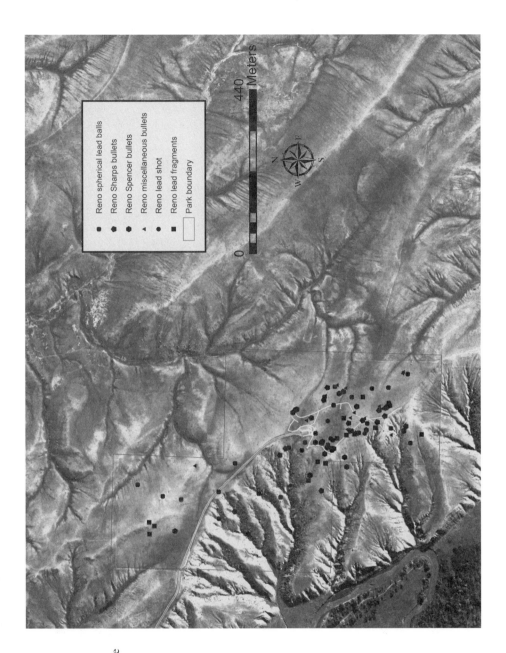

Figure 30.
Distribution of
warrior-fired
miscellaneous
caliber bullets
at the Reno-
Benteen defense
site.

Figure 31.
Distribution
of army-fired
.45–55-caliber
cartridge cases and
bullets at the Reno–
Benteen defense
site.

Figure 32.
Distribution
of army-fired
.45 Colt-caliber
cartridge
cases and
bullets at the
Reno–Benteen
defense site.

suggests that some element of the command attempted to provide covering fire to their comrades during their helter-skelter rush up the hill. The matching firing pin marks indicate that the firing came from a mixed group, with matches to finds in the traditional locations of Companies B, M, and H.

THE RENO-BENTEEN DEFENSE AND WEIR POINT EPISODES

When those of the Reno command who survived the river crossing and upslope climb to the bluff tops gathered, there appears to have been little attention given to organizing a defensive perimeter (see figures 27–32). Capt. Frederick Benteen and his battalion arrived from the south about the time Reno's command gained the heights. Benteen was moving north to join Custer's command after receiving a communication from Custer via messenger. As Benteen joined Reno, some warriors situated in nearby ravines commenced firing into the command's position (Stewart 1955:391). Company D threw out skirmishers under Capt. Thomas Weir and returned fire. With this, the warrior fire slackened. This skirmish line has not been identified archaeologically.

A discussion ensued among several of the officers concerning the appropriateness of attempting to join Custer's command. Major Reno apparently decided not to attempt to find Custer until the pack train carrying the command's extra ammunition could join his command. That train had been following Captain Benteen's battalion. In the meantime, Major Reno and several others attempted, unsuccessfully, to recover 2nd Lt. Benjamin Hodgson's body. Hodgson had been killed crossing the river.

Captain Weir, demonstrating a great deal of impatience, mounted his horse and set out to the north to determine the whereabouts of Custer. 2nd Lt. Winfield Edgerly, assuming Weir was under orders, mounted Company D and followed Weir. Captain Weir and Company D reached a high point about one mile north, where they stopped to observe the country. The point is now known as Weir Point. Lieutenant Edgerly moved north with Company D about one-half mile before he was signaled to return by Captain Weir (Sills 1994:45–46). Lieutenant Edgerly testified at the Reno court of inquiry that Captain Weir signaled him to swing around to the right (east) and return to Weir's position. Edgerly also testified that in the advanced position his men fired individually at hostiles who were within 150–200 yards of their position (Nichols 1992:444–46). It is unclear whether Edgerly was referring to the advanced Company D position or the firing from Weir Point proper.

When the pack train reached Reno's position, Reno sent 2nd Lt. Luther Hare to tell Weir that the rest of the command was about to follow him. Companies H, K, and M, under Benteen, joined Weir while Reno and the rest of the command transporting the wounded began to move north. 2nd Lieutenant Varnum also rode to Weir Point, and he recalled that Weir's company was dismounted and firing at warriors, "who seemed to be coming out on the prairie and turning back. It was quite a long range, but there were a good many shots being fired at him and he was firing away, a slow firing, a shot now and then at quite a little distance" (Carroll 1987:117; Nichols 1992:144–45). In other testimony, Varnum recalled that the ranges were 700–800 yards (Carroll 1987:143; Nichols 1992:161).

Pvt. Edward Pigford recalled, many years after the event, that he and two other Company M men advanced ahead from Weir Point to a small hill where they saw the last of the Custer fight. He also said that the other two soldiers were killed on the movement back to the hill (Stewart 1955:403–404). His information seems to be of questionable value since it is so inconsistent with other testimony and there is no other record of any men being killed forward of or on Weir Point. The only man lost was farrier Vincent Charlie during the retrograde movement back to the Reno-Benteen defense site.

There is little doubt that Sioux and Cheyenne warriors began to move to the south from their victory over Custer. The soldiers at Weir Point saw this movement and began to withdraw to their first position. Companies M and D covered the rather unorganized withdrawal until a few hundred yards north of the first position. 2nd Lt. George Wallace testified at the court of inquiry that the movement back was under heavy fire (Nichols 1992:80). Near the present monument's gate on the tour road, Company K dismounted and deployed in skirmish order to cover the retreat. 1st Lt. Edward Godfrey and his men began to withdraw slowly to the south, covering the other companies' retirement. The soldiers' fire slackened and they bunched up, but Godfrey reestablished skirmish order and continued the withdrawal in good order until within a few yards of the defensive position, when Godfrey told the men to make a dash for the lines.

Within a short time the command was under fire from all sides, as the warriors took cover on hilltops, in ravines, and wherever they could to shoot into Reno's position. It was on June 27 that the combined column of General Terry and Colonel Gibbon arrived to relieve the besieged Reno.

The 1985 investigations took in the entire Reno-Benteen area owned by the NPS, including portions of Sharpshooter Hill (Scott et al. 1989). In 1994 and two subsequent years much of the land between Reno-Benteen and Medicine Tail Coulee was also inventoried with metal detectors (Scott 1996b, 1998b; Scott and Bleed 1997). And an intensive metal detecting inventory was completed in 2004 along the entire asphalt tour road as part of a mitigation effort in preparation for rebuilding the road. The 2004 inventory was limited to 20 m on either side of the road. At the Reno-Benteen defense site the inventory entailed work around the parking lot as well as along the road all the way to Last Stand Hill (Scott 2006).

There is archaeological evidence for the Weir Point episode (figure 33) that supports Lakota and Cheyenne oral traditions as well as the statements made by the officers and men. In addition, the archaeological data identify the movement north of Weir Point, fighting around the point, and the route of the retrograde movement back to the Reno-Benteen defense site. The archaeological evidence is not extensive, but the limited data available are patterned.

The historical documents related to the action at Weir Point suggest that until the retrograde movement began there was only intermittent firing at long range between the opposing forces. It is known that Companies M and D covered the retrograde movement until Company K formed a skirmish line and covered the final elements of that movement. Historical documents suggest that the Company K covering fire began near Sharpshooter Hill, and there is ample archaeological information found during previous investigations (Scott et al. 1989) to support the Company K skirmishing efforts (figures 27–32).

The upper end of the coulee on the south side of Weir Point yielded, during a 1996 inventory, a curry comb, a spur and buckle, nine .45-caliber carbine bullets, two .50-caliber bullets, an unfired

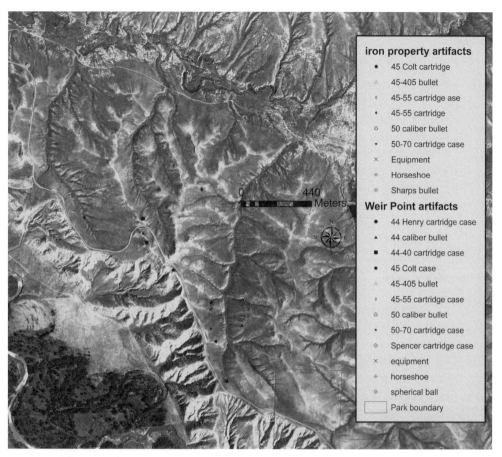

Figure 33. Distribution of army and Indian artifacts found on and around Weir Point and the route of advance and retreat to the Reno-Benteen defense site.

Colt .45 cartridge, an unfired .45–55 Springfield cartridge, and an iron arrowhead. These items found on the west slope of Cedar Coulee and below the modern park tour road probably indicate the line of Weir's retrograde movement to the defense site. The bullets are the physical evidence of the covering fire of one of the companies, perhaps Company M, during the retreat. The 2004 investigations (Scott 2006) found additional cartridge cases and bullets fired by the soldiers and warriors during the retreat episode from Weir Point to the defense site as well as an iron arrowhead.

The cartridges, spur, and curry comb suggest some of the haste inherent in the retreat. Although the artifacts may have all originated from a single individual, more likely they represent discrete episodes of rearing and plunging horses disgorging a curry comb from an unsecured saddle bag, a dismounted man catching and losing his spur, perhaps in the haste of remounting, the discard of a carbine round after the bullet nose was deformed in a hurried attempt to reload a carbine, and a fumbled attempt to reload a revolver. All of this gives the impression that the soldiers passing along this sideslope during the retreat did so in haste. The bullet distribution also gives the impression that after the soldiers retreated the pursuing warriors crossed the same ground, but under fire from the companies providing covering fire to the retreating soldiers.

Also in Cedar Coulee a single Colt cartridge, a carbine tool, and carbine bullet were found in proximity (Scott and Bleed 1997). The meaning of this pattern is not clear, but it leaves an impression of a discrete event occurring at that location. One possible interpretation, but not necessarily the only interpretation, is that these artifacts are associated with the wounding or death of farrier Vincent Charley. The fate of Charley is no longer in doubt. His remains were reported as having been dug up in 1903 and removed to the Custer National Cemetery. During the work to identify the 1903 and 1928 remains (Scott et al. 1998), one set of bones was shown to be those of a robust male about 28 years old and about 70 inches tall. A bullet wound to the right hip was evident in the bone, and it was in such a position that it must have come from the back right. Abdominal wounds were so serious in the nineteenth century that over 80 percent of those with this type of wound died. Charley was 27 years old and about 70 inches tall when he died of a gunshot wound to the hip. In all likelihood, the bones that we examined are those of Charley.

The finds along the west slope of Cedar Coulee as well as south of Sharpshooter Hill within the park boundary clearly indicate the route of the retrograde movement from Weir Point to Reno-Benteen. They also indicate that the area was subsequently used by warriors as they fired on the troops during that movement or while in the defense site. These data are entirely consistent with the analysis and results presented for the 1985 archaeological investigations at Reno-Benteen (Scott et al. 1989).

The warriors used at least ten Sharps or Remingtons and one

Model 1868 or Model 1870 Springfield rifle in .50–70-caliber when firing on the soldiers during their retreat from Weir Point and after they returned to the defense perimeter. The .44-caliber cases represent at least sixty-one individual lever action repeating guns that were used in the fighting around Reno-Benteen. Four Model 1873 Winchesters have now been identified as being used by warriors against the soldiers at Reno-Benteen, as well as at least one Joslyn carbine.

The .44-caliber and .50–70-caliber data indicate that the warriors did utilize Sharpshooter Hill, a long ridge north of the defense perimeter, and the ravines south of the defense perimeter as firing positions. The cartridge case concentrations in these areas suggest that they tended to take advantage of the same general locales, perhaps the best cover available. The isolated cases also indicate that almost every area of the battlefield was used. The distribution of warrior-associated cartridge cases confirms the historical accounts that the warriors surrounded the command and poured heavy fire into the defense perimeter. The cartridge case concentrations also indicate that the survivors' accounts of directions of fire are also accurate.

The Springfield carbine case distributional evidence is complicated, so it is perhaps best to begin with the least complicated portion. The ridges and bluffs surrounding the retreat ravine contained a few Springfield cartridge cases. The cases and warrior-associated bullets found impacted in the vicinity indicate that the retreat was under fire. The Springfield cases found along the ravine correlate with those found in the defense perimeter. The ravine cases match cases found in the Company B, D, K, and M positions.

The gross distribution analysis identified three discrete areas of Springfield carbine case concentrations north of the defense perimeter: on the west flank of Sharpshooter Hill, between the hill and a low knoll, and in the vicinity of the knoll about half the distance between the army defensive perimeter and Sharpshooter Hill. The carbine cases found on the flank of Sharpshooter Hill have firing pin marks that match cases found in the other positions and in the defense perimeter. The cases in the two concentrations between the hill and knoll also have firing pin imprints that match cases at the knoll and in the defense perimeter. This strongly suggests that the carbine cases found north of the defense perimeter are associated with the movement to and from Weir Point. Further corroboration is found by analyzing the specific defense perimeter match locations.

The majority of the carbine cases found north of the perimeter have firing pin imprints that match cases found in the northeast perimeter area. Those cases found around the knoll and some to its immediate north correlate with the historically documented Company K position. It was Company K, commanded by Lieutenant Godfrey, that formed a skirmish line to cover the latter part of the retreat from Weir Point. The cases found near Sharpshooter Hill match cases found on the northwest part of the perimeter. This area was occupied by Companies B and D during the fight. They also covered the early part of the Weir Point retreat. In this situation it is not just one or two case matches but evidence for the use of twelve different guns moving from Sharpshooter Hill to the knoll, and finally to the Company K position in the perimeter.

The hilltop position was anything but secure when it was reoccupied by the troops falling back from Weir Point. The officers deployed their men in a roughly shaped oval around the lip of a large depression and along a ridgetop that became the Reno-Benteen defense site. There the Reno command was besieged by warriors on the high ground and other advantageous cover around the soldiers' position. Throughout the siege, defenses were improvised by piling hardtack boxes and saddles to form breastworks. Shallow trenches, formally called "hasty entrenchements," or rifle pits were scooped into the hard Montana prairie with cups, knives, boards, and a few shovels. Dead animals also served as protection. Three of the rifle pits were excavated by Bray (1958) and restored as interpretive devices along the Reno-Benteen walking trail. During the tour road mitigation project, Steven DeVore (2005) of MWAC employed ground-penetrating radar and electrical resistivity as remote sensing techniques to uncover any anomalies in the proposed right-of-way area around the Reno-Benteen parking lot and trail head. Several anomalies were noted. One is likely the original site of the Reno monument, which was relocated sometime in the 1960s to its present position on the edge of the parking lot. DeVore also identified other anomalies on the north side of the parking lot. Two are relatively small and rectangular and are postulated to be soil disturbances that may be associated with rifle pit locations. These locations have not been validated by archaeological testing since they will not be impacted by the rehabilitation of the tour road, but their signature in the geophysical records suggests that DeVore's techniques are viable for finding other buried rifle pits in the Reno-Benteen defense site.

The abundant archaeological evidence of the Reno-Benteen defense shows that it was a spirited fight. The Lakota and Cheyenne held the most advantageous positions surrounding the soldiers. These positions provided excellent cover and commanded an excellent field of fire into the soldiers' positions. Many cartridge cases were found on Sharpshooter Hill, in the swales, and behind the knolls that surround the army positions. Among some .44-caliber Henry cartridge cases at one knoll was a brass bracelet, probably lost by one of the warriors. The tip of a gold-painted knife blade that once was part of a war club was found in another location.

Literally hundreds of bullets fired from the Lakota and Cheyenne guns, including many captured from the defeated Custer command, were found imbedded in the Reno-Benteen defense position. Relic evidence of those captured guns being used by the warriors was reportedly found on the long ridges 200–600 yards east of the park boundary (B. William Henry research notes, Oct. 5, Nov. 8, 1969, LBNM files; Rickey 1956; Vaughn 1956; Weibert and Weibert 1985). These finds indicate that the warriors used the available high ground and associated cover to pour a plunging fire into the Reno-Benteen defense. Such a position to the east also allowed them to see into the hospital area, where the soldiers used dead mules, horse tack, and ration and ammunition boxes as barricades to protect themselves and the wounded. Ample evidence of the barricade is evident in the form of box nails, iron buckles from the horse tack, a picket pin, and even horse and mule bones found along the barricade line.

Among the more poignant reminders of the power of the missiles fired by the warriors into the Reno-Benteen defense perimeter are the remains of six of the men who died. One showed dramatic evidence of a gunshot injury to the head. His yet unidentified remains show that a tumbling bullet struck him on the right side of the head and passed through his skull, exiting on the left (Scott et al. 1998).

Another set of remains had a skull with many fillings of gold and tin in the teeth. The victim's age and height are consistent with those of Cpl. George Lell, but DNA analyses of blood samples from his maternal great-grandnieces did not match. Either these remains are not Lell's or the genealogical information is incorrect (Scott et al. 1998; Willey et al. 2004).

THE MEDICINE TAIL COULEE EPISODE

There is essentially no evidence of Custer's movements until he arrived at Medicine Tail Coulee. In the lower reaches of Medicine Tail and at Nye-Cartwright Ridge, along Deep Coulee, and on to the north there is abundant evidence of the beginning of the final phase of the battle.

Battle events in Medicine Tail Coulee and the cavalry's movement to Calhoun Hill are some of the most difficult to reconstruct from the historical record. It is now fairly well agreed that Custer halted in upper Medicine Tail Coulee and divided his command into two wings, a right wing consisting of Companies C, I, and L and a left wing composed of Companies E and F under the command of Capt. George Yates (Fox 1993; Gray 1991:360). It is Gray's (1991:360–70) assumption that Custer's purpose in dividing the command was for the left wing to conduct a feint to the mouth of Medicine Tail Coulee while the remainder of the command moved along the ridges to the north in an attempt to ford the Little Bighorn and attack the north end of the village. Gray (1991:362–63) cites the R. G. Cartwright and Joseph Blummer cartridge case finds on Nye-Cartwright Ridge as well as cartridge case finds on Luce Ridge as support for this argument. He also uses other Cartwright and Blummer artifacts found along a line from Nye-Cartwright to Calhoun Hill and from Deep Coulee to Calhoun Hill as further evidence of the reconvergence of the two wings.

The Crow scout Curly (Gray 1991:360–72) described Yates's wing as moving down Medicine Tail Coulee to its juncture with the Little Bighorn, where members of the command fired at the enemy on the river's west bank. At one point Curly, who presumably observed the left-wing movements from his position with Custer, suggested that Yates's command dismounted and fired into the village on the opposite side of the river, while in another narrative he claimed that Yates did not dismount but fired across the river while mounted, then turned to move up Deep Coulee and reunite with Custer's command.

Curly indicated that two soldiers rode into the river but returned to the command before the movement up Deep Coulee. He also reported only light firing at the coulee's mouth. The warriors on the west bank fired at the soldiers, who were apparently in column, with perhaps only the column's front ranks firing on the west bank. The historical accounts generally agree that the movement to the mouth of Medicine Tail Coulee was of short duration with only limited firing on either side. 1st Lt. Oscar Long reported that his Sioux informants mentioned only one man killed at the ford (Brust 1995:8). The Sioux identified him as an officer who had a compass and field glasses. Gray (1991) cited a burial party account indicating that the man was a noncommissioned officer who was found on the west bank in unmutilated condition. His horse was found near the body. Long's informants also mentioned that to them it appeared that one company near the river mounted on bay horses tried to run away but were fired upon by their own men and forced to return to the command (Brust 1995:8). Perhaps this incident could also be interpreted as a company moving to the mouth of the coulee and retiring with the support of covering fire by another company or group held in a reserve position.

As Yates's wing moved northeast, presumably along the west bank of Deep Coulee, to reunite with the right wing and Custer on or near Calhoun Hill, warriors crossed the river and engaged the rear of Custer's command (Gray 1991:366) as well as his right flank. Fox (1993:143) argues that Yates's wing made the movement dismounted, but this is at odds with Curly's statements regarding the Deep Coulee movement. White Cow Bull, a Sioux, reported that before the soldiers dismounted they delivered an intense fire that drove the warriors back (Fox 1993:144). Curly said (Gray 1991: 366) that by the time the command reunited near Calhoun Hill the Sioux and Cheyenne were in their front, in both ravines (presumably Deep Coulee and Calhoun Coulee) and a strong force in their rear. Gray (1991:370) and Wells (1989) reconstruct the reunion near the park's southern boundary fence and suggest that one or more companies dismounted and deployed in the vicinity of the so-called Finley marker. There the soldiers tried to drive the warriors from a ravine in their front, but with men killed to their rear that attempt failed and the warrior advance was not checked. Fox (1993) places this event in Calhoun Coulee with Company C charging the warriors in the ravine. The charge failed in the face of overwhelming numbers of warriors and precipitated the collapse of the Company L position because 1st Lt. James Calhoun had to split his force to support the Company C retreat.

The 1994 (Scott and Bleed 1997) and 2004 (Scott 2006) archaeological evidence for combat at the mouth of Medicine Tail Coulee is meager but definitely present (figure 34). The area has been heavily collected, as indicated by J. W. Vaughn (Vaughn to historian Andrew Loveless, July 3, 1965, Acc. 278, Field Notes) and by Greene's (1986) summary of previous collecting efforts. The area has also been the subject of many other uses. Its primary use is grazing land, but at least one movie (*Little Big Man*, 1970) was filmed

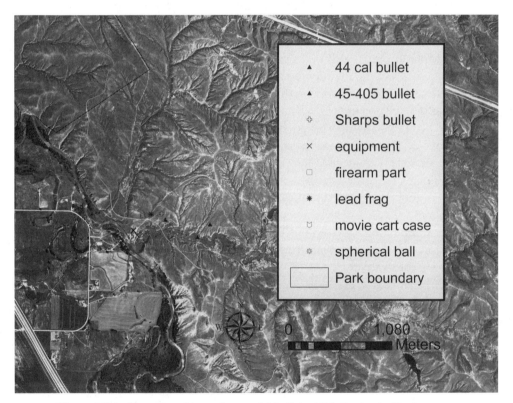

Figure 34. Artifacts found in and around Medicine Tail Coulee indicating a light action in the area, and the site of the filming of the Last Stand sequence of the movie *Little Big Man*.

along the tour road at the coulee's mouth. Archaeological evidence of the movie making was recovered in the form of 5-in-1 movie cartridge cases (a blank cartridge designed for use in .44-caliber and .45-caliber firearms) and various other caliber blank cartridge cases. The "Last Stand" sequence was filmed on a cutbank east of the tour road at the mouth of Deep Coulee. Ample evidence of that scene's filming was recovered there, including hairpins used to secure wigs to the actors' heads. The charge to the river was filmed at the mouth of Medicine Tail Coulee where it joins the Little Bighorn River, and movie debris was recovered there as well.

It is interesting that the locations used in the movie to represent battle sequences were in fact set on sites actually used in the battle. The area along the tour road where the "Last Stand" sequence was filmed yielded lead balls and Sharps bullets fired by the warriors and a .45-caliber carbine bullet probably fired by a soldier. These data alone indicate that there was combat in this area. The warriors' bullets impacted in areas on the east side of Deep Coulee. They may have been shots fired in the direction of retreating soldiers, or they may have been shots fired at Yates's wing as it moved to the mouth of the coulee during its movement toward the river. Many of the earlier collected relic locations as compiled and mapped by Greene (1986) are distributed in the same area.

The mouth of Medicine Tail Coulee, at the ford, also yielded period artifacts during the 1994 investigations (Scott and Bleed 1997). There were also numerous post-battle .45–60 caliber cartridge cases found in this location, intermixed with the battle period items. These cases are both headstamped and non-headstamped, but all were fired in Winchester Model 1886 firearms. These clearly postdate the battle. The reason for the clustering at the ford is not known, although they may be associated with one of the earlier reenactments or filming episodes.

The 1994 investigations did, however, recover two pieces of a broken Model 1874 army mess knife, a period butcher knife of the type that might have been carried by a soldier or a warrior as a sheath or belt knife, a lead rifle ball, the cylinder pin to a Colt revolver, and a .30-caliber Remington Smoot revolver cartridge case. Don Rickey and J. W. Vaughn (Greene 1986:20–25) also reported finding a few .45-caliber army carbine cartridge cases, some equipment and personal items, bullets, and warrior-related caliber cartridge cases at or near the ford. Greene's assessment of the earlier relic collection efforts and the 1994 archaeological data are entirely consistent in type and quantity. Those data are also consistent with the historical accounts that a small action with only limited firing occurred at the ford. The finds of soldier equipment indicate that some items were lost at or near the ford and are consistent with the conclusion reached by Rickey and Vaughn (Greene 1986:23) that at least one cavalry horse may have been hit and, in plunging around, scattered items attached to the saddle. Rickey and Vaughan also recovered some split Berdan primed .45-caliber cartridge cases. Unfortunately, these are not available for examination, but they may well be post-battle .45–60-caliber cases like those found in 1994.

DEEP COULEE TO CALHOUN HILL EPISODE

Rickey and Vaughn (Greene 1986:33–34) found cartridges, cases, bullets, and equipment pieces in their research around Deep Coulee. Greene's compilation of other finds also generally mirrors the archaeological finds. The distribution of the earlier finds is along the south side of Deep Coulee and adjacent and parallel to the park's boundary fence from Greasy Grass Ridge to Calhoun Hill. This is essentially the same distribution as the 1994 and 2004 artifact finds.

The 1994 archaeological investigations near Calhoun Hill took place in the upper portion of Deep Coulee in that area adjacent to the park's southeast corner (figures 35–38). Artifact recovery consisted of eighty-eight items, the majority bullets and cartridge cases. Only two cartridge cases are .45-caliber army carbine, but there are four unfired cartridges. In contrast to the number of army cartridge cases, twenty-eight .45-caliber bullets were recovered. There are eight .44-caliber rimfire cases, five .44-caliber bullets, four cartridge cases and two cartridges in .50–70-caliber, eleven .50-caliber bullets, one .40-caliber Sharps bullet, and one lead ball. Two .50-caliber bullets were fired in Sharps sporting rifles. Each was fired in a different gun. Several items of army equipment were also recovered, including two brass spurs (one a regulation spur and the other an earlier model army spur), a picket pin, and a currycomb. A single iron arrowhead was also recovered, as was an iron awl. One of the .44-caliber rimfire case's firing pin imprint matches a case found in

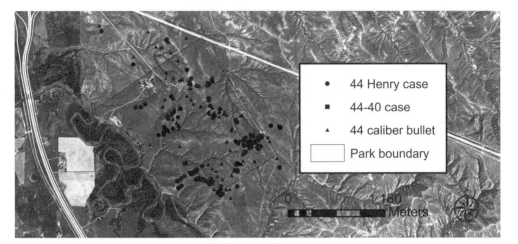

Figure 35. Distribution of .44-caliber warrior-fired weapons, including Henry rifles and Model 1866 and Model 1873 Winchesters at the Custer battlefield.

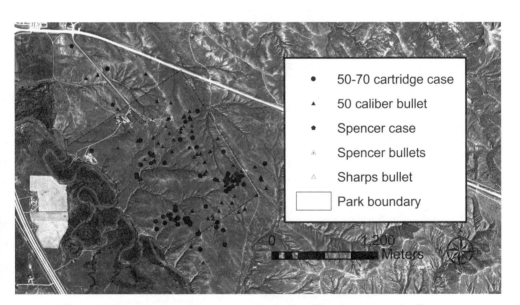

Figure 36. Distribution of the warrior-fired .50-caliber firearms at the Custer battlefield.

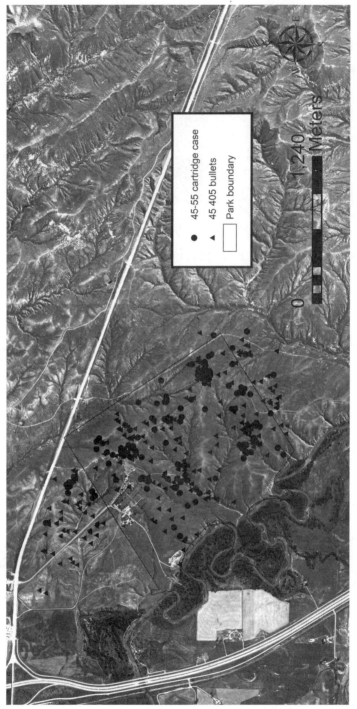

Figure 37. Army- and warrior-fired .45–55 caliber cartridge cases and bullets at the Custer battlefield.

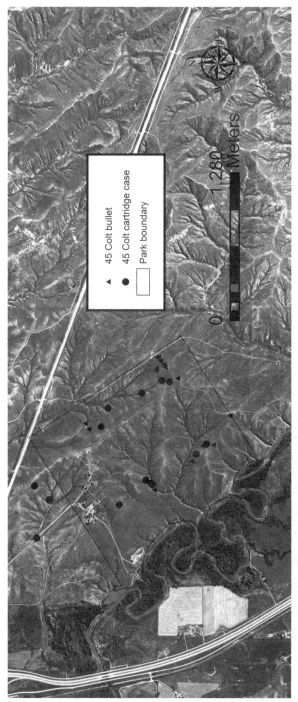

Figure 38. Distribution of the few army- and warrior-fired .45-caliber Colt cases and bullets at the Custer battlefield.

1985 at the Reno-Benteen defense site. Clearly that Henry or Winchester Model 1866 was used at both battlefields.

The artifact patterning and distribution give the impression of soldiers moving up Deep Coulee toward Calhoun Hill (Scott and Bleed 1997). The expended army cartridge case distribution indicates that there was some firing as the movement took place, but it appears light or at least limited in scope. The distribution of warrior-related caliber bullets also gives the distinct impression that the army movement was under fire. Most army bullets were found around the park's boundary fence near Calhoun Hill. The same is true of most of the cartridge cases attributed to the warriors (.44-caliber, .50-caliber, and others). This bullet distribution is consistent with firing by Companies C and L after their deployment at the south end of Custer (Battle) Ridge. Some army caliber bullets (.45-caliber Springfield and Colt) were also found northeast of the fence corner. These may have been fired toward warriors on or near Henry Ridge. One of those warriors may have been Gall, who stated that he joined the battle at Calhoun Hill via a route through Henry Ridge (Fox 1993:143).

Although the cartridge case and bullet evidence suggests only limited fighting during the movement from Medicine Tail Coulee to Calhoun Hill, the distribution of equipment in the Deep Coulee area indicates some loss (Scott and Bleed 1997). Spurs, picket pins, and a curry comb finds suggest enough haste in the movement to cause the loss of items from the horse equipage or from individual soldiers. An alternative interpretation of these data is that they represent killed or wounded soldiers or horses. Some support for this supposition comes in the form of skeletal remains found in this general area. A soldier's skeleton was found by Frank Bethune in the Deep Coulee area in 1928. Willey (1993) examined that skeleton, which had been reburied in the National Cemetery, and found it to be that of a 35-year-old white male about 68 inches tall. He had a gunshot wound to the head, evidence of blunt force trauma, and at least ninety-eight cutmarks on his bones, indicating that the victorious Lakota and Cheyenne mutilated him. Evidence of such ritual mutilation was seen on many of the skeletal remains from the Custer battlefield. No identity has been established for this man.

In addition, Cartwright and Blummer (Greene 1986:28) reported finding the skeletons of as many as four cavalry horses still partially outfitted with saddle gear near Deep Coulee. The horse remains could also represent wounded horses that got loose during the battle and died in this area.

In any event, the archaeological and relic evidence consistently point to a movement of soldiers to the mouth of Medicine Tail Coulee, where a small and perhaps brief action occurred between the soldiers on the east bank of the Little Bighorn River and warriors on the west bank. After this skirmish the cavalry withdrew and moved up the east bank of Deep Coulee to reunite with the rest of the command at or near what is now the park's south boundary fence. During the movement up Deep Coulee the cavalrymen were under some fire, but perhaps not intense. It appears from the finding of human remains in 1928 that one or more soldiers was lost in this movement. Presumably the movement represented by the artifacts is that of the left wing rejoining the remainder of the command as they passed from Nye-Cartwright Ridge to Calhoun Hill. The two wings apparently rejoined at or near the present park boundary fence, probably not far from where the modern tour road breaks the fence line. From there Custer deployed Companies C and L on Calhoun Hill, where heavy fighting ensued. The warriors used Deep Coulee, Calhoun Coulee, Greasy Grass Ridge, Henry Ridge, and other available cover to fire into the front and right and left flanks of the soldiers posted at Calhoun Hill.

GREASY GRASS RIDGE AND CALHOUN HILL

Upon gaining the ridge, Custer, or someone else in command, deployed a group of men on a line facing in a southerly direction. Traditionally the men deployed are assumed to have been from Company L and possibly some from Company C, owing to the presence of identifiable remains of men of these two companies and their respective officers in this location after the battle. This includes ground at and surrounding the area traditionally known as Calhoun Hill. The soldiers on this line faced intense fire from enemies south and east of their position. The deployment probably protected the southern end of Custer Ridge. There is evidence of at least fifteen Springfield carbines and three Colt pistols in use in the Calhoun position, based on the analysis of the recovered cartridge cases and bullets. Historical and relic evidence presented by Greene

(1986) and artifacts subsequently collected by Weibert and Weibert (1985) and other amateurs suggest that the warriors attacked from the south and southeast. They found cover below the tops of ridges 100–800 yards away. Once the warriors advanced on the soldier position, they were able to bring a diverse variety of firearms to finish off the surviving soldiers, including several .50–70-caliber rifles and carbines, at least one Joslyn carbine, and several .44-caliber Henry or Winchester 1866 rifles (see figures 35, 36).

Another area of heavy Sioux/Cheyenne fire came from south and west of the Calhoun position on a lower portion of Greasy Grass Ridge (see figures 35–38). The 2004 investigations (Scott 2006) added to the number of guns used on Greasy Grass Ridge by the warriors. At least thirty .44-caliber rimfire lever action weapons, one .44–77-caliber Sharps, one Smith and Wesson American .44-caliber revolver, sixteen .50–70-caliber guns, four Spencers, a Ballard .50-caliber rimfire, and two .44–40-caliber Model 1873 Winchesters were used in this area against the soldiers, a total of at least fifty-five different firearms. The heavy fire must have aided in the annihilation of Calhoun's men. From the cartridge case distribution matches, it appears that Calhoun's position was overrun by the same warriors who fired at the soldiers from Henry Ridge and Greasy Grass Ridge.

Two Springfield carbine cartridge cases found in the Medicine Tail Coulee area in 2004 had firing pin marks that matched cartridge cases found in the Finley-Finckle and Calhoun Hill areas. Custer's left wing that went to the mouth of Medicine Tail Coulee is presumed to have been composed of Companies E and F, and the units known to have fought in the Finley-Finckle area and on Calhoun Hill are Companies C and L. The cartridge case matches are inconsistent with the traditional historical view without alternative explanation. One explanation may be that members of Companies C and L were under fire in Medicine Tail Coulee before deploying to Nye-Cartwright Ridge. Alternatively, members of Companies E and F returned fire as the command reassembled on Calhoun Hill before the deployment of Companies C and L by Custer to hold the ground to the south while he took the remainder of the command farther north. This second scenario seems to be the more plausible explanation, suggesting that the entire command was under some hostile fire as it gained the Finley-Finckle area and Calhoun Hill.

CALHOUN HILL TO KEOGH AND LAST STAND HILL

Neither the mid-1980s (Scott and Fox 1987; Scott et al. 1989) archaeological investigations nor the 2004 (Scott 2006) investigations recovered substantial numbers of cartridge cases or bullets from either side of Custer Ridge adjacent to the current tour road. Only twenty-eight artifacts were collected between the end of Calhoun Hill loop road and the parking lot at Last Stand Hill (see figures 35–38). Five of these finds are post-battle items. A canteen stopper ring, a horse bone, and a possible American Indian ball-shaped button constitute the personal items. Four .45-caliber 405-grain army bullets and four warrior bullets (.44 and .50-calibers), one .45-caliber Colt cartridge case, seven .45–55-caliber cartridge cases, and four warrior cartridge cases (Henry, 1872 Colt, and a Joslyn carbine) clearly demonstrate both soldier and warrior activity along the ridgeline, but not in significant numbers. However, it must be remembered that Last Stand Hill, the Keogh area, and Calhoun Hill are among the most heavily trafficked areas and likely the most subject to uncontrolled individual collecting efforts over the years, so a conclusion must be drawn carefully.

Capt. Myles Keogh and the men of Company I deployed below the ridgetop on the east side of Custer Ridge. Perhaps they were being held in reserve, perhaps they were on their way to aid Calhoun, or perhaps they were positioned to cover Calhoun's withdrawal. In any event, they were not sent along the ridgetop but along Horse Holders Ravine and the eastern slope of Custer Ridge. The archaeological data do not support the theory that Keogh and his men were pushed from the ridgetop to the base of the ridge where they were killed. The spatial distribution of army-related artifacts clearly indicates very few battle-related artifacts on either side of the ridgetop above Keogh's position.

The Keogh position yielded ample evidence of combat in that area. Impacted warrior bullets, expended army cartridge cases, as well as soldiers' equipment and even human remains (Scott et al. 1989) all attest to the intensity of the fighting in the Keogh sector. Much of the warriors' gunfire probably came from the high ridges east of the current park boundary. That area has not been investigated archaeologically, but relics have been collected there. Greene (1986) and Weibert (1989) document large numbers of cartridge cases along the ridgetops and slopes that may well indicate warrior positions during the early phases of the fighting on Calhoun Hill and in the Keogh sector.

Cheyenne oral tradition places the Lame Whiteman death site on the west side of Custer Ridge and above the Keogh sector (Stands in Timber and Liberty 1972). Lame Whiteman was part of a war party coming up from the Little Bighorn River valley and entering the battle by rushing over the top of the ridge and crashing into Keogh's position. With the effective warrior fire from the ridges to the east and the attack from the west, Keogh and his men were caught in a pincher that resulted in the annihilation of the command in this area.

LAST STAND HILL AND CUSTER RIDGE EXTENSION

Recent analysis of Lakota and Cheyenne accounts of the battle (Fox 1993:173–94) strongly suggest that the left wing under Yates with Custer and his staff moved from Calhoun Hill through the Keogh sector past Last Stand Hill and continued in a westerly direction toward a river ford north of the village site. Fox argues that the left wing and Custer followed Custer Ridge beyond the present northern park boundary. Custer Ridge does not terminate at Last Stand Hill but drops away to the northwest (see figures 35–38). Fox (1993:176) argues that the left wing followed this ridge until the men were near present Highway 212, where the command turned west to move to the Little Bighorn River ford in what he terms the Cemetery Ridge episode. He cites several Cheyenne and Sioux accounts to establish this movement.

Simply stated, Fox argues that the left wing moved north to the far end of Custer Ridge, then westerly to the river. There they may have halted for a brief period. Then, perhaps under some fire, the left wing moved north once again, this time across the flats below what is now the modern park housing area and through that area to the current vicinity of Custer National Cemetery. There the command halted for some undetermined time. Fox's (1993:180–84) analysis allows him to argue that at the cemetery area the command divided again. He places Company F in a shallow basin between the upper branch of Deep Ravine and Calhoun Coulee. He has Company E with Custer and his staff move back to Last Stand Hill, where they were killed along with the remnant of the now nearly annihilated right wing.

Fox acknowledges there is little in the way of archaeological evidence to support his arguments since so much of the area has been disturbed (the National Cemetery, visitor center, maintenance shop, and housing area) by park facility development. Although the park development zone is too disturbed to yield archaeological patterns, the privately held and Crow tribally owned lands between Highway 212 and the park boundary did yield archaeological evidence of the battle (Scott and Bleed 1997). However, portions of this area were also impacted by later activities. Among the documented disturbances are the old park entrance road, now abandoned, which ran from near the present housing area to the old Highway 87; the present park entrance road running from north of the housing area to Highway 212; and a large quarry scar that nearly covers the western third of the lands northwest of the park boundary near the river. These disturbed areas did not yield any battle period artifacts. If they were ever present, they are no longer there today due to the various earth-disturbing activities of the recent past.

Even though there has been some prior ground disturbance, the 1994 archaeological investigations did yield patterned battle-related artifacts in nondisturbed areas. There is clear evidence for combat actions on the northern extension of Custer Ridge, in the ravines below the Custer Ridge extension, and along an extension of Cemetery Ridge adjacent to the old park entrance road. There were more than forty .45–55 cartridge cases, more than forty .45-caliber Springfield carbine bullets, a few Colt .45-caliber cartridge cases and bullets, a number of .44-caliber rimfire cartridge cases, eight .44-caliber bullets, two Spencer cartridge cases, a few .50-caliber bullets, a .50–70 cartridge case, a Springfield carbine butt plate and trigger guard assembly, and an army curry comb found in this Custer Ridge extension.

All of the .45–55 carbine and .45-caliber Colt revolver cases were recovered north of the present park entrance road. Bullets of various calibers were found south of that road but are generally limited to the Cemetery Ridge extension and its associated ravines. A large number of post-battle .45–70 cartridge cases were found along a ravine on the north side of the Cemetery Ridge extension. Only two guns are represented by these later cases. The cases are dated, and most postdate 1884.

If it is assumed that the majority, if not all, of the .45-caliber Springfield bullets were fired by the cavalrymen, then it appears that the two ridges were used by the Sioux and Cheyenne warriors. The orientation of the bullets, as recorded at the time of discovery, gives the impression that most were fired from the Last Stand Hill vicinity. In contrast, the warrior caliber bullets (.44, .50, balls, etc.) are widely distributed over the area, and there are fewer than fifteen artifacts altogether.

The distribution of warrior caliber cartridge cases follows a similar pattern (see figures 36, 37). They are few and widely distributed. The .44-caliber rimfire cases indicate that three Henry or Winchester 1866 rifles were in use as well as one Ballard rifle and a Model 1872 Open Top Colt revolver. One .44-caliber Henry case matches a cartridge case found on Calhoun Hill in 1984. This demonstrates movement of this firearm from Calhoun Hill to the Custer Ridge extension during the battle. The two Spencer cartridge cases indicate that one Spencer and one Ball carbine were used on these two ridges.

By far, the largest quantity of artifacts were army type cartridge cases. Colt revolver cases were found in two concentrations and one isolated case. At least six separate revolvers are represented, as indicated by the firearms identification. One case matches a case found in Calhoun Coulee in 1984. The .45–55 carbine cases were concentrated along the ridgetop of the Custer Ridge extension. At least ten carbines are indicated by the firearms identification. Four of these match cases found on Calhoun Hill in 1984, and cases representing one gun also came from the Keogh area. The 1994 matches to the 1984 finds indicate movement of those firearms across a one-mile area (Scott and Bleed 1997:72–75).

The archaeological and historical evidence indicates that the army cases deposited on Calhoun Hill and in Calhoun Coulee were most likely deposited by members of Companies C and L. There is no historical evidence that any member these companies was part of the movement to the north; in fact, there is evidence to the contrary. It is generally accepted that Companies C and L were annihilated at or near Calhoun Hill while the remainder of the command was moving north. Assuming this is the situation, the cases found on the Custer Ridge extension that match those on the south end of the field probably represent army carbines, Colt revolvers, and ammunition captured by the Sioux and Cheyenne and turned on the left wing and Custer at the north end of the battlefield.

It appears reasonable to conclude that the left wing and Custer did move north through Last Stand Hill and northwesterly along the Custer Ridge extension at least one-quarter mile. The presence of scattered warrior caliber bullets on the ridge and in adjacent ravines suggests that the soldier's movement was under fire by a few warriors. One interpretation of this event is that Custer and the left wing attempted to move north and west to ford the river and continue the attack on the village from that direction, but as the movement on the Custer Ridge extension began he was observed and fired upon by several warriors—perhaps a small group that moved north and finally surrounded Custer's command. From positions at the Custer Ridge extension some of those warriors may have used army weapons and ammunition captured on Calhoun Hill only a short time before.

Traditionally (Stewart 1955) this northern route has been presumed to be warriors led by Crazy Horse. Fox (1993:166) and Michno (1993) counter this argument by reconstructing Crazy Horse's movements up Deep Ravine through Calhoun Hill and then to the north. It is also well documented that Crazy Horse and many other warriors were involved in the valley fight with Reno, and it is likely that some army firearms were captured there as well. Whatever route Crazy Horse took, it appears Custer's left wing movement met with opposition. It is possible that some of Custer's men returned fire and may have deposited a few of the army caliber cases found on the Custer Ridge extension. Still, the archaeological context and association are a compelling argument for most of the cartridge cases being deposited by warriors using captured army weapons. Custer may have retraced his movements back along the ridge or perhaps swung to his left and across a ravine onto Cemetery Ridge and thence to Last Stand Hill after running into these warriors moving along the ridge and ravines outside the present park boundary. The swing to Cemetery Ridge, perhaps near the what is now the National Cemetery, as is posited by Fox (1993), is supported by a variety of oral testimonies. Gall told noted frontier photographer D. F. Barry during the battle's tenth anniversary ceremony in 1886 that a location downslope (near the modern visitor center) was where Custer stopped before he came back to Last Stand Hill (notation in Barry's hand on the back of a photograph depicting Capt. Frank Baldwin's Fifth Infantry company conducting firing demonstrations on the battlefield in 1886; original photograph in the possession of Douglas Scott).

Archaeological evidence suggests that when Custer made the movement to Last Stand Hill numerous warriors gained the Custer Ridge extension and began firing at the remaining members of the command. They used some Henry and Winchester rifles as well as many army carbines, revolvers, and ammunition just captured from the fallen men of the right wing. Custer's remaining men returned fire until they were overrun and killed. Much of Custer's fire must have come from Last Stand Hill. The bullet orientation strongly suggests this, even though there were very few corresponding army caliber cartridge cases found on Last Stand Hill during the 1984 investigations (Scott et al. 1989). It seems likely that one reason cartridge cases were not recovered in corresponding quantity is that they were souvenired from the field in the ensuing decades, for this area was heavily visited. As noted earlier, P. W. Norris on his 1877 visit to the battlefield collected about one hundred army cartridge cases from Last Stand Hill, likely beginning the relic collection of the area that continued for decades. Thus the absence of army cartridge cases and other artifacts on and around Last Stand Hill should not be construed as a lack of evidence of fighting, only that the area has been compromised by early relic collecting.

Fox (1993) interprets this absence of army cartridge cases here and in the Keogh position as evidence of the command's reorganization and redeployment, but without tactical prescription, arguing that there was no formal last stand as such. He suggest that tactical disintegration occurred as the command structure broke down during the battle. Tactical disintegration of the then surviving elements of the command most likely occurred. Fox's work is an excellent example of how analysis of archaeological data, historical records, and oral history can combine to provide new insights into past events. The caution is one of vetting data sources carefully. Although the archaeological record is important, it too has been affected by indiscriminant collecting. There have been many people over many decades who walked that ground and picked up cartridge cases and other relics. Care must be exercised in devising interpretations based on the presence or absence of cartridge cases alone. The data must be assessed holistically, such as including the distribution of impacted army bullets found on the Custer Ridge extension. The number of army caliber bullets found in the surrounding areas, particularly in the face of the slopes on the Custer Ridge extension, is prima facie evidence that far more fighting occurred on and around Last Stand Hill than the cartridge cases recovered from that locale suggest.

DEEP RAVINE

Just what happened along the Deep Ravine Trail (aka South Skirmish Line) is open to several interpretations. The archaeological materials show that horses died there, men died there, and there was fighting along the trail where the white marble markers now stand. It was probably a breakout attempt, as the oral accounts suggest. The issue is whether it was organized or helter-skelter. The archaeological evidence is not strong enough to refute or support either assumption (see figures 21, 35–38). The human skeletal remains do not appear to be from E company men, although they are not definitively identified at this point. The bullets, cartridge cases, a rather poignant man's wedding ring, and some other personal items, as well as evidence of cutmarks and crushing blows on the skeletal remains, certainly indicate that the victorious Lakota and Cheyenne had time to utterly destroy those soldiers who ventured toward Deep Ravine.

The archaeological evidence for combat is well established all along and in and around the marble markers that dot the length of the trail. Though some marker locations are likely spurious, such as those found in pairs that have been investigated (Scott and Fox 1987; Scott et al. 1989; Scott et al. 1998), the vast majority likely represent a location where a soldier fell. The excavated makers (2, 7, 9–10, 33–34, 42, 52–53) all revealed human remains consistent with only one soldier at each marker or pair of markers. Over the ensuing years isolated exposures of human bone at other markers along the Deep Ravine Trail indicate that far more than six men's remains were covered over in that area in 1876.

The question of the soldiers' remains in Deep Ravine itself remains unanswered. The geomorphological work by C. Vance Haynes (1989) and subsequent geophysical investigations (Josten and Carpenter 1995) all point to one area of the ravine where there is a geophysical anomaly (see "Geomorphology of the Little Bighorn Battlefield," below). Whether this will prove to be the burial site of up to twenty-eight men or some other feature is entirely open to future resolution. Regardless, the archaeological evidence of combat and soldiers' resting places is compelling and clear all along the Deep Ravine Trail. Michno's (1994) argument that Cemetery Ravine is the true Deep Ravine burial site is a misinterpretation of the documentary and archaeological evidence. Michno ignores the absence of archaeological materials in Cemetery Ravine and that Cemetery Ravine has not been an active erosional feature for several thousand years. Geophysical investigations (Josten and Carpenter 1995) in Cemetery Ravine revealed a few small near-surface magnetic anomalies that are likely iron artifacts and natural magnetically susceptible soils. But no anomalies that could be even remotely construed as burial sites were identified. The only anomaly consistent with such an interpretation is the one in Deep Ravine proper.

The gross distribution of army-related artifacts on the Custer field provides some idea of the combatant locations during the battle. The positions of cartridge cases, buttons, spurs, equipment, and human bone indicate that soldiers fought and died along the east side of Custer Ridge from Calhoun Hill to the Keogh position, and to Last Stand Hill. There was also fighting at the northernmost extent of the Deep Ravine Trail (aka South Skirmish Line). These troop positions are further corroborated by the presence of impacted bullets from warrior-associated weapons.

At least seven discrete warrior positions can be discerned on the basis of the variety of cartridge case types and government bullets impacted around these positions. Two positions are on Greasy Grass Ridge. Another is on Henry Ridge, where numerous .44 Henry cartridge cases were found southwest of Calhoun Hill. Yet another is a knoll 660 feet northeast of Last Stand Hill. In addition to a variety of nongovernment cartridge cases found at the knoll, also found were split .45–55 government cases, which probably represent captured government ammunition fired from .50 caliber weapons.

THE RENO-BENTEEN EQUIPMENT DUMP SITE
AND HORSE BONE GRAVE SITE

Aside from the extensive evidence of the combat at Little Bighorn, there is a wide variety of other archaeological evidence related to the aftermath of the battle. Some of that information is related to army and NPS administration of the site; other artifacts relate to the untold thousands who have visited the site or to artifacts that evoke the various memorial and film-making activities that have taken place at or near the park.

Three data sets illustrate what happened after the victorious warriors left the field. One records the remains of the men buried on Custer battlefield, in the valley, and at the Reno-Benteen defense site. They tell the tale of hasty, but not uncaring, burial in the face of uncertainty about when or if the enemy would return. They also tell the tale of the men's lives, the manner of their deaths, and the burials and reburials those remains have endured (Scott et al. 1998). These are discussed in more detail in chapter 6.

Additionally, the Reno-Benteen equipment dump was excavated in 1989 (Scott 1991a, 1991b, 1992b). It may be but one of several equipment disposal areas. The investigations yielded evidence of the deliberate burning and destruction of ammunition and ration crates or boxes, some guns, and a large number of saddles and other horse tack. The army held the field of battle, but they had suffered an ignominious defeat, and they simply destroyed what equipment they could not salvage to render it unserviceable to the enemy.

Perhaps of greatest interest is the horse bone grave. In addition to soldiers and American Indian combatants killed at Little Bighorn, perhaps as many as ninety horses were killed during the battle or wounded and later destroyed by the troops burying the dead.

Through natural erosion and some human vandalism, human skeletal remains were exposed in the years following the first hasty burials of June 1876. Horse bone continued to litter the field as well, giving rise to speculation of poorly treated and unburied human remains. In April 1879, Capt. George Sanderson was ordered with his company of Eleventh Infantry from Fort Custer to rebury the exposed remains. He also constructed a cordwood memorial near the top of Last Stand Hill. Sanderson noted that he believed the reports of unburied dead resulted from misidentification of horse bones for human remains. To forestall further problems, he had the horse bones gathered together and placed in the cordwood memorial, giving the field "a perfectly clean appearance, each grave being re-mounded and all animal bones removed" (Sanderson cited in Gray 1975:37).

In 1881 a detail of soldiers commanded by 1st Lt. Charles Roe, Second Cavalry, was sent to disinter the remaining soldiers' remains and rebury them in a mass grave. Lieutenant Roe was also to erect a granite memorial shaft to commemorate those who had fallen in the battle. He moved the pieces of the monument to the site on sledges, erected the granite shaft on the top of Last Stand Hill at the site of the Sanderson cordwood marker, and then had his detail disinter the remains from around the field. A mass grave, 10 feet wide, was dug surrounding the memorial shaft (Charles Roe letter, October 6, 1908, to W. M. Camp, LBNM files), which now lies under the sidewalk surrounding the memorial on Last Stand Hill. Roe made no mention of the horse bones that were in the center of the cordwood monument his men disassembled, but it is presumed that he had his men dig a pit and bury the horse bones not far from the site of the monument.

That was certainly superintendent Edward Luce's assumption when the laying of a water discharge line from a large water tank on Last Stand Hill revealed a pit containing a large number of horse bones (Luce 1941a). Luce also thought he identified human bone comingled with horse bone when he inadvertently cut into the horse bone grave pit.

The water tank, of 20,000 gallon capacity, on Last Stand Hill was the primary water reservoir for the National Cemetery irrigation system and for potable water to the residences. The tank was installed on the northeast side of Last Stand Hill immediately east of the Seventh Cavalry monument placed by Roe. The tank's date of construction is not precisely known, but it may have been around 1911 (Doerner 2002). Water was pumped to the tank from the Little Bighorn River and from there delivered by gravity-fed lines to the cemetery irrigation system and to a hypochlorinater that filtered the water for the drinking fountain and residences (Hommon 1940).

Apparently the reservoir tank overflowed from time to time, and in April 1941 Superintendent Luce installed an overflow drain on the tank and a drainage line that discharged to the east. During the digging of the trench for the drain line a large quantity of horse bone was encountered. The discovery of the horse pit during the overflow line trenching was excitedly reported by Luce (1941a) on April 9, 1941. On April 18, bypassing the normal NPS chain of command, Luce (1941b) wrote directly to the U.S. Army quartermaster general to inform him of the discovery of human remains in the horse pit. Luce conducted an informal investigation of the pit at the time of its discovery and placed some of the recovered items in the museum collection, where they remain today.

Luce's agenda in writing to both the Yellowstone superintendent and the quartermaster general appears to have been to generate interest and funding to excavate the horse pit for research purposes. He couched his request in terms of recovering and reburying any associated human remains, but the broader purpose seems to have been to have Col. Elwood Nye (figure 39), one of the discoverers of Nye-Cartwright Ridge and an army veterinarian stationed at West Point, detailed to the park to excavate the horse pit. Luce made that request to his superiors in a memorandum dated May 6, 1941 (Luce 1941c).

Luce was in routine correspondence with Nye concerning the issue of excavating the horse pit, for in a letter to Nye dated May 27, 1941, Luce (1941d) reported that the park service lacked the funds to examine the horse cemetery at that time. He further expressed to Nye his desire for the study to proceed at some point in the future. World War II intervened, and it was not until 1946 that the horse pit work again surfaced.

In July 1946, Nye, along with Luce and several local men, dug into the horse pit (Nye 1946). Photographs in the park collections indicate that they dug a hole at least 4 feet in diameter, and they recovered a variety of horse bones including ribs, vertebrae, and limb bones (figure 40). Study of the available photographs does not show any readily identifiable human bone comingled with the horse bone. The photographs show Luce and Nye examining the horse bones, a large pile of disarticulated bone elements, and an excavation scene taken from atop the 20,000-gallon reservoir tank in which there is clearly a group of horse bones being arranged in anatomical order. Nye apparently had permission to study some of the horse bones, and it also appears from the correspondence that Nye returned those from the horse grave. The Larimer County,

Figure 39. Lt. Col. Elwood Nye, whose interests in the Little Bighorn story helped stimulate work on the horse bone grave. Little Bighorn Battlefield National Monument.

Figure 40. The crude excavations of the horse bone grave, probably taken at the time of its discovery in 1941. Little Bighorn Battlefield National Monument.

Figure 41. Robert Nickel employs a ground-penetrating radar unit in the initial search for the horse cemetery. Geophysical investigative techniques have good potential at Little Bighorn to find buried features such as riflepits at the Reno-Benteen defense site. Midwest Archeological Center, National Park Service.

Colorado, museum has some of Nye's personal collection, including some revolver and carbine cartridge cases and horse hoof bones collected at the Reno-Benteen defense site before it became NPS property (William Schneider, personal communication, February 9, 2012).

During planning for the Indian Memorial sidewalk, it became apparent that the sidewalk would be very near the presumed location of the horse pit. Since the precise location was not well documented and could not be precisely verified with the available photographic evidence, it was decided to use archaeological methods to locate the horse pit.

Steven De Vore (2002a, 2002b) undertook geophysical investigations using a magnetometer and electrical conductivity meter, and Robert Nickel (2002) used ground-penetrating radar (figure 41); both identified anomalies within the suspected area. Most were interpreted to be associated with natural features and water runoff from the nearby Last Stand Hill parking lot. One was rectangular in shape and thought to be consistent with the horse pit location as seen in the 1941 and 1946 photographs. The size was somewhat smaller than Luce's 1941 description—about 5 m by 2 meters—and only 2 m from the abandoned overflow drain outlet feature.

Subsequent archaeological investigations did locate a pit (Scott 2002c) containing disarticulated horse bone elements at the anomaly location (figure 42). The feature is substantially smaller than the pit originally reported by Superintendent Luce in 1941. It is suspected that Luce only guessed at the size of the pit found during the trenching for the overflow drain line. It is also suspected that Luce exaggerated the pit's size and contents to engender support for its investigation. The discovered feature yielded evidence of one or more disturbances during the twentieth century as revealed by artifacts found mixed in the pit fill and the evidence of mechanical abrading and bone breakage. It seems likely that the most significant disturbance was not the 1941 finding of the pit or the 1946 digging but an undocumented disturbance probably related to 1950s or 1960s era construction projects carried out on Last Stand Hill associated with construction work to support increased visitation.

The sidewalk construction that leads to the Indian Memorial from Last Stand Hill did not affect the horse bone pit location. The

Figure 42. Horse bone grave pit during excavation. Little Bighorn Battlefield National Monument.

pit was bypassed, and a marble marker commemorating the horses and their burial site was erected along with an interpretive panel that discusses the horses and the pit excavation as part of the interpretive exhibits along the walk (figures 43, 44).

Geomorphology of the Little Bighorn Battlefield

During the 1984 fieldwork, Richard Fox supervised the excavation of several soil mounds and disconformities in Deep Ravine in the hopes of finding some of the soldiers thought to be buried there. The testing effort revealed only sterile deposits, and the mounds appeared to be natural slumping of soils from the nearby ravine banks (Scott and Fox 1987). He also used a power posthole digger or augur in an attempt to locate buried soils and remains in the lower reaches of Deep Ravine. The augur was unable to reach sufficient depth to ensure that all soil deposits were sampled.

In 1985, C. Vance Haynes of the University of Arizona joined the team to conduct geological investigations in Deep Ravine (Haynes 1989). Of particular interest were the bodies of a score or more of troopers reported in several historical accounts to be located in the steep-walled gully and buried where they had been found (Scott et al. 1989). Soil auguring and trenching in Deep Ravine revealed five strata of Holocene alluvium separated by four disconformities, most of which are erosional. Of the stratigraphic units identified, three are prehistoric in age and two are less than a century old. The conformable contact at the base of unit F_1 was the floor of Deep Ravine at the time of the 1876 battle; it was examined in six backhoe trenches placed across the ravine in 1985. Five other trenches exposed the erosional contact at the base of unit F_2 and on top of unit C (of prehistoric age). An area, designated unit X, was postulated to be the fill of a buried ravine headcut that could host the missing remains a few meters downstream of trench 11.

In 1989, Haynes (1991) tested the postulated unit X area by placing three lines of auger holes across the floor of Deep Ravine near the lower trail crossing. The hand augering was hampered by a high water table in Deep Ravine but did prove the presence of unit X, although no battle-related remains were found. Unit X was found to contain a clear geophysical anomaly when geophysical investigations

Figure 43. A stone marker commemorates the horses lost in the battle. The stone was designed by chief historian John Doerner and placed on the site of horse grave pit.

of the area were undertaken in 1995 (Applied Ground Imaging 1996; Coleman Research 1996; Josten and Carpenter 1995). The association of the anomaly with 1876 events cannot be proven without extensive and expensive excavations of the area.

In addition to the work in Deep Ravine, three soil test pits up to 60 cm deep were placed in the vicinity of archaeological excava-

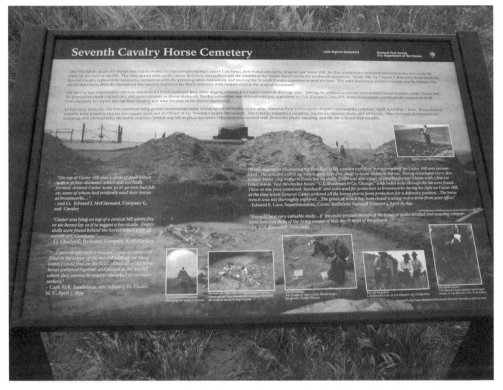

Figure 44. Interpretive panel featuring the archaeological investigations and historical accounts of the horse grave pit.

tions in the Reno-Benteen dump area (Haynes 1991). These were to determine the sedimentary substrate, evaluate slope processes, and relate these to alluvial processes in gullies such as Deep Ravine. The findings in the dump area are consistent with those of the 1984/85 archaeological work (Scott et al. 1989). Cartridge cases from the 1876 battle showed no preferred orientation even on relatively steep slopes (up to 20 degrees) and no abnormal concentration in drainages as would be expected if significant slope washing had occurred. The conclusions were based upon a qualitative assessment of the cartridge case plots in relation to the topographic maps with a 2-foot contour interval.

Repeat photography also undertaken in 1989 showed no significant changes in vegetation type since 1877, the earliest photographs of the battlefield. These early photographs indicate slightly less dense grass and sagebrush and a few more eroded patches than today, suggesting slightly drier conditions at the time. The steepness of Water Carrier Ravine precludes typical fluvial aggradation as the origin of prehistoric soil units C and E. Their presence on the adjacent slopes as alluvial aprons and the presence of pebble lines are deemed compelling evidence for accumulation by washing from higher slopes during late glacial (Wisconsin) time. Essentially there is no evidence of significant erosion or aggradation of soils on the Little Bighorn battlefield since 1876, except for infilling and headward cutting in Deep Ravine and in those active drainages such as Deep Coulee, Medicine Tail Coulee, and along the Little Bighorn River course.

Beyond the Events of Battle

Aside from allowing a great deal more to be inferred about the way the battle played out, the artifacts recovered from the battlefield area provide details about what was actually worn, carried, or used by the battle participants. The range and extent of what the artifact studies have shown about clothing, equipment, ornaments, and weaponry used at the battle are reported in detail in Scott et al. (1989) and further revised in Scott and Bleed (1997). This section summarizes that information.

CLOTHING AND PERSONAL ITEMS

The number of artifacts representing clothing and sundry items used by the combatants is relatively small. This is not unexpected given the nature of the battle and the historical accounts of scavenging the battlefield. The clothing worn by the battle participants has been the subject of several studies (Hutchins 1976; Reedstrom 1977). The archaeological project recovered only a few American Indian personal items, and no clothing items whatever, so that category of attire cannot be addressed with the archaeological data. Army clothing and equipment-related artifacts were, however, recovered in moderate quantity.

Archaeological evidence for the soldiers' clothing consists of general service buttons, an infantry "I" button, trouser and under-wear buttons, cloth fragments, hooks and eyes, a chinstrap slide, a trouser buckle, a suspender grip, boots, and boot nails. The apparel artifacts support Hutchins's (1976) findings. Hutchins's analysis of contemporary and survivor accounts contains more detailed infor-mation on clothing than the archaeological data. But he does not document the use of the forage cap, and the chinstrap slide found during the archaeological investigations does suggest that the forage cap was present at the battle.

A few personal items were recovered. Four five-cent pieces, two dated 1869 and one each dated 1870 and 1876, were found. All four coins exhibit very little wear, which is consistent with their loss in 1876. Two of them were found in one of the marker excavations, in association with human bone. Their position suggests that they were in a trouser pocket or a bag.

A gold watch chain from the Calhoun position on Custer bat-tlefield and an almost complete gold-plated brass, imported Swiss hunting case watch from Reno-Benteen attest to the presence of timepieces.

Tobacco was definitely present at the battle. The historical rec-ord documents that some warriors recovered tobacco from the dead soldiers at both the Reno-Benteen and Custer battlefields. The presence of tobacco is also documented in the archaeologi-cal record. Three tobacco tags were found, two at Custer and one at Reno-Benteen. Indirect evidence for pipe smoking is present in one set of human remains. The teeth of the individual found at the Marker 33-34 excavation exhibited extensive wear. Tobacco stains were also noted on the teeth of several of the remains recovered (Scott et al. 1998). A recent study (Vihlene 2008) of tobacco use by the Seventh Cavalry during the nineteenth century expands the archaeological information and places army tobacco consumption in the context of tobacco use and smoking habits in the nineteenth century.

Perhaps the most poignant personal item recovered was a silver-plated brass wedding band. The ring was found on the south skir-mish line still encircling a joint of the left third finger. Over the years, other rings, like 2nd Lt. William Van Wyck Reilly's, were recovered and returned to the family (Hutchins 1976:17). 1st Lt. Donald

McIntosh's ring was found in the Reno-Benteen valley fight area by Pitsch (Swanson 2004:101; 2011:150–51), as was a "gutta percha" or vulcanized rubber button that helped his fellow officers identify his body in the field.

Several artifacts can be ascribed to the American Indian combatants. One is a Hudson's Bay style trade fire steel. Two ornaments were also recovered. One from the Reno-Benteen defense site is a brass bracelet found in a warrior position and associated with a group of .44-caliber Henry cartridge cases. The other is an ornament made from two cartridge cases and a piece of lead; its purpose has not been identified. Ball-shaped brass buttons were recovered during B. William Henry's 1969 metal detecting work and the 2004 tour road mitigation effort (Scott 2006) and are assumed to be Native clothing ornaments given their positions at Greasy Grass Ridge and the Reno-Benteen defense site. Many other indigenous objects were found by Pitsch in the village areas of the Little Bighorn valley. Among those finds were scrapers and fragments of cast iron kettles as well as other camp debris. Personal items included a variety of trade buttons, brass bracelets, a necklace with a crucifix, and decorative conchas (Swanson 2004:275–78).

SOLDIER'S EQUIPMENT

The average cavalryman carried a variety of equipment during a campaign. He, of course, carried weapons, but he also had a cartridge belt with a buckle, a holster for his revolver, and a carbine sling. He wore spurs and would have had a canteen, mess gear, and haversack. Hutchins (1976:33–55) addresses the type of equipment carried by the Seventh Cavalryman in excellent detail.

The archaeological evidence for equipment is limited in number but diverse. Several firearms parts were found. Three screws are associated with the carbines used by the command, and a backstrap, cylinder pin, and ejector rod button are from three of the command's Colt revolvers. Lock retaining screws found in the Reno-Benteen dump indicate the presence of a .50–70-caliber rifle at that site. A trigger guard, tang screw, and butt plate from a Springfield carbine were found in 1994 on the Custer Ridge extension. Another two parts represent warrior firearms: the loading lever from a Model

1858 New Model Army Remington percussion revolver, and a trigger from a shotgun. The valley fight area yielded several additional firearm parts and a nearly complete Colt Model 1873 revolver to Pitsch's metal detecting efforts (Swanson 2004:279).

No field glasses or compasses were recovered archaeologically, but the eyepiece of a telescope was found at the Reno-Benteen defense site. The eyepiece is very similar to that of French-made telescopes of the era.

Several army issue brass 1859 pattern spurs were recovered as well as three iron spur strap buckles. The iron buckles suggest that the 1859 or Civil War–period spur and strap were used on the campaign. A single brass private purchase spur was found at the Reno-Benteen defense site. Another equipment item recovered was the carbine sling snap swivel. Two were found, one each at Custer and Reno-Benteen, and others in the valley fight area.

There is direct and possibly some indirect evidence of the use of belts. An adjustment hook for a Model 1851 waist belt was recovered on the Custer battlefield. A small fragment of black buff leather was also found. The leather is the style that was used in manufacturing the Model 1851 waist belt. The fragment is too small to be positively identified, however. Indirect evidence for a thimble belt may also exist. Two unusual .45–55 Springfield carbine rounds were found on Last Stand Hill. Both rounds were unfired, but each had been damaged when struck by a bullet. The rounds were found near one another on the ground, suggesting that they were in the same thimble belt when struck.

A few mess items were recovered at the Reno-Benteen defense site. An iron spoon was found in the June 23 camp, an iron-handled three-tined mess fork was found in the Reno-Benteen June 27 camp area below the defense site, as was a fragment of a nonissue three-legged cast iron cooking pot. One nearly complete and one fragmentary issue tin cup were also found. The nearly complete cup was crushed flat and appears to be the 1874 pattern cup, although no U.S. stamp is present on the handle. Three crudely scratched block letters (KKK) were noted on the cup's bottom. The letters' association has not been determined. Several canteen stopper rings have been recovered and could be from either the Model 1858 canteen or the Model 1874 canteen.

MISCELLANEOUS EQUIPMENT

A sectional tent pole ferrule was found at the Reno-Benteen defense site and is likely associated with a shelter half. Other tent-related artifacts, also found at Reno, are grommet stiffeners. The recovery of these items confirms the presence of shelter halves with the command during the battle. Wall or A tents or ground cloths may be responsible for the grommet stiffeners, for there is mention of using canvas of some sort to protect the wounded from the ground surface in the defense site hospital area.

Another group of items with exclusive Reno-Benteen affiliation are the ammunition box nails and screws and ration box nails. These artifacts were recovered in large quantities near the barricade area and in the camp of June 26–27 as well as in the excavated equipment dump site (Scott 1991a, 1991b; Scott et al. 1989). These nails and screws indicate where these boxes were discarded or broken up for fuel. Their presence helps to define the barricade and camp areas more precisely than has been possible in the past even with the available survivor accounts.

HORSE-RELATED EQUIPMENT

Artifacts related to horses, saddles, bridles, and other equipment were found in larger quantities than was soldier-related equipment (figure 45). A poorly preserved Model 1859 carbine socket was found at the Reno-Benteen defense site. Several buckles of the size found on carbine sockets were also recovered. This buckle size was also found on other horse-related equipment.

Also found at Reno-Benteen were a hand-forged hoof pick and several Model 1859 picket pins or parts. Horseshoes and horseshoe nails were found on both battlefields. Saddle parts found include brass saddle plates, foot rings, and foot ring staples from Model 1859 McClellan saddles or the 1872 modification. Halter and bridle buckles were found on both battlefields, as were other buckles in sizes used on harnesses and other equipment. Several sizes of girth rings were recovered at Reno-Benteen. The context of recovery suggests association with pack animals' saddles and harness.

A few recovered tack items indicate that some of the command's horse-related tack met the specifications of 1874. A brass staple was

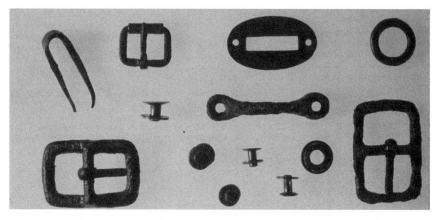

Figure 45. Tack buckles, saddle plates, staples, and harness rivets all aided in the identification of the army saddles used at the battle as McClellan models 1872 and 1874. Artifacts like these are the physical evidence of the event that goes beyond the battle itself to tell the story of the individuals who participated in the battle. Midwest Archeological Center, National Park Service.

found at the Reno-Benteen defense site, as was a iron girth ring for the near side. Two side-line (hobble) snap hooks were also found at Reno. This indicates that the new model items had reached Custer or that the company saddlers were making up items to meet the then new specifications.

Some nonmilitary but battle-associated horse-related materials were also found. A nickel or tinned buckle may indicate an officer's private purchase bridle or possibly an army experimental buckle. A large iron girth ring may also represent an officer's private purchase or a company saddler's modification of an issue saddle to accept a horsehair cinch. Finally, a small iron ring from Custer battlefield may represent either a civilian's saddle rigging or the rigging from a Lakota or Cheyenne pony.

FIREARMS

Along with the aforementioned gun parts, bullets, cartridges, cartridge cases, arrowheads, and knives are the direct evidence of the weapons used during the battle. During the archaeological investigations the Little Bighorn battlefield was viewed much like a crime scene. By employing forensic techniques such as studies of firing pin marks on cartridge cases and rifling marks on bullets (Fox 1984; Scott 1989b; Scott and Haag 2009), it was possible to determine the variety of weapons used by the various participants. Firearms examiners at the Nebraska State Patrol Criminalistic Laboratory in Lincoln were instrumental in mentoring project personnel in the techniques of cartridge case and bullet identification and comparison.

By combining firearms identification methods with the archaeological constructs of spatial patterning and individual artifact analysis, it was possible to discover evidence for the movement of individual firearms over the field of battle, verify cavalry positions, and define previously unknown fighting areas, which was an important advance in battlefield interpretation. Prior to this time static distributions of artifacts such as cartridge cases or bullets were used in concert with historical documents to reconstruct fighting positions and movements during a battle. With the application of firearm identification coupled with spatial patterning, actual movements of firearms on a battlefield were shown for the first time, which led to a significant advance in the interpretation of physical evidence independent of documentary or oral history evidence. Comparing data sets, a richer and more accurate understanding of the events could be reconstructed.

Firearms identification procedures applied to archaeological evidence are the same as those applied to a criminal investigation. One archaeological specimen is placed on one stage of a comparison microscope and another archaeological case of the same caliber is, in turn, placed on the adjacent stage, and the two are compared visually. Two types of characteristics are identified during the process: class characteristics and individual characteristics. Class characteristics indicate that a given case was fired in a specific firearm type. If the class characteristics match, then individual characteristics are examined. These included depth of firing pin mark, size of the mark, breech face marks, manufacturing tool marks, and other conditions like evidence of firing pin drag. Each firearm is unique in these characteristics, and any case fired in a specific gun shows the same set of microscopic characteristics. This technique of firearms identification has been used by law enforcement agencies since the early 1900s to prove that a cartridge or bullet was fired in a particular gun.

The results of the Little Bighorn firearms analyses are nothing

short of incredible. Forty-seven different types of guns were identified as used by warriors. The cartridge case and bullet analyses demonstrated evidence for the use of more than three hundred specific
and individual firearms by the warriors at the battle (figures 46–49).
These figures are considered a minimum, since not all cartridge
cases or bullets collected from the field of battle are available for
comparison.

This stimulating data also brought about, through a Kinnican
Arms Chair Grant from the Winchester Gun Museum in Cody,
Wyoming, an opportunity to search out and study actual firearms
used in the battle. The effort required finding well-documented
battle-attributed firearms from which firing pin impressions were
taken. More than 130 firearms were examined and firing pin
impressions made and compared with the archaeological specimen
cartridge cases. Sixteen firearms have now been documented as seeing service in the Battle of the Little Bighorn (Scott and Harmon
2004:289–324).

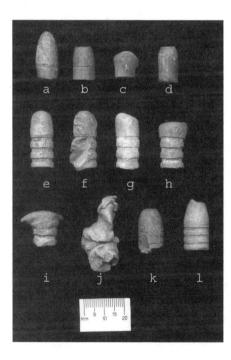

Figure 46. Examples of .44-
and .45-caliber bullets from
the battlefield: (a) .44 Sharps,
(b) .44 Henry single crimping
groove, (c) .44 Henry deformed
by impact, (d) .44 Henry
raised base variety, (e) .45–405
Springfield, (f) .45 Springfield
with side impact damage, (g) .45
Springfield with slight nose
deformation, (h) .45 Springfield
with medium nose deformation,
(i) .45 Springfield mushroomed
by impact, (j) unidentified
impact damaged bullet, (k) .50–
450 bullet with three land and
groove rifling impressions,
(l) .50–450 bullet. Midwest
Archeological Center, National
Park Service.

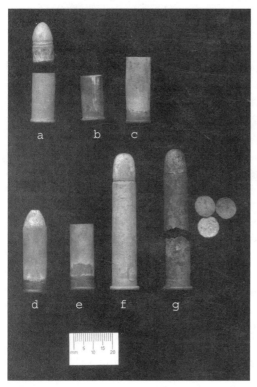

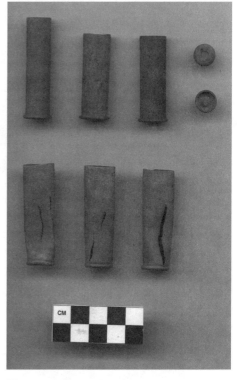

Figure 47. Examples of .44-caliber, .45-Colt, and .45–55-caliber cartridges and cartridge cases found during the inventory work: (a) Smith and Wesson Russian bullet and case, (b) Smith and Wesson American cartridge case, (c) .44–40 cartridge case, (d) .45-Colt misfired cartridge, (e) .45-Colt cartridge case, (f) .45–55 unfired cartridge, (g) .45–55 unfired cartridge broken by oxidation and exposing the cardboard wads used to fill the case. Midwest Archeological Center, National Park Service.

Figure 48. Examples of .45–55 cartridge cases and .50-caliber cartridge cases, Benet primers, and .45–55 cartridge cases damaged when fired in .50-caliber firearms. All are believed to have been fired in warrior-used weapons. Midwest Archeological Center, National Park Service.

Firearm Types

The different firearms types and their quantity, particularly those used by warriors, has intrigued Little Bighorn enthusiasts for years (du Mont 1974). One of the first to use physical evidence to deter- mine the type of firearms used in the battle was B. William Henry, Jr. He evaluated and described the variety of bullets and cartridge

Figure 49. A .50-caliber bullet with bone embedded in the body after cleaning and conservation, found on the Custer battlefield in 1984. Midwest Archeological Center, National Park Service.

cases from warrior positions around the Reno-Benteen defense site and Custer battlefield. Henry's (du Mont 1974:55–56) analysis of 1,672 artifacts identified thirteen different types of cases and bullets representing thirteen different battle-related firearm types. The archaeological projects recovered 2,665 cartridges, cartridge cases, and bullets: 166 cartridges of various calibers, 927 cartridge cases, and 1,572 bullets. The .44-caliber Henry and Model 1873 Winchester cases represent about 27 percent of the total, and .45–55 Model 1873 Springfield cases account for another 54 percent. Corresponding bullet types were found in similar quantities, with over 17 percent and 46 percent, respectively. The Little Bighorn Battlefield museum collection also has similar quantities of .45–55 cases (1,069) and .44 rimfire cases (222). The sheer number of these cases indicates the prominence of the Model 1873 Springfield single-shot and Winchester-manufactured repeating firearms in the battle.

Firearm identification analysis has found evidence for at least 371 individual guns among the forty-seven firearm types used in the battle. The archaeological data provide the direct physical evidence of the guns used on the battlefield site. Three other types—

.44-caliber rimfire used in the Frank Wesson guns, the .44-caliber centerfire Colt, and .58-caliber muzzle-loaders—were identified by Henry from one artifact each, but these types were not seen in the archaeological collections.

The cavalry utilized the .45-caliber Model 1873 Springfield carbine and the .45-caliber Model 1873 Colt revolver. Some army participants are also known to have utilized personal firearms during the battle. Even taking these into account, the warriors had at least forty-five firearm types at their disposal at the battle's beginning. As the battle progressed, the warriors took carbines and revolvers from dead soldiers and eventually utilized all forty-seven types against the cavalry.

Among the ammunition identified is shot from shotguns or other weapons firing shot and eleven types of nonmetallic cartridge firearms types along with metallic cartridge firearms. The nonmetallic cartridge and muzzle-loading firearms include at least three types of revolvers, five types of long guns, and three unidentified types. Of the long guns, at least three are military types: Maynard, Starr, and Smith carbines. The other two types are .58-caliber balls and the .577-caliber Enfield, which could have been fired in either a military musket or a commercial weapon such as a trade musket. The three unidentified types are .44, .45, and .50-caliber balls. The rifling marks on these balls have not been identified, but they may be from plains rifles or trade guns.

The thirty-three types of metallic cartridge weapons represent eight revolver types, fifteen single-shot long gun types, four repeating long gun types, and seven as yet unidentified cartridge bullet types. Among the cartridge firearms identified are the Springfield Model 1866, Model 1868 or 1870 rifle, Spencer carbine, Joslyn carbine, Ballard carbine, Ball carbine, Sharps .50-caliber, Sharps .44–77-caliber, Springfield Model 1873 carbine, Colt Model 1872 revolver, Colt Model 1873 revolver, and the Remington .50-caliber rifle. The firearms are an impressive array of weaponry. This archaeologically identified group can be compared to the list of weapons turned over to the army in 1877 when some Sioux and Cheyenne bands returned to the reservation. These bands surrendered 410 guns (War Department 1879), including 160 muzzle-loaders. The rest were cartridge guns. These guns may not have been used at the Battle of the Little Bighorn, but they do represent the variety of firearms available to the tribes of the Northern Plains. The archaeological sample does not correspond to the surrendered guns one for one, but the comparability is excellent.

Issues of Extraction Failure

Some Lakota/Cheyenne accounts of the battle (Marquis 1976), as well as comments by Major Reno (Hedren 1973:66), suggest that many of the soldiers' carbines jammed in the process of extracting the spent case. Some authors have even gone so far as to speculate that Custer's defeat was, in part, due to extraction failures (Graham 1953:146–47). There is no doubt that some carbines failed to extract their case properly, as the historical and archaeological evidence clearly indicates. The archaeological data provide more direct evidence to clarify the role of extraction failure. Hedren (1973) examined all of the available .45–55 carbine cases from the park and private collections in 1972. Three cases of the 1,625 he examined had evidence of extraction problems.

Evidence of case extraction problems is present in the archaeological sample. The microscopic examination of the cases from the Custer battlefield identified two with scratch marks on the head. These could have been caused by prying the case from the carbine chamber with a knife. A third case has two gouges in the rim, which could have been the result of prying the case from the chamber. These three cases were fired in different weapons. Six cases from the Reno-Benteen defense site exhibit extractor problems in four different guns, with two different ones exhibiting extraction failure at least twice each.

The number of cases exhibiting extraction failure amounts to 2 percent of the total number of archaeologically recovered specimens (1.8 percent at Reno-Benteen and 3.3 percent at the Custer battlefield). Taken with Hedren's data the extractor failure rate amounts to 6 percent of all examined .45–55 cases. The archaeological cases represent sixty-nine different guns from the Custer battlefield and sixty-two different guns from the Reno-Benteen defense site. The extraction problems represent 4.3 percent and 5.6 percent failure rates for the two battlefields, respectively, or an average of 5 percent overall failure rate. Since the cartridge cases represent 131 guns—about 22 percent of the carbines used by the army in the battle—a 5 percent failure rate mean that about thirty total battle carbines would have failed (ten on Custer battlefield and twenty at Reno-Benteen).

If the army had extractor failure problems, did their enemy face a similar problem? The archaeological record indicates that about 8 percent of the .50–70 and Spencer cases have pry or scratch marks on them. These figures exclude the .45–55-caliber army cases that were fired in .50-caliber arms. Those cases all exhibit extraction failure, as might be expected with a ruptured case. From the archaeological data, then, it appears that the case extraction failure rate during the battle was about the same on both sides, reinforcing the argument that extraction failure did occur, but not to a large degree. That extraction failure did occur is not debatable, but it was not significant to the outcome of the battle.

Brass Cases and George Custer's Guns

For many years it was assumed that George Custer was the only person to use .50-caliber brass cartridges during the battle. This unfortunate notion has crept into the literature on the battle and been used to reconstruct Custer's personal movements (Weibert and Weibert 1985). Custer is known to have possessed a .50–70-caliber Remington sporting rifle that may have utilized a brass case (du Mont 1974). He also may have used one or a brace of Royal Irish Constabulary pistols that used a brass case (du Mont 1974; Palmer 1975). Brass cartridge cases began to come into use in the 1870s and were commercially produced. In fact, the government bought several million rounds for their .50–70 military models in 1874 and 1875 (Lewis 1972:19). Brass cartridge cases were also produced for several other weapons, such as the Model 1873 Winchester and the Evans Old Model.

Several dozen brass archaeological cases were recovered on both battlefields. The archaeological case types include the .44-caliber Evans and the .44–40-caliber Model 1873 Winchester. The only other brass cases found were .50–70-caliber. The Winchester-Millbank primer type cases are brass and were found on the Custer battlefield and Reno-Benteen defense site. A total of twenty-one brass .50–70 cases were recovered. Firearms identification analysis indicates that they were fired in fourteen different Springfield, Sharps, or Remington guns. The distribution and context of the brass cases suggest use by warriors on the Custer battlefield and by both sides at the Reno-Benteen defense site. Clearly these brass cases cannot be associated with Custer's Remington sporting rifle. Nor can the presence of brass cases in other contexts be the primary evidence to support the reconstruction of Custer's personal movements.

NONFIREARM WEAPONS

Weapons other than firearms used at the Battle of the Little Bighorn are limited to cutting and crushing implements: knives, spears or lances, tomahawks or belt axes, and war clubs. The archaeological evidence for the use of such items is both indirect and direct. The number of nonfirearm artifacts is low, particularly based on direct evidence, but indirect evidence conclusively supports their use and corroborates the historical accounts.

Historical accounts indicate that the bow and arrow were significant in the fight. The archaeological evidence for the use of the bow is limited to twelve arrowheads (figure 50). Indirect evidence of bow and arrow use is present on the human remains (Scott et al. 1998). At least two, and possibly three, bones from different bodies exhibit cutmarks that could have been made by arrows.

Knives, spears or lances, tomahawks or belt axes, and war clubs are also mentioned in the warriors' accounts. The archaeological evidence for the use of tomahawks and war clubs is indirect. The human remains bear the marks of crushing by heavy blunt instruments, such as war clubs, and at least one soldier was decapitated by a blow to the neck with a heavy edged instrument like a belt axe. There is direct archaeological evidence of knives. One nearly complete sheath knife, three blade fragments, and three complete folding or pocket knives demonstrate the use of knives by the soldiers. There is also some indirect evidence too. Several .45–55-caliber cartridge cases retain evidence of being pried from a carbine chamber by pointed instruments. Only one sheath knife fragment attests to warrior use of knives in the battle. The blade fragment, found in a warrior's position at Reno-Benteen, is a large butcher knife style. It is painted gold and closely resembles a Green River Russell trade knife. Blades of this type are also known to have been set into Sioux war clubs of this period. Although this evidence is not striking, it does confirm the recollections of the battle participants.

Figure 50. Four of the twelve iron arrowheads found during the archaeological investigations. Midwest Archeological Center, National Park Service.

The ability to identify individual weapons is an important achievement in the study of the Battle of the Little Bighorn. It helped to address questions about the numbers and armament of the Lakota and Cheyenne. But coupled with the piece-plotted data, which located precisely where cartridges and bullets were found, this capability became even more important by allowing tracing of individual movements during the battle, which in turn allows a reinterpretation of the chronology of events of that short span of time. When all the firearms data are taken into account, it becomes readily apparent that Custer and his men were outgunned by the warriors, if not in range or stopping power then certainly in firepower.

| Bones on the Battlefield

Since the Battle of the Little Bighorn there have been three major episodes of reburial of the soldiers' remains. In 1877, 1879, and again in 1881 burial details went to the field specifically to reinter remains exposed by the elements and scavengers (Dustin 1953; Gray 1975; Hardorff 1989). Human remains have been found, collected, or formally recovered from the battlefield since 1877. No formal professional examination of any of the remains occurred until 1984. Since then there has been a concerted effort to find and analyze human remains associated with the Battle of the Little Bighorn. This is done in part to learn more about the lifestyle and manner of death of those who died in the battle.

Another goal of the studies of human remains is to determine if any are American Indian, and if so to ensure that they are repatriated to the appropriate tribe or group. In addition, human remains are examined to identify individuals represented by the bones, which has been only partly successful. Studies of the human remains found on and around the battlefield have been the subject of several reports (Scott et al. 1998; Snow and Fitzpatrick 1989; Willey 1993, 1997). This chapter utilizes those sources and others to document the human remains recovery and analysis efforts.

Early Burial and Reburial Efforts

The first of the human remains recovery and reburial episodes began in the spring of 1877 when Gen. Phillip H. Sheridan ordered his brother and aide to exhume the remains of the fallen officers and return them to the East for proper interment. Lt. Col. Michael Sheridan reached Fort Abraham Lincoln on May 21, 1877, and soon started for the Little Bighorn escorted by Company I of the Seventh Cavalry. The expedition quartermaster in 1876 was 1st Lt. Henry Nowlan, who had staked the officer's graves and made a sketch map of their locations. In 1877 he commanded Company I.

On July 3, Colonel Sheridan had his men exhume the bones of the identified officers and placed them in pine boxes, with the exception of those of Lt. John Crittenden. At the request of his father, Crittenden was reinterred on the field where he fell. A fatigue party also reinterred some exposed remains of the men. Apparently they removed what dirt had been placed over the bones and then heaped three feet of earth over the bones they uncovered. In a *Chicago Times* account of July 15, 1877, Sheridan stated very clearly that his men found only bones, with all traces of flesh gone.

2nd Lt. Hugh Scott, a member of the detail, recalled years later that where he found bones exposed he had the men gather them up into a small pile. He then had them buried in a hole dug for the purpose (Scott 1928). By noon on July 4 the officers' bones, in their boxes, were on their way back to Post No. 2 (soon to become Fort Custer) to await shipment downstream.

There was, at the time, and certainly since, a question as to whether the body of George Custer was correctly identified (Hardorff 1989). Apparently the first set of bones uncovered was found with a corporal's blouse and was thought not to be those of Custer. A second grave was exhumed and those bones were assumed to be Custer's.

Another 1877 human remains recovery effort was spearheaded by P. W. Norris, who in early July found and removed scout Charley Reynolds's skeletal remains. After Norris departed the battlefield with Reynolds's remains, a severe thundershower and hailstorm struck the site on July 6 and washed away much of the newly heaped-up earth. Within two weeks General Sheridan arrived on an inspection tour and hunting trip. His party visited the battlefield and found some human bones eroding out of their newly constructed graves. Sheridan ordered a police of the field, and sixty troopers spent four hours again reburying the dead.

Because of natural erosion and some human vandalism, bones were exposed again over the next two years. In one case a stage station operator, living near the site of the current Garryowen post office, was formally castigated in a letter from Fort Custer for removing a soldier's skull from the field. Apparently the station keeper had collected the skull for presentation to the director of the stage line.

Skeletal remains continued to be exposed, and in April 1879 Capt. George Sanderson was ordered with his company of Eleventh Infantry from Fort Custer to rebury exposed remains once again. Sanderson reported that he found very few exposed remains. He gathered together remains of parts of four or five bodies, by his estimate, and buried them on Last Stand Hill. He then proceeded to build a cordwood mound on that site. Sanderson noted that he believed the reports of unburied dead had resulted from misidentification of horse bones for human remains (Gray 1975:37). Stanley Morrow's famous photographs of the Keogh area graves, Crittenden's grave, and the mound of horse bone (figure 51) were taken at this time, and some were even attached to Sanderson's original report to his superiors.

In 1881, a detail of soldiers commanded by 1st Lt. Charles F. Roe, Second Cavalry, was sent to disinter the rest of the soldiers' remains and rebury them in a mass grave. He was also to erect a granite memorial shaft to commemorate those who had fallen in the battle. Lieutenant Roe moved the pieces of the monument to the site on sledges. He erected the granite shaft on the top of Last Stand Hill at the site of the Sanderson cordwood marker and then had his detail disinter the remains from around the field. A mass grave, 10 feet wide, was dug surrounding the memorial shaft (Charles Roe letter, Oct. 6, 1908, to W. M. Camp, LBNM files).

It was not until 1890 that the marble markers that now dot the battlefield were placed to commemorate locations where soldiers fell, making the Little Bighorn battlefield the only battlefield in the world where markers denote where men fell or were found after the battle. The party to erect the headstones, under the command of Capt.

Figure 51. This photograph of Last Stand Hill taken by Stanley Morrow depicts the nature of the battlefield in 1879, with stakes marking soldiers' graves and scattered horse bones. The horse bones were collected and placed in a cordwood monument on the top of Last Stand Hill just after the image was taken. The cordwood monument was replaced by the granite Seventh Cavalry memorial in 1881, and the horse bones were reburied in a separate grave nearby. Little Bighorn Battlefield National Monument.

Owen Jay Sweet and supervised by 2nd Lt. Samuel Burkhardt, Jr. (Greene 2008:276n), arrived fourteen years after the battle, nine years after the soldiers' remains were reinterred in a mass grave.

A daily skirmish line searched over an area of about 2 square miles of the battlefield and the last of the 29 missing bodies were found and buried and the last headstone erected. During the search [four] bleaching skeletons of men were found and for some reason of neglect had remained unburied and with God's canopy alone to cover them for fourteen years. ... On examination of the field it was found that the resting places of only 217 officers and men had been marked, exclusive of the places where Boston Custer and Arther (Autie) R. Reid [Reed] fell, a difference of 29 graves. Lieut. Porter's not inclusive. This necessitated additional and trying work in an attempt, if possible, to discover and verify the resting places of the 29 missing bodies. (Official report of O. J. Sweet 1890, LBNM files)

Thus, in 1890 there were 246 markers on the field. It was Lieutenant Burkhardt's assumption that there should be 246 markers on the Custer field that led the men to search for missing graves. Burkhardt had confused the number of men who died in the overall battle with those who died under Custer's immediate command and thus added the Reno-Benteen dead to the number on the main battlefield. In fact, of the 249 headstones the party was given to erect, only two were placed on the Reno-Benteen defense site, "making a total of 246 officers and men over whom headstones were erected on the Custer field. Two headstones, one for Lt. McIntosh and the other for Dr. DeWolf being erected on the Reno field, and that of Lieut. Porter being returned to the post and turned over to the Post Quartermaster, accounts for 249 headstones" (Official report of O. J. Sweet 1890, LBNM files).

Sweet's report and Burkhardt's observations also document another feature of the markers that students of the battle have discussed at length: "all parts of the field show evidence of a large number of men who fell by two's or as comrades in battle" (Official report of O. J. Sweet 1890, LBNM files).

There are, indeed, forty-three marker pairs scattered over the Custer battlefield. Explanations like Sweet's and Burkhardt's have been proffered, such as that the pairs represent where "bunkies," men who bunked together, fought and died together. An alternate explanation is that each pair represents only one soldier. In the original 1876 burials and probably during the 1877 and 1879 reburials, dirt was scooped up from either side of the deceased and piled on top. This left shallow indentations on both sides of the burial. Later burial parties, seeing a scatter of human bone and two shallow indentations, may have assumed that each indentation represented a burial and therefore placed two markers at that site.

The creation of the Custer National Cemetery in 1879 afforded a measure of protection to the Little Bighorn battlefield that was unprecedented in the trans-Mississippi West in the era of westward expansion. It reflects a mix of cultural philosophies, that of memorializing fallen heroes and allowing them to rest in the securely enclosed confines of a national cemetery. The hasty burial of the dead at the Little Bighorn, when viewed in the context of the history of warfare, was not uncommon. The concept of military dead being treated with respect and being reverently buried grew out of the American Civil War experience, which was a very visible extension of the Victorian era public mourning process and an extension of the secular and religious mores of that era (Scott et al. 1998).

Collecting Medical Specimens

Reburial episodes, as revealed by the archaeological investigations of 1958, 1984, 1985, 1989, and 1991, did not recover all the bones of soldiers who died there. Continuing to the present, bones of dead soldiers have eroded to the surface. Undoubtedly nature is more to blame than scavengers and relic collectors for the exposed skeletal elements observed by visitors in the late 1870s and 1880s (Hardorff 1984; Taunton 1986).

Shortly after the battle, some remains were collected and documented to enhance nineteenth-century scientific knowledge. During the third quarter of the century, medical science was advancing rapidly in its ability to diagnose disease. But lack of full understanding of the germ theory of disease and causes of infection led medical scientists, particularly the surgeon general of the U.S. Army, to collect for study examples of trauma, disease, and infection in tissue and bone. Pvt. Frank Braun (also listed as Baum and Brunn) of Company M, who was wounded in the face and left thigh on June 25 during the Reno engagement, posthumously contributed one of those examples to medical science (Scott and Owsley 1991).

Braun was wounded while in a stooped position, the bullet entering the lower leg, traveling a tortuous route up the thigh, and lodging in the head of the femur. He was treated by Dr. Henry Porter in the field hospital and transported on the steamer *Far West* to Fort Abraham Lincoln for further medical treatment in the post hospital. Private Braun died of his wounds on October 4, 1876, and was buried in the fort cemetery. When the fort was abandoned, his remains were reinterred in Grave 571A at Custer National Cemetery.

Apparently, Dr. J. M. Middleton, the Fort Abraham Lincoln post surgeon, was intrigued enough with Braun's case to excise part of the dead man's wounded femur and innominate and send them to the Army Medical Museum (the repository of such specimens), where they remain today as a part of the extensive wound trauma specimen collection of the National Museum of Health and Medicine, Armed Forces Institute of Pathology.

Private Braun's contributions to medical science are the bones of his innominate and the femur head that still retains the ball that caused the wound. The specimen shows good progress in the healing of the wound, but the bone also shows necrosis, which means that the bone itself was affected to the extent that alteration of its structure began. Private Braun probably died of the effects of his wound, possibly the debilitating effects of the subsequent infection that resulted from it. Private Braun's bones testify to the state of medical science in 1876—ignorance of not only the causes of infection but also the medications suitable for healing. At the same time, they illustrate physicians' attempts to learn the causes of the illnesses they faced, the way such illnesses affected the body, and effective methods of treatment.

The earliest record of bone actually collected from the battlefield was made by a medical doctor, assistant surgeon Robert W. Shufeldt, who visited the battlefield in June 1877. He collected a human skull not as a souvenir but as a medical specimen. Shufeldt's regular report to the surgeon general stated that he was the senior medical officer with a battalion of the Fifth Cavalry in June and July 1877 and noted that he was with Company I scouting along the base of the Bighorn Mountains to the Custer battlefield during that time (Shufeldt to Surgeon General, Box 521, Papers of Medical Officers and Physicians, Adjutant General's Office, National Archives).

The skull and mandible Dr. Shufeldt collected were sent to the Army Medical Museum in Washington D.C. in July 1881 (Army Medical Museum record 2120, National Anthropological Archives, Smithsonian Institution). According to Shufeldt the remains were pointed out to him by a Sioux who had seen the man killed during the Battle of the Little Bighorn, reportedly among the first killed in the charge on the Indian camp. After he was killed, the report continued, the man's face was mutilated by a war club wielded by a woman. Shufeldt presumed the man to be a bugler because of the double yellow stripes found on his rotting trousers, and he further assumed him to be a trumpeter of Company M, killed in Reno's charge on the camp. The basis for these assumptions is not indicated.

Shufeldt (1910:123–24) described the finding of the skull in a medical journal article, providing some additional information on the actual recovery site:

> This was where Reno lost his men, for I found the skeletons of the unburied dead, just where they had fallen, and everything on "the hill" practically as the command had left it at the time of the arrival of the relief. At an easy pace for our ponies, my lone scout and I passed into the bottom at one end of which the enormous camp of Indian hostiles had been. We came opposite the bluffs where Reno threw up his entrenchments, below which we could see the winding river. Almost level, the great broad area over which we cantered grew great patches of tall prairie grass. As we were passing through one of these, the Indian that was with me suddenly halted. . . . He requested me to look down and note what I saw upon the ground, partly hidden in the tall grass. It was the skeleton of a soldier in a cavalry uniform.

Shufeldt clearly and unequivocally placed the remains' location in the Reno valley position, probably on the retreat line from the skirmish line to the timber. He noted that the remains were unburied when pointed out to him, and in fact he removed one or more iron arrowheads from the body's chest cavity.

The double yellow trouser stripe for field musicians was not authorized until 1883, although some commanding officers did allow their use among band members. Custer apparently allowed such a deviation; Lt. Charles DuRudio testified during the Reno court of inquiry (Nichols 1992) that one trumpeter was identified "from the marks on the pants." An 1875 photograph of Seventh Cavalry soldiers shows a musician with the double stripes (McChristian 1995:64, 1996:65). It is also possible that a year's decay of a solid trouser stripe would allow it to appear as a double stripe. Only officers, sergeants, and corporals were authorized to wear a trouser stripe, each of a different width.

Shufeldt donated the skull and mandible to the old Army Medical Museum, where they resided for over fifty years before being moved to the Smithsonian Institution. In 1988 a request was made of Dr. Douglas Owsley of the Smithsonian's Physical Anthropology section to view and study the remains with the goal of identifying the remains. Owsley determined that the skull and two uppermost vertebrae were from a white male with gracile features (Scott and Owsley 1991). He was between 27 and 35 years of age. He had suffered from dental problems. Three teeth were lost before death, and caries were present in five molars. The skull exhibited blunt instrument trauma to the left frontal and temporal areas, and there was evidence that a blow from a heavy sharp instrument was directed to the left cheek area.

The skull was sent to Sharon Long of ID Images, who specializes in facial reconstruction of forensic cases. It was hoped that a facial approximation might lead to a match with another soldier's photograph and thus aid in the identification of the remains. The completed facial approximation was compared to known photographs of the men, but no similarities were noted. Based on age and the elimination of known photographed individuals, there are twelve soldier candidates for the identity (Scott and Owsley 1991).

Little Bighorn researcher Walt Cross became intrigued with the story of the skull and devoted a book-length treatment to the story of one of the officers, 2nd Lt. Henry Harrington, one of the few unidentified officers (Cross 2006, 2011). Cross devotes a fair amount of his work to proving that the skull is that of Lieutenant Harrington. He even illustrates a photographic facial superimposition of the skull over Harrington's photograph to prove his point. But Cross ignores historical facts in creating his reconstruction of the identification of the skull as Harrington. He employs a classic conspiracy theory approach, suggesting that Shufeldt lied about where he found the remains—they were not at the Reno valley fight area but farther north. The facial superimposition is likewise poorly done. The skull should not have been used for such a purpose until it could be properly reassembled by professional anthropologists. Such was suggested to Cross, who refused to accept the fact that the remaining skull fragments are wired together, and it is clear from looking at the skull or an image of it that several pieces are incorrectly aligned, giving a false impression of the face. In addition, a careful study of the published photographic superimposition clearly shows that several features on the skull do not align correctly with Harrington's image. Cross's conclusions are not supported by the physical evidence, which indicates that the skull recovered by Shufeldt has not even a remote possibility of being that of Harrington.

2nd Lt. George S. Young, Seventh Infantry, was another early collector of human bone at the battlefield. During a trip to the battlefield in 1878 or 1879, he collected a .45–55 cartridge case, an iron arrowhead, and a human cervical vertebra transfixed by an iron arrowhead (see figure 5). The arrow entered the vertebra at an angle that suggests the individual was shot from the front and above—that he was lying on the ground when the arrow entered his body or was shot by a mounted assailant. The items were retained by Young's family for many years and were finally donated to the Smithsonian Institution in 1967 (correspondence relating to Accession 275426, Smithsonian Institution).

In another early case of recorded finds a party of five men, driving horses from Nevada to the Tongue River, passed by the battlefield on August 25, 1884. They came upon a human skeleton in a ravine 400–500 yards southeast of the monument, probably in the Keogh area or in the vicinity of the ravine between the Keogh area and Calhoun Hill. According to a short article in the *Army and Navy Journal* (September 20, 1884:148), they collected the skull. Four of the teeth were filled with exceptionally fine gold dental work. The teeth were examined by a Dr. C. S. Whitney, who pronounced the individual to be between 35 and 40 years of age. The skull was thought to be that of an officer because it was assumed that the quality of dental work observed could not have been afforded by an enlisted man. The disposition of the teeth and skull are unknown, so unfortunately a modern examination of the remains cannot be made. However, these same teeth may have been examined by a dentist and forwarded to Dr. William Saunders, who did dental work on West Point cadets. An analysis of this story by Hyson and Whitehorne (1993) led them to believe these might have been the remains of Lieutenant Harrington.

Another find occurred in April 1886, when hospital steward James Carroll of Fort Custer discovered an incomplete skull, which he donated to the Army Medical Museum in 1889 (National Museum of Health and Medicine, Armed Forces Institute of Pathology records relating to specimen 1001064). Carroll discovered a skull cap in a ravine 2,000 yards from the Last Stand Hill monument, probably Deep Ravine (Scott and Owsley 1991).

At the same time the Shufeldt skull was being examined by Dr. Owsley, this skull fragment was studied. The skull cap had extensive evidence of trauma, including a large-caliber gunshot entry wound in the back of the head, with an exit wound in the middle of the forehead over the left eye. The size of the exit wound was much larger than the entrance opening in the occipital bone. In addition, there were cutmarks on the top of the skull indicating that the individual was scalped, and the tip of an iron arrowhead or knife was embedded in the bone. The skull cap is from a 27–35-year-old white male. Of the men who died with Custer, there are more than eighty possible candidates who fit this age range, so it is unlikely that, with the available information, he can be identified.

Other Early Bone Discoveries, with Modern Analyses

Since 1877 there have been at least twenty other documented discoveries of assemblages of human bone on the battlefield (Greene 1986:59), exclusive of the formal archaeological investigations. In four separate episodes at least ten skeletons were found on the battlefield and reburied in graves marked "Unknown" in the National Cemetery. None of the remains received any scientific analysis before they were reburied.

Walter Camp recorded in an interview with battle survivor Henry Mechling (Mecklin or Mechling) (Hardorff 1997:76) that he and national cemetery superintendent Andrew Grover uncovered several graves on Reno Hill. Four bodies were uncovered in one grave and were assumed by Camp to be Corp. George Lell and Pvts. Thomas Meador, James Tanner (aka Jacob Gebhart), and Henry Voight.

Camp further noted that Grover and Mechling (Hardorff 1997: 77) also found the presumed body of Vincent Charley in a swale between Weir Point and Sharpshooter Hill. These remains were reinterred in the National Cemetery within a few days of their discovery.

Custer National Cemetery records indicate that five bodies from the Reno-Benteen site were interred in Section A Graves 453–456 and 458 in 1903.

An unidentified newspaper account in the Elizabeth Custer file at Little Bighorn Battlefield National Monument dated November or December 8, 1905, may refer to another recovery effort or perhaps one of the 1903 disinterments:

> Such was the case recently when one of Reno's men was dug up, somewhere in the wild stretch of country between Custer hill and the bluffs where Reno's command held their savage foes at bay. This man was a sergeant, a crack shot, who had been despatched by Reno to find out what had become of Custer and to carry news of Reno's own desparte plight. The sergeant was caught midway between the two commands and was finally killed, but not until he had reckoned with many of his savage foes. When he was found his body was literally surrounded with shells and his comrades knew of the man's ability as a shot to swear that every shell represented a casualty on the Indian side. A comrade who assisted in burying the man where he fell only a short time ago headed a party to the spot, and the remains were disinterred and brought to Custer Cemetery.

Rickey (1967:72) believed that the article referred to the recovery of Sgt. James Butler's remains, but the National Cemetery records do not indicate that any remains from the battlefield were interred in 1905. The only battle-related interments to occur in the 1895–1910 era were those in 1903. A review of the National Cemetery registers identified no battle participants registered at the site in 1905. However, Henry Meckling did visit the site on June 25, 1903. Meckling, a Medal of Honor awardee, had been a Corporal in Company H and was with Captain Benteen during the battle. He had, in fact, assisted in the burial details at the Reno-Benteen defense site and on Custer battlefield.

It is quite probable that the newspaper article quoted above refers to the 1903 disinterments by casual reference to "recently." It is also possible that Meckling did identify a burial location between the two fields as well as those on the Reno-Benteen defense site. If so, then as many as six individuals were buried in the five grave sites.

Such an interpretation may explain why Grave 458 is separated from the others by a single intervening unassociated burial.

In May 1992, volunteer Dick Harmon, park historian Douglas McChristian, maintenance man Cliff Arbogast, and Douglas Scott exhumed these skeletons with the intent of completing proper osteological examinations and attempting to identify the remains. The skeletons were analyzed (Willey 1997) and reburied in the same graves in the National Cemetery in August 1994.

The five graves dating to 1903 were the first excavated. The remains (Graves 453–456 and 458) were buried in a relatively consistent manner. Each grave contained a small wooden box, which held the bones. The buried boxes were encountered at a depth of 30–34 inches below present ground surface. Army quartermaster reburial boxes or coffins for skeletal remains were prescribed as being 10 inches high, 12 inches wide, and 24 inches long (Col. George S. Young, June 13, 1911, Walter M. Camp Collection, Henry Lee Library, Brigham Young University), and the rotten box remains found in the graves approximated these dimensions.

Grave 458 was separate from the other 1903 graves. The reason for the separation is unknown. It may have been a happenstance that Grave 457 was already occupied, or it is possible that the bones were actually recovered and reinterred at a different time than Graves 453–456. It is possible that this grave is related to skeletal remains found between the Reno-Benteen defense site and the Custer battlefield.

The remains in Grave 458, designated Burial 1, were a nearly complete, well-preserved skeleton. Many of the smaller bones of the wrists, hands, ankles, and feet were absent, but all of the larger elements were present. Parts of the right tibia and fibula were sunbleached and weather-checked, indicating exposure above ground, and this exposure may have led to the skeleton's discovery and reburial in 1903. The absence of other individuals' bones in this grave and the grave's discontinuous number suggest that it was recovered separately from the rest of those exhumed and reburied in 1903.

There were numerous cuts on the bones. A cut on the left side of the skull suggested scalping, cuts near the right shoulder indicate arm dismemberment, and cuts in the pelvic area and thigh may have represented slashing mutilations. These and other cuts on the skeleton suggested severe mutilation, although surprisingly there were no indications of gunshot wounds or blunt trauma.

The skeleton was that of a white male about 68.5 inches tall and 20–25 years old. He had a stressful growth period. His dental health was poor; he had several active caries when he died and had already lost nearly a quarter of his teeth. Brown stains on some teeth suggested coffee drinking and tobacco use. There were many indications of traumatic injuries before death and degenerative joint disease, the most notable being a possible healed shoulder separation and back problems. And there was a possible nasal passage lesion, perhaps resulting from snuff use. Articular facets adjacent to the hip and lower leg ankle joints indicated hyperflexibility at those joints.

Considering the information gleaned from this skeleton and assuming that the individual fell on the Reno-Benteen fields, there are five possible identities for the skeleton. It seems likely, considering the number of cuts present on the skeleton, that the body came under the warriors' knives. If the man fell on the Reno-Benteen battlefield, the most likely identities are David Summers and John Meyers. Summers was reported falling in the valley battle (Blake in Hardorff 1989:145), where his body would have been vulnerable to being dismembered and disfigured. Meyer died during Reno's retreat, about halfway up the bluff toward the hilltop defense area (Morris cited in Hardorff 1989:140). Both Summers's and Meyer's bodies (Slaper cited in Hardorff 1989:140, 145) were "in an awful state of mutilation." Either of these identifications, however, is far from certain.

Although the Reno-Benteen association is likely, it is also possible that these remains are from or near the Custer battlefield. If so, then there are numerous candidates for the identity of Burial 1. The extensive number of cutmarks on the bone is consistent with the descriptions of mutilations seen on the bodies on the Custer battlefield. If these bones were uncovered in a separate episode from those in the nearby cemetery graves, then a separate burial location seems a logical conclusion as well. These bones may be the remains referred to in the 1905 newspaper article describing the finding of a skeleton somewhere between the two battlefields.

There were parts of at least three individuals included in Grave 453, designated Burial 2, the extra bones later associated with the individuals in Graves 454 and 455, although some elements cannot be associated with any of the other National Cemetery burials. Those unassociated elements may indicate that other skeletal parts were exposed and removed at the same time the other individuals were exhumed in 1903; some of the unassociated elements displayed possible canine chewing and considerable weathering, supporting this interpretation. A couple of elements belonging to the Burial 2 individual were located in the adjacent Grave 454. This mixing may have occurred during or immediately after the original exhumation, but before reburial in the National Cemetery.

Burial 2 was one of the most fascinating skeletons found on the Little Bighorn battlefield. It consisted of a nearly complete, generally well preserved skeleton, missing only some of the ribs, vertebrae, and smaller bones of the wrists, hands, ankles, and feet as well as a few other bones. Unlike Burial 1, all of the nicks and cuts on the Burial 2 bones appeared to be from postmortem events, such as the 1903 exhumation. There were no indications of gunshot wounds or perimortem mutilations.

These remains were those of an older white soldier, probably between 30 and 35 years or perhaps even older. He was gracile, so gracile in fact that many of the skeletal sex indicators suggested a female. This gracileness was in part due to his small size, and this smallness is reflected by his stature. At 65.3 inches tall, he was among the shorter casualties. His size may have been caused, in part, by fairly numerous growth interruptions. There was an old, small, well-healed cranial fracture above his right eye. Numerous degenerative changes were present. The upper neck demonstrated arthritic changes, but, as with the other National Cemetery specimens, the most marked joint changes were in the mid- to lower spine. He had temporomandibular joint problems, suggesting that he ground his teeth while sleeping.

Unlike the other National Cemetery specimens, Burial 2 had good oral health. With the exception of a lateral maxillary incisor, all of the teeth were present, with few caries and slight periodontal disease. The left lateral maxillary incisor was unerupted and diminutive, most likely a congenital anomaly, and was absent occlusally but not lost through dental disease.

His dental health was surprising because he was an older member of the Seventh Cavalry, and oral disease, especially in those days, tended to increase with age—an accumulative process. The most likely explanation for his healthy teeth was dental care. He had at least six fillings—a unique discovery among the specimens recovered archaeologically from the Little Bighorn, although there are historical accounts of filled teeth being found in the 1870s and 1880s (for reviews, see Glenner et al. 1994; Hyson and Whitehorne 1993).

These restorations provided a unique opportunity to examine dentistry techniques and materials during a formative period of American dentistry. We were able to involve Dr. Richard Glenner, a clinical dentist practicing in Chicago with a long-term interest in the development of the practice of dentistry, who welcomed the opportunity to examine the fillings. There were two tin foil fillings in the occlusal surfaces of the maxillary right first and left second molars. The other four fillings were gold amalgam or gold foil. Gold foil fillings were present in the occlusal surfaces of the maxillary left first molar and the buccal (cheek) surfaces of the mandibular first molars. The mandibular fillings were amazingly small, and it was likely that the pits they filled were naturally occurring and noncarious. The gold amalgam filling was in the maxillary right third molar. Two other teeth appeared to have had fillings at one time (occlusal surfaces of the maxillary right first and third molars) but lost at least a portion of them.

The combination of tin and gold restorations in the same mouth are interesting. The poor and good materials together suggested that the dental work was performed in different settings, most likely at different times in this person's life. Given the poor condition of the other troopers' teeth, it is likely that Burial 2's fillings were placed earlier in his life, before his military career commenced.

This individual's excellent oral health occurred despite one nearly ubiquitous oral devastator of the cavalrymen—tobacco consumption. His teeth displayed moderate staining, with particularly heavy brown stains on the right posterior teeth. The location of the stains and the associated dental wear indicated tobacco chewing.

The identity of this fascinating skeleton remains uncertain. Assuming that the skeleton came from the Reno-Benteen defense site, based on the historical data associated with its burial in the National Cemetery, and considering the information gleaned from the bones, there are six possible identities. The dental restorations suggest that the man had access to excellent medical care, either through being from a higher socioeconomic group or being associated with a dental school or dentist. An additional two individuals, who fit both of the general skeletal parameters and would have had access to better dental care, were eliminated by photographic superimposition: Lt. Benjamin Hodgson and acting assistant surgeon James DeWolf.

There are six remaining possible identities for Burial 2. Considering the absence of perimortem injuries, the most likely possibilities are three who fell in or near the Reno-Benteen hilltop: Sgt. DeWitt Winney, who was born in New York and died in the hilltop fight (Godfrey in Hardorff 1989:1677); Pvt. Elihu Clear, who was born in Indiana and died on the east side of the river at the foot of the bluffs (John Creighton in Hardorff 1997:71); and George Lell, who was born in Hamilton County, southwest Ohio, and enlisted in Cincinnati in 1873 (Carroll 1993:147). Cincinnati was the location of the second dental college in the world, where many of the most important figures of the day taught. Once enlisted, Lell quickly rose to the rank of corporal, his rank at the time of the battle. He was shot in the stomach during the first day of the hilltop defense and was taken to the field hospital, where he died the following day. Windolph (in Hardorff 1989:147) described Lell's death: "I will never forget Sgt. [*sic*] Lell. He was fatally wounded and dragged to the hospital. He was dying and knew it. 'Lift me up boys,' he said to some of the men. 'I want to see the boys again before I go.' So they held him up to a sitting position where he could see his comrades in action. A smile came to his face as he saw the beautiful fight the Seventh was making. Then they laid him down and he died soon after."

Lell's age was similar to Burial 2's skeletal age, and his photograph matched Burial 2's skull and mandible. The only marked discrepancy was stature: Lell's enlistment record indicates that he was 69 inches, but Burial 2's stature was 65.3 inches or perhaps even shorter. Subsequent research located two female descendents of Lell's sister who provided DNA samples for comparison to DNA derived from one of the skull's teeth. The two DNA sets did not match the skeletal DNA, and Lell is currently excluded as a candidate

As with the previous grave, Grave 453, Burial 3, contained the remains of at least three individuals, based on the presence of three left tibiae and other duplicated elements. A few of the extra bones belonged to Burial 2, most to Burial 4, and some to Burial 5. Parts of Burial 3 were found mixed with Burials 2 and 4. Also as in the previous grave, some elements in this grave did not belong with Burial 3 or any of the other assigned individuals.

The well-preserved skeletal remains of Burial 3 indicated a robust, medium-size individual and included most of the major elements, except a portion of the right innominate. Many bones of the wrist, hand, ankle, and foot were missing, as well as some vertebrae and ribs.

There were some alterations to the bones, including cuts and stains. Most of the cuts were consistent with being made during the first exhumation, although a cut on the right navicular might have been a perimortem wound. A fabric pattern stain on the skull suggested burial in rough-woven cloth, such as burlap, and there was a blue-green stain on a lumbar vertebra indicating that copper or brass had been in contact with the bone at one time.

This was a young, white adult male, about 18–23 years and most likely 19–21, and at 69 inches he was medium tall for the Seventh Cavalry casualties. The most striking injury was a gunshot wound to the head (Willey and Scott 1996). There was a rectangular entrance hole (28 mm by 14 mm) in the right parietal (figure 52). The shape of the entry was unusual; usually they are round.

The rectangular entry wound suggests that the bullet was in yaw or tumbling when it struck the skull. There are several possible explanations for this lack of gyroscopic stability. The bullet may have hit something and passed through it or ricocheted off an object before penetrating the skull. Another possibility is that the bullet was improperly loaded. Also, the bullet may have been fired from an unrifled gun, or it may have gone its maximum distance and lost stability in the process. A smaller bullet fired from a larger-caliber gun is a final possibility; because of the loose seal around a smaller bullet, it would lack the normal spin rifled barrels provide and thus tend to tumble. The bullet may have been in mid-tumble when it struck the skull. Firing smaller bullets from larger rifles has been recorded and demonstrated by archaeological work on the Little Bighorn battlefield (Scott et al. 1989).

Associated with the entrance wound were radiating and concentric fractures surrounding the hole. After entering the right side and passing through the brain, the bullet exited from the left side, leaving a "keyhole"-shaped wound. The direction of fire, from the

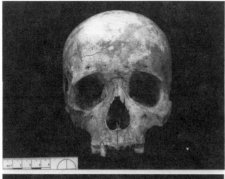
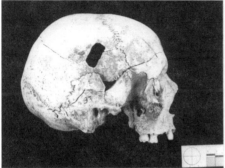
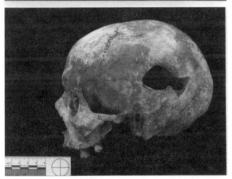

Figure 52. This skull of a soldier found originally in 1903 and reburied in the National Cemetery in Grave 454 shows how one member of the Reno-Benteen defense died of a right-to-left through-and-through gunshot wound to the head. The bullet was tumbling when it struck this young man. Midwest Archeological Center, National Park Service.

person's right to the left, under other circumstances would be consistent with a suicide wound. However, to tumble, the bullet must have passed through an intermediate target or traveled a considerable distance, in neither case a muzzle-skin contact as expected in a suicide. The wound would have caused death quickly, assuming the person was alive when the shot occurred.

There were are several behavioral alterations indicated by the skeleton. There were facets on the femoral necks and talocrual (lower ankle) joints indicating hyperflexibility at those joints. The big toe was deviated toward the outside of the foot. Degenerative joint changes (arthritic) were slight in the elbows and marked in the mid-spine. Jaw clenching was suggested by developed muscle markings. Oral health was poor, with before-death tooth loss, active carious lesions and alveolar resorption, and calculus present. Many teeth were stained, suggesting tobacco use. His growing years, however, were apparently healthy, at least as indicated by the absence of growth interruption lines.

Identification of the individual was attempted. Assuming that the person died on the Reno-Benteen field, there are four possible identities based on the osteological data. The three most likely identities, considering the gunshot wound to the skull, are packer Frank Mann, Pvt. Richard Dorn, and Pvt. Patrick Golden. Mann was described as receiving a fatal head wound (Taylor in Hardorff 1989:168) or a temple wound (Roy in Hardorff 1989:168) on June 26 while in the Reno-Benteen hilltop fight. According to Captain McDougall, Dorn was attempting to wake the captain when he was struck in the head and killed (Schoenberger 1990:237). Golden received a fatal head wound the same day and in the same fight as Mann (Hardorff 1989:161–63). One of the observers (Thompson in Hardorff 1989:162) recounted that Golden received four wounds before being hit with the fatal head wound, although the skeleton showed none other than the head wound. Dorn, Golden, or Mann remain the most likely identities of Burial 3.

Grave 455, Burial 4, contained at least three individuals based on triplication of metatarsals. A few specimens in Grave 455 belonged to Burials 3 and 5, and some bones from Graves 453 and 454 belonged to Burial 4. In addition, there were other elements that did not belong to any of these skeletons and were unassigned.

Burial 4 was moderately well preserved, consisting of all of the larger bones and most of the smaller ones. Some of the bones of the wrist, hand, ankle, and foot and some of the ribs and vertebrae were absent. Although there were many cuts on the bones, most appeared to be from the exhumations, and there was only one old cut from around the time of death in the iliac fossa, which might have been from a mutilation.

He was a large, robust, white young adult about 25–35 years old, most likely 25–30. He was 70.7 inches, a rather tall stature for the casualties. Indications of behavioral alterations included articular facets on the femur neck, suggesting hyperflexibility of the hip, and the large toes turned toward the smaller ones. He did lack articular facets near the talocrural joints. There were numerous pathological lesions. He had a healed fracture of the radius midshaft and a possible healed fracture of a metatarsal. He had spinal problems, both degenerative disks and articular facet osteoarthritis. Even the atlanto-occipital (skull-neck) joint displayed degenerative changes. There was only one possible indicator of growth delay. His oral health was particularly poor. Many of the maxillary posterior teeth were missing before death, alveolar resorption is extensive, carious lesions common, and calculus moderate. Two mandibular molars were lost a year or two before his death; perhaps they were diseased or impacted teeth that had been extracted.

A gunshot wound (hole 13 mm by 19 mm) was in the right ilium (hip). The bullet came from the back (posterior) right side, and assuming he was alive when it occurred the wound would have probably caused death, at least eventually.

Considering the skeletal assessments and assuming that the body was on the Reno-Benteen field, there are five possible identities, with one likely. Of these five, the best fit is farrier Vincent Charley (Scott and Willey 1996). Charley was born in Lucerne, Switzerland, immigrated to the United States, and his first enlistment began in Chicago in 1871. He was in his second enlistment at the time of the battle (Hammer 1995).

Burial 4's robusticity and healed injuries are consistent with the active life of a farrier. In addition to the similarities between the skeletal determinations and Charley, particularly age and stature, the gunshot wound in Burial 4's innominate is in keeping with Charley. Charley, who was struck and abandoned while retreating from Weir Point, was described as being "shot through the hips" (Harrison in Hardorff 1989:160) and "hit in the hips" (Winfield in Hardorff 1989:160). Charley was with his company during the retreat, and Sgt. Thomas Harrison of Company D (Liddic and Harbaugh 1995:97) stated that Charley was shot about a quarter mile south of Weir Point, but on the slopes above the ravine. Pvt. John Fox, Company D, recalled that when Lt. Winfield Edgerly stopped to examine the wound and tell him to take cover until his comrades could return for him, Charlie implored his comrades to not leave him behind (Liddic and Harbaugh 1995:96).When Edgerly and Sgt. Thomas Harrison left Charley, they were followed by two hundred warriors, and they had to use their revolvers to extricate themselves from the body of warriors. As they looked back, they saw warriors swarming over Charley, apparently finishing him off (Harrison in Liddic and Harbaugh 1995:97).

One historical source (Edgerly in Hardorff 1989:160) claimed that when troops returned to recover and bury Charley's body they found a "stick rammed down the throat." The skeletal evidence on this point is ambiguous. A final point is that Charley was said to have been exhumed early in this century, and Burial 4 was placed in the National Cemetery in 1903. All lines of evidence considered, Burial 4 is Charley. A headstone was made with Charley's name and rank and placed on his grave after the remains were reinterred, and a similar stone was placed south of Wier Point at a pullout on the park tour road.

Grave 456, Burial 5, contained at least two people, based on duplication of the innominate. This duplicated element is not assignable to any of the other burials. There were parts of the main skeleton of Burial 5 in Graves 454 and 455. The Burial 5 skeleton was poorly preserved, most likely from the grave's proximity to a sprinkler head in the National Cemetery and the greater moisture retained there than in the other graves. The poor preservation likely explains why the skeleton was partial and the elements present more fragmentary than the other skeletons from the adjacent graves.

Most of the larger bones were present, lacking some lower arm bones and a fibula. Among the missing smaller elements were many ribs and vertebrae and some bones of the wrists, hands, ankles, and feet. Of the bones that were present, a tibia may have had carnivore chewing and a clavicle had a blue-green stain suggesting contact with copper or brass.

Cuts were present. Although two of the cuts were probably from the 1903 exhumation, other cuts suggest mutilation. A cut on the cranial vault may have been associated with scalping, and three cuts near or on the femoral head suggested dismemberment of the thigh from the torso. In addition to the cuts, there were metal fragments in the upper end of the humerus, which suggested a gunshot wound at or near that location.

This was a young adult white between 20 and 30 years old, most likely 20–25. At 69.5 inches tall he was a medium-to-tall Seventh Cavalry trooper. There were numerous indications of disease. Both tibiae had slight inflammations on the medial midshaft, suggesting a low-grade body-wide infection. Many of the thoracic and lumbar vertebrae had degenerative lesions. There were numerous indications of growth interruptions. Dental health was good, but the poor preservation made observations difficult. The femur head and the distal tibia had extra-articular facets, indicating hypermobility at those joints.

Using these skeletal determinations and assuming the skeleton was buried originally on the Reno-Benteen field, there are nine possible identities. The most likely candidate, considering the mutilation cuts, may be Pvt. William Meyer, who was killed retreating up the bluffs toward what would become the Reno-Benteen entrenchment. Slaper (in Hardorff 1989:141) recounted that Meyer was "in an awful state of mutilation."

After the 1903 remains were found, no further record of bones from the battlefield are recorded until 1926, when human bone was found during excavation for a culvert or a borrow pit for construction of a road. According to Crow Agency superintendent C. H. Asbury (letter to Custer Battlefield National Cemetery Superintendent Eugene Wessinger, May 28, 1926, Little Bighorn National Monument files), a nearly complete human skeleton was uncovered in the valley 500–600 feet from the McIntosh marker and in line with the Reynolds marker. The skeleton was thought to be essentially complete except for the skull. Two bullets were found with the remains, one in the hip region and one near the shoulder, and were thought to be the cause of death. Five or six buttons were also recovered and were thought to be trouser buttons.

Henry Weibert (Weibert and Weibert 1985:134) disputes the circumstances of the finding of this unknown soldier. He says it occurred in 1925, when he and his father were putting in a culvert along the road to the Reno retreat crossing. Weibert and Weibert (1985:134) claim the remains were found about one-quarter mile east of the Garryowen store. Joseph Blummer recollected that the bones were found by a county road crew along the Reno retreat route (Joseph Blummer manuscript, 1959, Little Bighorn National Monument files). The body was reburied in 1926 in a specially prepared cenotaph near the Garryowen store during an impressive fiftieth battle anniversary celebration (McChristian 1996). When the highway was realigned in the 1950s, the cenotaph was removed to its present site near the Garryowen store. The bones buried in 1926 were exhumed and reburied under the cenotaph at that time (administrative files, 0752-0764, LBNM files).

The year 1928 saw two more sets of remains recovered from the battlefield and reburied in the National Cemetery. On October 3, Superintendent Asbury wrote a letter to the War Department Cemetery Section (LBNM files) in which he discussed the finding of a skeleton some two and one-half years earlier, presumably the remains just discussed. He noted that he had recently been taken to the same spot and found more human bones and thought he saw evidence of three other graves. He wanted the bodies removed to the National Cemetery. In a follow-up letter October 26, 1928, to the quartermaster general, Custer Battlefield National Cemetery superintendent Eugene Wessinger stated that on October 24 he went to the Reno valley fight area near the crossing and on unplowed land 300 feet from the river found one skeleton buried about a foot deep. Wessinger further remarked that he had the skeleton exhumed and removed to the National Cemetery and interred as an unknown in the same grave as another unknown found close to Custer battlefield on August 1, 1928.

Indeed records for Grave 942 Section A of the National Cemetery note that it held the burials of two unknowns. One was found 300 yards south of the Custer battlefield boundary fence and buried August 1, 1928, and the other consisted of the remains found October 24 and buried on the 25th.

The remains found in October may be same as those initially discovered by J. A. Blummer in 1927 (letter to R. G. Cartwright from J. A. Blummer, July 18, 1927, Little Bighorn National Monument files). Blummer wrote:

> Frank Bethune was here yesterday and I went with him to the Reno field he showed me the places that he says Goes Ahead told him that each place there was a soldier killed but I think they were buried All right but very shallow and the cyotes dug them up an[d] scattered the bones around. . . . Max Big Man told me when he was a boy there were

three graves near the river on the side next to the store only close to the ford that Reno retreated on. so I took a shovel [a]long yesterday and dug one of them up. I found a pair of boots in it also the two leg bones the large ones. some ribs and a few other small bones I reburied the bones the boots I have here.

Blummer again wrote Cartwright on June 3, 1928, regarding the same burial (Little Bighorn National Monument files):

also some digging I wish to do at the same place where I dug up the body last year there were some students and other people here Decoration day and I showed them the boots I found they said they were childs boots, which of course they thought by them being shrunk up so after 51 years so I had to take them down and dig up the bones again there were several doctors with them and as soon as they saw the bones they knew they were human bones, and he was a big man at that.

Yet another burial is represented by the August 1 find, also located by Frank Bethune: "the draw towards the Custer field from the Butler marker. Well Frank Bethune found a skeleton of a man in this draw. . . . This body had a arrow sticking in the back bone Also a scabbard for gun with, R.D. on it. . . . I forgot the body was found about 1/4 mile outside the fence" (J. A. Blummer to R. G. Cartwright, September 13, 1928, Custer Battlefield National Monument files).

Wessinger further elaborated on the Bethune find in a letter to Fred Dustin (Wessinger to Dustin December 17, 1928, #6075, LBNM files). Writing in response to a note from Dustin, Superintendent Wessinger indicated that the skeletal remains were shallowly buried and were found just south of the present battlefield boundary in an area of active erosion. Wessinger, who saw the skeletal remains, also remarked on the iron arrowhead that had transfixed one of the vertebrae.

A map in the Blummer files, in the Little Bighorn archives, shows the location of the body but also contains a note that states "body found by Frank Bethune also stirrup with J D on it." At some point since the discovery, the leather artifact has been interpreted as a boot upper, which was assumed to belong to Pvt. John Duggan (Greene 1986:39).

The skeletal remains in Grave 942 consisted of two reinterments, one found in the Valley (Burial 6) and this one found outside the boundary fence (Scott 1993b). Burial 7 was in a wooden box buried in the same grave but below Burials 6A and 6B. One white porcelain shirt or underwear button was found with Burial 7.

Burial 6A did not fit the profile expected of a trooper. It was not young, not white, and not male. It was a middle-age or old American Indian woman. Although not a member of the Seventh Cavalry, her inclusion in the National Cemetery is instructive for what it has to tell us about the battlefield and the value of skeletal analyses in interpreting the past.

Her National Cemetery remains consisted of a relatively complete, well-preserved skeleton, although missing a few ribs, vertebrae, and most of the bones of the wrist/hand and ankle/foot. A metacarpal and two cervical vertebrae, perhaps scattered by burrowing rodents, were found in the more deeply buried Burial 7. There were cuts and gouges on the skull and innominate, most likely made during the 1928 exhumation, and fabric stains on many bones, perhaps from a cloth bag that contained her remains when she was buried in the National Cemetery.

A coincidence happened during the analysis of the National Cemetery skeletons. Jason Pitsch, whose family has farmed the Little Bighorn Valley for decades, found military buttons near the timber and the Reno retreat crossing in 1993. Watching the spot carefully, later that same year he discovered human bones. The NPS sent Melissa Connor and Dick Harmon to excavate the remains of what was presumed to be a cavalryman. Assisted by then park historian Douglas McChristian, they recovered metal buttons, glass beads, and some smaller human bones, the sort of specimens that might have been easily overlooked during an exhumation. No large, major elements were found.

Thinking that what was dubbed the Pitsch Burial might be the left-behind parts of one of the National Cemetery specimens, the two sets of elements were compared. The kinds of elements, the general biological parameters (e.g., age and sex), the size and shape of matching bilateral elements, and the articular surfaces of adjacent bones were compared with the National Cemetery specimens. With a few minor exceptions, all of the characteristics of the Pitsch Burial matched those of the National Cemetery Burial 6A. They were from the same individual. The details of the Pitsch Burial recovery and the skeletal analysis are presented by Connor (1994) and Willey (1994). The reunited skeleton was returned to Montana in May 1994 and interred in a more appropriate cemetery on the Crow Reservation.

The important message of this story is that not all skeletons on the battlefield are troopers, not all burials necessarily date to the battle, and skeletal analysis can help resolve these issues.

Unlike the other skeleton in this burial, Burial 6B was consistent with being from a trooper. Only a few bones, however, were present: two upper and several lower limb long bones, two ribs, and one thoracic vertebra. These bones were generally more weathered than those of Burial 6A, suggesting that Burial 6B was partially exposed above ground at one time. This exposure may have led to their discovery and recovery, perhaps at the same time and from the same general location where Burial 6A was being exhumed.

The scanty remains made skeletal estimations less certain than they might have been had more elements been present for analysis. This was a male, 20–35 years old and 70.2 inches tall—tall for the Seventh Cavalry casualties. Determining race was especially difficult because few definitive parts were present and those available were ambiguous. Using a discriminant function for postcranial measurements, he was classified as white, but his tibia-femur ratio suggested that he was black. Although there are no indications that he was American Indian, race is otherwise uncertain and may be either white or black.

A few behavioral and disease modifications were present. The femur head had an extra-articular facet suggesting hyperflexion of the hip. There were slight inflammations on the tibia shafts, indicating a possible infection. And there were growth interruptions. Considering the osteological conclusions and assuming that the skeleton was buried in the valley, there are five possible identities. None of these can be considered the most likely.

There is a sixth possible individual, omitted from the list because neither his stature nor his age were recorded, although he is known to have been a middle-age adult. That person is interpreter Isaiah Dorman, who was the only black to die in the battle. He was killed in the valley fight. There are accounts that his body was mutilated, including multiple gunshot wounds in the lower legs (Herendeen in Hardorff 1989:149), which Burial 6B lacked. The identification of Burial 6B as Dorman is extremely tenuous but cannot be excluded.

Included with Burial 7 were several small bones that apparently were parts of Burial 6A and were included with that burial for the purposes of analysis and reburial. In addition, some human ribs included with Burial 7 apparently did not belong to Burials 7, 6A, or 6B.

Burial 7 consisted of a partial skull and mandible, most of the axillary skeleton, and most of the limb bones. Few of the smaller bones of the hands and feet were present. These absences occurred despite the excellent preservation of the elements. There was a blue-green stain on the mandible, perhaps left by a brass button or cartridge, and a fabric pattern was present on the skull, suggesting that a rough-woven cloth was once included in the burial.

He was white, 25–45 years old and most likely around 35—considerably older than most of the cavalry casualties. He was 68.4 inches tall. There were many indications of trauma. There were bony "spurs" on his right first finger, probably from an injury occurring long before his death. Trauma from around the time of death included a gunshot wound, blunt force trauma, and many cuts.

The bullet entered the skull vault from the back, fractures radiated from the entrance, and the bullet exited near the nasal bridge. The trajectory indicated a back-to-front path. Blunt force trauma was evident to the left side of the cranial vault, apparently after the gunshot. The blunt force may have been from falling, counting coup, a coup-de-grace, or perhaps a mutilation, because the gunshot wound would have been sufficient to kill the trooper.

As a part of the mutilation process, there were many marks, at least 98 cuts on the bones. The vertebral column displayed hacks, stabs, or jabs. There were cuts near the right shoulder, left elbow, left wrist, and left hand that suggested dismemberment or at least dismemberment attempts. There were a multitude of cuts on the left innominate and femur consistent with thigh removal. And the innominate had cuts that suggest castration.

There were behavioral and degenerative modifications and dental problems. The femora had extra-articular facets, although the tibia displayed no "squatting" facets. Degeneration was visible in the shoulders, elbows, spine, and knees. Dental health was poor, with several teeth missing before death and many of the remaining teeth with carious lesions. One of the carious lesions was so bad that it occupied nearly the whole crown, and the root tip had an abscess. Calculus was prevalent on most of the teeth. There were dark stains on the teeth, consistent with smoking a pipe.

Based on the skeletal assessments and assuming that this is the body found in August 1928 by Frank Bethune near Deep Coulee, there are many possible identities. Assuming that this was a member of Company C or L, the number of possibilities is reduced to ten individuals, none of whom have initials J. D. or R. D., as reported on the piece of leather found with the skeleton. Based on the initials, some believe the remains to be those of Pvt. John Duggan, but his enlistment records indicate that he was somewhat younger (27 years old) and somewhat taller (69.5 inches) than the Burial 7 skeleton. No most-likely identity can be established.

One intentional recovery of human remains occurred in the 1930s: the excavation and removal of Lt. John Crittenden's remains. The *Sheridan Press* (September 20, 1931) reported that the skeletal remains were found in a grave, with the left temporal bone detached from the skull, denoting that he had been "tomahawked." His body was removed, under protest, from where it had lain on Calhoun Hill since 1876 to the National Cemetery. Ostensibly the remains were removed to make way for construction of the new tour road (Rickey 1967:75). The *Sheridan Press* stated that the remains had to be removed because they were in the line of the highway. Cemetery superintendent Victor Bolsius reported to the Office of the Quartermaster General, Ninth Corps Area (letter of September 11, 1931), that Crittenden's remains were buried that day in the National Cemetery with full military honors "due his rank, supplied from the American Legion, of Hardin, Montana," and he further reported: "I have also removed his private monument with his remains."

The next report of human remains comes from superintendent Edward Luce (letter to Regional Director May 21, 1941, Little Bighorn National Monument files), who thought he identified human bone comingled with horse bone when he inadvertently cut into the horse cemetery near Last Stand Hill during a 1941 waterline trenching operation. A review of the photographs taken of the open trench and in the Little Bighorn Battlefield National Monument files failed to identify any human bones comingled with the horse bone. As late as the 1970s, bones were reported found during the laying of a waterline between the Crow Agency and the now abandoned Sun Lodge (King 1981:4–5). The whereabouts of those bones and associated artifacts are unknown.

The National Cemetery records indicate that two unknowns from the Custer battlefield area are buried in Grave 517A. The records cite an Office of the Quartermaster General Memorandum N-293 dated May 22, 1941. That memorandum has not been located. However, a letter from R. G. Cartwright to Superintendent Luce (October 10, 1943, Little Bighorn National Monument files) may refer to these remains. Cartwright says, "One skeleton was found on the right bank of Medicine Tail proper. This you should find in your interment records for I believe it was placed in the Cemetery. I recovered a tibia of a human which jutted from the right bank of Medicine Tail. Marquis identified this as a human bone."

Grave 517, Burials 8A and B, was the most shallow of those exhumed. The wooden box containing the remains was encountered only 10 inches below present ground surface. The grave contained at least two individuals, based on element duplication. Both skeletons were incomplete, fragmentary, but otherwise well preserved.

Burial 8A elements included a mandible with teeth, vertebrae, ribs, right clavicle and scapula, both forearms and innominates, sternum, and other smaller bones. This collection is an odd set of remains, but it provides many of the crucial bones for assessing the basic biological parameters.

He was a young adult male between 17 and 25 years, with a most likely age around 19 years. And he was a short 65.9 inches. Race was not determined. He was particularly healthy. Other than a few indications of slight spinal deterioration, there were no health problems, not even growth interruptions. This good health extended to his teeth, which, with the exception of a molar and an incisor, were present at death. Those that remained were free of caries. Most of the teeth were stained brown, probably caused by tobacco consumption.

Based on the skeletal assessments and assuming that the person died on the Custer battlefield, there are nine possible identities and doubtlessly more individuals would be included if misrepresentations of youths' enlistment ages could all be identified. Of these people, the most intriguing—although no more likely—one is Harry Armstrong Reed, Custer's nephew and civilian guest. Reed's body was found near Last Stand Hill, buried in 1876, and likely recovered around 1878 for reburial in Monroe, Michigan. There is, however, no single most-likely identity for Burial 8A.

The kinds of elements representing Burial 8B were similar to those in Burial 8A. Burial 8B's bones included a mandible and teeth, both clavicles, radius, ribs, vertebrae, innominate, sacrum, and a few bones of the wrists and hands. The duplication of Burial 8A and 8B's elements is interesting. Both specimens had mandibles, clavicles, vertebrae, ribs, radii, innominates, and bones of the hands. Both lacked skulls and bones from the lower limbs. The only major elements that Burial 8A had that Burial 8B lacked were a scapula and part of an ulna. It is difficult to imagine that the similarities are due to chance alone. Presumably the similarities reflect the finders' identification and choice of parts, or perhaps the parts that had been left behind by a previous exhumation.

There was damage to some of the Burial 8B bones. A left rib and a radius had what may be old cuts associated with mutilation. There were also cuts and hacks from the exhumations. The x-rays displayed metal fragments on the left innominate, a thoracic vertebra, and a rib fragment. These metal pieces suggest a gunshot wound or wounds to the abdomen and thorax, or perhaps the adjacent areas. He was 30–45 years, most likely 35–40, and a tall 71 inches. No race identification was possible with the remains present.

There were many indications of degenerative changes and trauma. There were two healed rib fractures. Slight degenerative joint disease was evident in the radius. The vertebrae had moderate osteoarthritis and osteophytosis, and intervertebral disk deterioration was severe. Of all the degenerative changes, the most severe were in the mandibular condyles and ascending ramus. The temporomandibular joint degenerative changes were severe enough to reduce the height of the ascending ramus.

His dental health was also poor. Many teeth were missing before death, and those present displayed much calculus and many carious lesions, especially at the gum level. One carious lesion was apparently so extensive that the tooth crown was destroyed and only the roots remained. The teeth displayed tobacco use. The left premolars had a "pipe stem" groove, indicating where a pipe had been habitually held. The teeth were also stained.

Based on the osteological conclusions and assuming that the person died on the Custer portion of the battlefield, there are four most likely identities. Being so tall and old effectively eliminated most of the dead from consideration. The most intriguing identity is none other than George Armstrong Custer himself. And the skeletal age, stature, and gunshot wound to the chest fit him as well as or better than any of the other casualties. There are contraindications, however, with this identification. The indications of tobacco use are inconsistent with Custer. He had apparently abstained from tobacco. It is, however, possible that the groove and stains persisted from the time before his vow through the decades until his death (R. A. Glenner and B. Reuben, personal communication, December 1993). Further, there are no accounts that Custer suffered from temporomandibular, dental, or back problems. The identification of Burial 8B as Custer is tenuous, but the possibility cannot be excluded and deserves further consideration.

The Bray Excavations

In 1958, the NPS constructed walking paths for visitors at the Reno-Benteen defense site. These facilities were adjacent to areas where the historical record documented battle-related features such as the field hospital, a barricade, and rifle pits. Robert Bray, an NPS archaeologist, was detailed to conduct investigations of the site before the commencement of construction, and in the process of his investigations he found human bones (Bray 1958). All of the remains discovered by Bray were buried in a single grave in the National Cemetery without analysis or attempts at identification. Because the grave was to be used to rebury the human remains from the 1984 and 1985 investigations and other miscellaneous remains found over the years that were in the park collections, it was exhumed by Melissa Connor and the remains given a formal examination (Connor 1986; Scott and Connor 1988; Scott et al. 1988). The remains were reburied with a formal military funeral in June 1986.

BARRICADE BURIAL

Bray found one skeleton in the area of the barricade east of the field hospital. The historical record (Gray 1976; Nichols 1992) indicates that Company A was posted along this area of the barricade. After the battle, this barricade rifle pit depression had apparently been used as a grave for one of the fallen soldiers. The burial Bray found was badly disturbed. The left half of the body was almost totally missing, although a left humerus was found a short distance away mixed with some horse bones. The body was lying face up, and along the left side of the upper portion of the body was a line of nine uniform blouse buttons. Some were still attached to blue cloth. Bray also found a few other military buttons in the soil around the body and some small iron rings, which were probably grommet stiffeners from canvas tenting. At the time of the excavation, Bray thought that the poor condition of the burial was due to disturbance of the grave relatively soon after the battle by rodents, dogs, or wolves.

The analysis found the skull and mandible both present, along with the hyoid bone. The mandible was in good condition, with most teeth present. The upper jaw had lost many teeth before death, at least three teeth had cavities, and several teeth displayed small grooves that suggested growth interruption during his youth, possibly a prolonged high fever. The result of the childhood problem manifested itself in the adult years with poor dental development and the early loss of teeth. The skull was elongated, indicating scaphocephaly, which is considered a congenital defect.

The infracranial skeleton consisted of fifty-five individual bones, including two vertebrae, both clavicles, several ribs, a complete right arm, and the left humerus found with the horse bone. The right and left humeri were the same size and of equal robustness. The left humerus probably belonged to this individual. The lower half of the body was represented by the sacrum and right innominate, a complete right leg and foot, a left femur, and a few left foot bones. The axis vertebra and sacrum had some minor osteoarthritic lipping. Otherwise the bones were from a moderately robust male of about 21 years, and the femur suggested a height of 67.75 inches.

The archaeological position of the bones of the barricade burial suggests that the body was laid on its back at burial with the legs flexed and up over the chest area. The several iron rings associated with the burial suggest that the individual was wrapped in a piece of canvas shelter half or some other type of tent at the time of interment. As Bray (1958) noted, the right femur, sacrum, and innominate were out of place. They appear from Bray's photographs to have been placed on top of the other bones when only partially desiccated. The left humerus was also found associated with horse bones several yards away from the primary interment site. The overall condition of the burial suggests that it was partially disturbed at one time and then the bones gathered and reburied. Gen. Hugh Scott, a young lieutenant in 1877, helped to rebury the dead at the Reno-Benteen defense site. He recalled (Scott 1928:48) gathering a burial's exposed bone and covering it with earth from the grave. In addition Charles Roe, who removed many human bones from the battlefield to the mass grave in 1881, recalled finding a few skeletons at the Reno site and removing them as well (Hammer 1976:250). It is possible this burial was reburied by Scott in 1877 but missed by Roe in 1881.

L-ENTRENCHMENT BURIALS

To the south and a little east of the field hospital, and on the hill occupied by Benteen's Company H, is what Bray called the L-Entrenchment, named for its shape. This is the southernmost defense perimeter. Prior to Bray's arrival, battlefield historian Don Rickey found several human hand and foot bones at this location, brought to the surface by rodent burrowing. Rickey's field notes state that he found three hand or foot bones, two trouser buttons, two military eagle buttons (one with a "C" for cavalry in the center of the eagle's shield), a bone button (probably from underwear), and a .50-caliber bullet. This entrenchment proved to be the final resting place for two soldiers.

One burial consisted of scattered bones: a skull, one tooth from the mandible, the hyoid, one cervical vertebra, the coccyx, left scapula, left humerus, left radius and ulna, three ribs, and the left femur. He was about 67 inches tall. The bones suggest an age of over 25 but under 30. Bray also found bits of blue uniform cloth, seventeen buttons, some bits of leather, and a cartridge scattered through the excavation. The second burial was even more disturbed. Both lower

arms and most of the hand bones were found in their correct anatomical positions, as were two vertebrae and four ribs. The burial
was lacking the other large bones such as those of the legs and the
skull. The bones indicate an adult male over 21 years of age with a
height of about 67 inches.

The bodies in L-Entrenchment Burials 1 and 2 were extensively
disturbed. But the disturbance left the remaining bones in nearly
correct anatomical position. This suggests that the disturbance was
after the flesh had completely decomposed and the bones could be
individually pulled from the earth. This is not likely to have been
done by American Indians or predators even up to six months after
burial. Some ligaments would still have been attached to the bone,
and more disruption to the anatomical order would have occurred.
The remaining bones in both burials suggest a formal disinterment
by untrained persons rather than random digging.

The burned wood, nails, and screws found in the entrenchment
during Bray's 1958 work have been identified as the remains of a
packing box. The presence of large screws suggests an empty ammunition box, which in that era used not only nails in the construction
but large screws to hold the bottom and top in place.

IDENTIFYING THE BARRICADE AND
L-ENTRENCHMENT BURIALS

It was decided to have molds made of the Reno-Benteen remains
before their reburial in 1986 so they could be studied further and
used for identification if additional historical information became
available. With the help of Greg Brown from the Nebraska State
Museum, molds and casts were made of each skull. The intent was
to use these facial approximations to determine if they might match
a photograph, and thus aid in the identification of the remains. If no
identification was forthcoming, at least there would be more por-
traits of the men who fought at the Battle of the Little Bighorn.
Betty Pat Gatliff, a renowned expert in facial reconstruction (Gatliff
1984), was asked to complete the facial reconstructions.

Comparisons of the sculptures were made to a published collection of photographs of the men who were in the Seventh Cavalry in
1876. One photograph was unmistakably similar to the man shown
in the bust sculpted from the Burial 1, L-Entrenchment skull. The

man was Sgt. Miles O'Hara. A review of O'Hara's military record showed that he was 68.25 inches tall and 25 years 8 months old when he died. The osteological data made O'Hara a definite candidate for the identity of Burial 1.

O'Hara had not been considered a candidate before the photographic comparison, because the historical record reported him killed in the valley fight and not at the Reno-Benteen battlefield. Walter Camp's (Hammer 1976) interviews with Pvts. Roman Rutten and James Wilber indicate that O'Hara was shot in the breast and fell on the valley skirmish line. However, Pvt. Edward Pigford told Camp that O'Hara was shot on the skirmish line but retreated with the others and was killed on the way to the timber. All accounts say O'Hara died or was wounded in the valley. There is no historical documentation of bodies from the valley being carried to the entrenchment for burial, with the exception of Lt. Benjamin Hodgson.

Further confirmation of O'Hara's identity was needed. A cast of the skull and the picture of O'Hara were taken to the Nebraska Educational Television studio for a photographic superimposition. It was an excellent match.

How, then, should the position of O'Hara's remains in the Company H position on Reno Hill be reconciled with the historical accounts of his death in the valley? Sgt. John Ryan remarked to Walter Camp (Camp Notes Envelope 130) that he had looked for O'Hara's body but could not find it and so assumed that it had already been buried. It is possible that his body was recovered along with that of Lieutenant Hodgson and possibly others, then buried on the hill after the battle and just not noted by anyone who wrote down their battle recollections or was later interviewed by various battle researchers. Or possibly O'Hara was one of the wounded who retreated to the top of the bluffs and died in Dr. Henry Porter's makeshift hospital, and his body was subsequently buried on the hill. Either scenario is plausible, and Ryan's observation to Camp could be interpreted either way—but without further historical evidence both remain speculation.

The other barricade burial represents a 21-year-old, who was about 67.75 inches tall and suffered from bad teeth; he remains nameless. Comparing the vital statistics of the known dead from the Reno-Benteen defense to the data from the barricade burial provides three possible candidates, if no one lied about their age at enlistment. One is Pvt. James Drinan of Company A, who was about 23 years old and 67.4 inches tall. Another is Pvt. Richard Dorn of Company B, who was also about 23 and 69 inches tall. The third candidate is Pvt. James McDonald of Company A, about 23 and 66 inches tall. Critically examining the evidence and comparing it to the historical record of enlistment, it is obvious that all three are about the right age to be in the barricade burial. However, McDonald and Dorn are too tall or too short to fit in the height range for the burial. This leaves Drinan as the most likely candidate. Company A did occupy the barricade line in the area where the burial was found. That fact adds strength to the argument that it might be Drinan, but this location is also close to the hospital, so anyone who died there might have been buried at this site. Unfortunately, there are no known photographs of Drinan, or the other possible candidates, with which to attempt a match. However, the facial approximation does not match any of the other individuals for whom there are photographs.

The second, incomplete burial in the L-Entrenchment presents even more of an identification problem than that of the barricade remains. The lack of a skull as well as most of the infracranial skeleton hamper the ability to age the individual accurately. All that can be reliably said is that he is a fully adult male over the age of 23 but probably under 35, and he was about 67 inches tall. He could be any one of the twenty-one men known to be in that age and height group who were killed with Reno. Excluding the men killed in the valley and the few known to have been buried under special circumstances that do not fit the excavation findings, the group can be narrowed to ten men.

There is a remote possibility that these are the remains of Lt. Benjamin Hodgson. The historical and firsthand accounts of Hodgson's burial are vague, but they may suggest a burial site in the general vicinity of the L-Entrenchment. Lt. Charles Varnum (Hammer 1976:62) stated that Hodgson's body was buried up the bluffs from the site of the June 26 circular entrenchment location. "Up the bluffs" could be Benteen's Company H position. Capt. Thomas McDougall (Hammer 1976:72) reported that Hodgson was buried above the position taken on June 26—the area of the circular entrenchment. McDougall with two enlisted soldiers actually buried

Hodgson. McDougall (Utley 1972:395) stated in the *Chicago Times* account of the 1879 Reno court of inquiry that "on the night of the 26th of June, 1876 I took privates Ryan and Moore of my company, and we went and got Lieut. Hodgson's body. We carried it up to my breastworks and kept it until the next morning. After sewing him up in a blanket and a poncho, we proceeded to a little knoll between my position and the works on the hill and those two men and myself dug his grave and buried him." Augustus DeVoto (Schoenberger 1990:70) stated in a 1917 letter to Walter Camp that he also helped to recover and bury Hodgson. DeVoto said that Hodgson's body was found about 20 feet from the water, naked and shot in the temple and groin. He further stated, "We laid Lt. Hodgson's body across our carbines and carried it to camp. We dug a grave, wrapped his body in a blanket, and buried it on the hill. We planted a sapling there to mark his grave." Saddler John Bailey of Company B told Walter Camp that Hodgson was buried 40–50 feet uphill from McDougall's entrenchment and under a little bushlike tree (Liddic and Harbaugh 1995:81–88).

Hodgson's body was removed from the field in June 1877, by the reburial party, and transported to his family (Graham 1953). The 1877 reburial detail apparently recovered the body from one of the rifle pits: "though killed at the foot of the ravine, was buried within the most southern line of rifle pits" (*New York Graphic*, July 1877). This location, along with the recollections of those of Reno's men, is consistent with the L-Entrenchment site.

Intriguing bits of corroborative evidence may support this thesis. Although not conclusive, the 1958 finds of a military button with a "C" in the center of the eagle's shield and the possible shelter half grommet stiffeners at the site of this burial suggest that the body was in uniform and wrapped in a shelter tent half or a rubber blanket. The only individuals authorized to wear the "C" button were cavalry officers, and the only officer buried known to be wrapped in a shelter half or rubber blanket, as well as being buried on the bluffs, was Hodgson. This tenuous link might strengthen the argument, but for the fact that older-pattern enlisted uniforms also utilized the button. Even though enlisted men were not authorized to wear the button in 1876, they did wear these older uniforms for field service. So the button could have come from one of those uniforms or been lost from another officer's coat. The grommet stiffeners might represent a tent fly that was used, along with a blanket, or perhaps instead of a blanket, as the shroud for Hodgson's body. There is little doubt the remains were disturbed, probably by one of the reburial parties, and that disturbance, like that on the Custer battlefield, is severe enough to make a positive identification most difficult without other lines of evidence. But the evidence that is available does not rule out Hodgson as the man who was buried in the L-Entrenchment with O'Hara.

Custer Battlefield Marker Test Excavations

One of the archaeologists' jobs during the 1984 and 1985 investigations was to determine why there were more markers on the Custer battlefield than soldiers killed in the battle, 252 markers versus 210 men. Two five-week field seasons were not nearly enough to excavate around all the markers on the main battlefield, although eight excavation units were completed during the 1984 field season. When planning the 1985 season, it seemed feasible to complete eighteen more units. This brought the total number of units excavated to twenty-six and yielded information from thirty-seven of the 252 markers, or about 15 percent of those on the main battlefield.

During the various nineteenth-century reburial details, separate work parties apparently reburied or exhumed bodies on different areas of the field. The differences in their treatment of partial remains, particularly after the remains decayed to leave only bone and teeth, may mean that some work parties could have been responsible for differential clearing of the field. This in turn may have led the 1890 marker setting detail to erect more spurious markers in one area over another.

To help reduce variation caused by differences in how the remains in each area were originally treated and to ensure that some markers from each area were archaeologically tested, the markers were divided into five spatially discrete areas to create a statistically valid sample of all markers on the field. These five areas were Calhoun Hill, the Keogh area, the Deep Ravine Trail (South Skirmish Line), Last Stand Hill, and isolated markers, those widely scattered across the southwestern area of the battlefield. These groups are relatively discrete spatial clusters of markers around the field and are defined simply by breaks in the clusters as seen on the marker distribution map. For details on the original sampling strategy and excavation techniques, see Scott et al. (1989:57–59).

CALHOUN HILL

> Each soldier [was] lying just where he had fallen, each with a small amount of earth thrown over him, with his head protruding from one end of the grave and his feet from the other. One very noticeable feature presented itself to me, the boot tops had been cut from the dead. Their skulls in many instances had been crushed and shot with pistol bullets after being killed. (Allen 1903:67–68)

The historical documents positively identified only four of the men in the Calhoun position. The body of Calhoun himself was recognized by a filling in his teeth (Taunton 1987). Crittenden was reportedly found nearby. He had a glass eye, by which he was recognized, which was shattered during or after the battle. His body was also reported to have been riddled with arrows. Two sergeants from C Company, August Finckle and Jeremiah Finley, were identified south of the two lieutenants, on Greasy Grass Ridge.

Five areas on Calhoun Hill and Greasy Grass Ridge were archaeologically investigated, encompassing a total of seven markers. An isolated marker to the west of Greasy Grass Ridge was also excavated. The archaeological resources were badly disturbed by the construction of the present road along the top of the ridge and the loop on the top of Calhoun Hill that gives tourists an overview of the area. One case of disturbance is certain. At the request of Col. Thomas Crittenden, Seventeenth Infantry, his son's body was not removed when the other officers were exhumed in 1877 but was left to lie on the field of battle. In 1931, however, with the construction of the road, the army removed the body. It was reinterred in the National Cemetery without benefit of an osteological examination to determine if the body is, indeed, Crittenden. However, a *Sheridan Press* (September 21, 1931) account of the disinterment reported that the skull exhibited a cutmark, perhaps made by a tomahawk. The reporter thought the cutmark was consistent with the identity of Crittenden, who was supposed to have been found with his skull cleaved by a tomahawk.

Two excavation units, around Markers 153 and 131, were sterile excavations, yielding no artifacts related to the battle. Although these may be spurious markers, it is more likely that they were originally in the path of the road and were moved to the side to make way for the road. The other three excavations each yielded a scattering of bone consistent with a single individual. In no case was there enough to determine the age, height, or identity of the individual involved. Paired Markers 152 and 155 did yield one interesting artifact, whereas most of the Calhoun Hill excavations yielded only bone. The excavation at Markers 152 and 155 recovered a few links of an elegant gold watch chain of a style consistent with the battle date. It is not possible to identify the owner with certainty, but an intriguing possibility is Lieutenant Crittenden. Crittenden's father described his son's watch and chain in a July 7, 1876, letter as "a chain made of gold coin, large, composed of several plates, and almost round" (Cecil 1995:38). The archaeological find is a finely crafted double round link gold chain. Whether it is the chain described by Colonel Crittenden is only speculation. However, warriors recalled finding and taking several watches from the dead (Graham 1953; Marquis 1931). Certainly this chain represents one of those watches if not that of Crittenden.

The excavation at an isolated marker, Marker 128, is the only one in this area that provided enough information for a detailed study of the remains (figure 53). The bones at Marker 128 were an unusual find, with most of the body present, except for the skull. The body had been reburied sometime after the flesh decayed, probably by the 1877 or 1879 party, before the mass grave was constructed. Differential weathering of the bones indicated that the left side was exposed at some time for several months.

The individual represented by the burial was a white male, about 19–22 years old and roughly 67 inches tall. Evidence of two gunshot wounds to the chest was found on the ribs. Both shots entered from the right side. A bullet fragment was also found embedded in the left lower arm. This may be a third gunshot wound or a fragment of one of the other two bullets. Both thigh bones showed three parallel cutmarks near the proximal ends. Another cutmark was found on

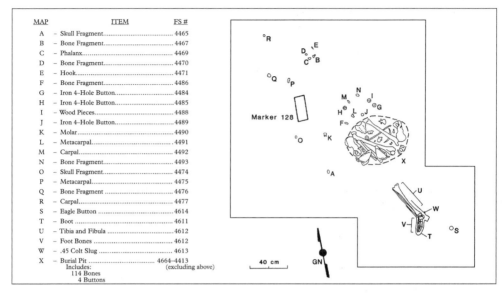

MAP	ITEM	FS #
A	– Skull Fragment	4465
B	– Bone Fragment	4467
C	– Phalanx	4469
D	– Bone Fragment	4470
E	– Hook	4471
F	– Bone Fragment	4486
G	– Iron 4–Hole Button	4484
H	– Iron 4–Hole Button	4485
I	– Wood Pieces	4488
J	– Iron 4–Hole Button	4489
K	– Molar	4490
L	– Metacarpal	4491
M	– Carpal	4492
N	– Bone Fragment	4493
O	– Skull Fragment	4474
P	– Metacarpal	4475
Q	– Bone Fragment	4476
R	– Carpal	4477
S	– Eagle Button	4614
T	– Boot	4611
U	– Tibia and Fibula	4612
V	– Foot Bones	4612
W	– .45 Colt Slug	4613
X	– Burial Pit	4664–4413
	Includes:	(excluding above)
	114 Bones	
	4 Buttons	

Marker 128

40 cm   GN

Figure 53. A typical excavation plan map of the archaeological finds located during the sampling of the marble markers. Here at Marker 128 an almost complete set of soldier's remains were found. The body was first covered over in 1876, then in 1877 or later parts of it may have been exposed and weathered. At that time the visible bones were collected and buried in a shallow hole dug for the purpose. The excavations here told the story of the death of this soldier, his initial burial, exposure, and finally reburial. Midwest Archeological Center, National Park Service.

the collar bone. And the few skull fragments indicate a forceful blow to the head (Snow and Fitzpatrick 1989:266–71).

The soldier suffered from a congenital defect of the lower spine; a portion of a lumbar vertebra had not closed properly. Although this would have little to do with the battle, it is likely that the trooper suffered frequent pain in his lower back, and particularly when riding for long periods of time.

The individual appears to have been originally buried in his clothes, a regulation uniform; buttons from his blouse and trousers were found, as were several fragments of army issue underwear cloth and hooks and eyes, possibly from his campaign hat. When excavated, one leg was in correct anatomical position still encased in its boot, indicating that it had probably not been moved since the original burial. However, the remainder of the body was in a jumbled pile that could only have occurred if the bones were redeposited after the flesh had decayed. The shallow soil covering the June 1876 burial probably eroded away, and by 1877 or 1879 the bones became exposed. One of the reburial parties, missing the lower right leg and foot, must have found the bones, gathered them together, and reburied them in a hole they dug for the purpose. Lt. Hugh Scott (1928) reported being detailed to bury exposed bones when he accompanied General Sheridan to the field in July 1877.

The enlistment records identify nine individuals killed in Custer's command that meet the age and height criteria of the bones found at Marker 128. None of the four people actually identified in this area meet these criteria. Of those possibilities, Nathan Short was purported to have been found some months later on Rosebud Creek, many miles away (Doran 1987). Three others are associated with remains purportedly in Deep Ravine, although one of the three was also identified on Last Stand Hill. Six privates from Company C also meet the age and height criteria, with J. Thadus's height matching the stature estimate. But, without further information, specific identification is impossible.

Fox (1988:200; 1993) suggests that this young man was one of the Company C individuals who charged the warriors hidden behind Greasy Grass Ridge and in Calhoun Coulee. Fox's scenario reckons that this soldier was killed in the charge or the subsequent retrograde movement. If this is the case, the pursuing warriors may have come upon the badly wounded man and with a swift and extremely forceful blow to the head with a war club dispatched him. The victorious warriors proceeded to slash the legs and perhaps shot an arrow into his shoulder. Again, if this scenario is true, then the man at Marker 128 would have been among the first to die and to suffer the mutilation that was so common among many of the dead soldiers.

KEOGH AREA

We went over the battlefield pretty thoroughly and located the spot where Captain Keogh and several of his men of Company I had followed Custer. Here was a slight depression in the ground. Evidently at one time it had been a buffalo wallow and the wind had blown out the dirt, forming a semicircular depression covering several yards. The graves were around this depression. The men were buried where they fell, which clearly showed that their position had been taken for defense. (Wheeler 1923:185)

Lt. Winfield Edgerly, assisting in the burial of the dead three days after the battle, noted that "Capt. Keogh had evidently been wounded as we found that his leg was broken and the sergeants of his company had got around him and were killed with him. There were no regular lines, but still evidence that there had been" (Graham 1953:166). The identities of only seven bodies are noted in the historical accounts as being in the Keogh group. Keogh was identified and noted to have had a broken leg. Hardoff (1985:50–51) suggests that Keogh was mounted during the battle, since information from the Camp manuscripts suggests that his leg was broken by a shot that struck his horse exactly where his leg would have been while he was sitting in the saddle. The wounded Keogh may have dismounted, or been thrown, and his loyal noncommissioned officers gathered around to receive orders and help defend him. He was found reportedly surrounded by approximately eighteen enlisted men.

The body of trumpeter John Patton was identified and found lying over Keogh's body. He may well have stayed close to the wounded Keogh to relay orders to the men using his bugle. The sergeants identified around Keogh included Edwin Bobo, James Bustard, and Frank Varden. Pvt. Charles Graham of Company L was found on a line between the Calhoun and Keogh positions.

In the years after 1890, Keogh's marble marker was somehow reset in an incorrect location, possibly in the 1940s. Extensive research by Brian Pohanka, using photographs from 1877 and the 1890s, showed the marker to be in the wrong location as of 1980 compared to early twentieth-century photographs of the field. In a field check of the area, Pohanka was able to find the brick base of the original marker. Keogh's marker was replaced in the correct location in 1981.

Five archaeological units were excavated in Keogh's position. One unit was placed around Marker 178—Keogh's marker, the site where Pohanka located it. The unit included a scatter of bone: a small piece of skull, one rib, a fragment of a wrist bone, a fragment of an ankle bone, and one toe bone. The only artifact found was a trouser button. This is not nearly enough material to confirm the location of Keogh's interment. Someone was buried there, but not conclusively Keogh. One the other hand, there was nothing recovered at this marker that would indicate it is not Keogh's grave. The original recovery team did a very thorough job.

Three of the other units (around Markers 200, 201 and 202, and 194 and 195) also exposed a light scatter of human bone and a few uniform-related artifacts. Although the excavations were not extensive enough to examine the distribution of bone throughout the area, the finds leave the impression that there is a light scatter of bone throughout the Keogh area, where there are about seventy marble markers today. At least nineteen markers are in the area directly around Keogh's marker. If these bodies were poorly buried, it is likely that coyotes and other predators dragged pieces of the bodies around the area. At roughly 206 bones per body, plus horse bones, there would have been a substantial quantity of bone scattered around the area. In no excavation was there evidence that more than one body was represented at any of those locations.

Excavations were also conducted around Marker 199. In an 1879 Sanderson photograph of Captain Keogh's marker there is a wooden marker labeled "Wild I," probably indicating the location of the grave of Corp. John Wild of Company I in approximately the same location that Marker 199 occupies today.

An articulated arm was found immediately north of the marker. All the bones in the arm, from the shoulder down, were present. The arm was extended, the two lower arm bones crossed, as when the palm faces behind the body. About 30 cm from the articulated arm lay a scatter of disarticulated bone representing most of the opposite hand. Found within and between these two concentrations of bone were a coccyx, eight trouser buttons, and two five-cent pieces. Also found in the excavation were fragments of skull, a mandible, teeth, and a scapula (Snow and Fitzpatrick 1989:264–65).

The bones found in this group did not have the ends fused with the shaft. When bone grows, the ends (the epiphyses) are separate from the shaft (the diaphysis) until the individual has completed growing. That the epiphyses are unfused on this individual means that the soldier was probably 15–17 years old, and almost certainly less than 19. Army enlistment records indicate that Corporal Wild was 26 at the time of his last battle. Either Wild was passing himself off as much older than he was, or, the more likely explanation, this individual is not Wild.

The only individual who died with Custer's battalion who claimed to be this young is Autie Reed. Historical accounts firmly place his body on or just below Last Stand Hill. The official enlistment age during the 1870s was 21, or 18 with parental or guardian's permission, so the enlistment records show few soldiers under the age of 21. Obviously, none of the bodies identified historically can be identified as this individual. It is unlikely that one so young, even by lying about his age, would have been a noncommissioned officer. Marker 199 appears to mark the remains of a young soldier so eager to go into service that he lied about his age when enlisting, a common ploy as established by looking at the actual ages of many of the enlistees.

One casualty is known to have lied about his age to enlist. Pvt. Willis Wright of Company C was just 17 when he died at the Little Bighorn. He was 66.5 inches tall. He fits the criteria well, but there were probably many others who also lied about their ages and forfeited their lives in the process. And Wright was reportedly identified on Last Stand Hill.

DEEP RAVINE TRAIL

> Most of the soldiers, either singly or in groups, have a stake driven where they rest. They are not in graves, but lie with a sprinkling of earth upon each or in groups as they fell last year. More earth was heaped upon them. Some were found this year that were not last. . . . Of course, where the remains were partly uncovered, an indescribable odor arose. (*New York Herald*, July 18, 1877)

The Deep Ravine Trail, South Skirmish Line, or whatever appellation a researcher chooses to apply to this line of markers running from below Last Stand Hill to Deep Ravine is subject to a great deal of controversy. Some theories (Fox 1993; Kuhlman 1951) hold that the line represents the attempted escape of some of the surviving soldiers, usually attributed to members of Company E. King (1981) argues that the markers along this line are spurious, because they represent the men buried in Deep Ravine. Michno (1994), on the other hand, completely dismisses the concept that Deep Ravine holds any remains and argues that the deep ravine mentioned by burial parties is closer to the National Cemetery. The archaeology proves that there are more than six soldiers buried along the line, and the physical evidence refutes both King's and Michno's arguments.

Estimates of the number of bodies scattered between Last Stand Hill and the head of Deep Ravine vary widely in the historical documents. Thomas McDougall told Walter Camp that there were less than a dozen men there and may not have been more than a half dozen (Hammer 1976:72). Richard Thomas told Camp there were nine or ten bodies (Hammer 1976:248). In Deep Ravine itself several bodies were reported, with estimates varying between eighteen and thirty-four. The problem is that there are no markers in Deep Ravine for men who were supposed to have been buried there.

Adding the estimates for men killed in the area between Last Stand Hill and Deep Ravine and the estimates for Deep Ravine itself, we come up with a range of twenty-seven to forty-four men. Today there are fifty-three markers on the Deep Ravine Trail.

Only twelve men were individually identified on the South Skirmish Line or in Deep Ravine. Only one identified soldier, Pvt. Weston Harrington, is associated with that line. His body was reportedly found near the top of the line below Last Stand Hill. Scout Mitch Boyer was identified in the recollections of those on the burial details as located not only in Deep Ravine but also in the river at Medicine Tail Coulee, between Custer and Reno, and several miles north of the battlefield.

Excavations in Deep Ravine are described in Scott and Fox (1987) and Scott et al. (1989). No human remains were actually found in the steep-sided gully known as Deep Ravine. Several excavations were undertaken at the markers that lie between the ravine and Last Stand Hill, and human remains were found at all marker excavation units. In addition, two subsequent surface finds of human bone in 1993 and 1995 at Markers 25 and 35 indicate that more remains are still buried on the field. None of the skeletal evidence matched the age and height of the men supposedly buried there. Six excavations associated with markers were completed in 1984 and 1985 where human bone was recovered.

Marker 2 is on the southeast side of Deep Ravine. The marker stands isolated from many of the others. The excavations uncovered cranial and mandibular fragments, a tooth, and a phalanx (Snow and Fitzpatrick 1989:260). The bones are consistent with those of a single individual of 25–40 years. The skull had been broken at or about the time of death, probably by a massive blow to the head by a blunt object. Three trouser buttons were also found in the excavations, confirming the individual's probable identity as a soldier. Scattered around the marker were bullets from six different weapons. Scott et al. (1989) speculate that he was killed late in the battle, when there were fewer troopers remaining to be shot.

Marker 7 was excavated in both 1984 and 1989. The marker is at the head of Deep Ravine. The additional excavations in 1989 became necessary because human remains were eroding out of the trail adjacent to the marker. In total, the bone assemblage consisted of about twenty skull fragments, teeth, several cervical and thoracic vertebrae, a nearly complete lumbar vertebra, a sternal body fragment, and several unidentified fragments (Scott and Snow 1991a, 1991b; Snow and Fitzpatrick 1989:258). A few horse bone fragments were also recovered. The human bone assemblage was consistent with the remains of a single individual 20–26 years old. As with many of the remains on the field, the skull appeared to have been crushed with a blunt instrument around the time of death. One cervical vertebra was from the lower portion of the neck, and the right portion of the bone was gone. It was separated from the rest of the bone by a single cut that bisected the bone. This would be expected if the trooper had been decapitated in a single blow with a sharp instrument like an ax or tomahawk.

The artifact assemblage at this marker yielded a variety of items: a trouser fly button, a canteen stopper top, an iron-backed rubber comb, and an 1876 five-cent piece. These items all indicate something of how the man was dressed, what he carried in his pockets, and what equipment he carried. All were fairly typical of a soldier's accoutrements. Something of how he died may be discerned from the bullets found near the bones. Two Colt .44-caliber pistol balls, one smashed flat on impact, were found adjacent to one another in the excavations. A Model 1873 Colt pistol bullet was close by, and a .45-55-caliber Springfield bullet was nearly in contact with a cervical vertebra.

Paired Markers 9 and 10 are near Marker 7, also located near the head of Deep Ravine. Fragments of the skull, ribs, vertebrae, scapula, sternum, hand bones, right foot bones, both humeri, a left radius, and a left ulna as well as some smaller bones were found in the unit (Snow and Fitzpatrick 1989:259–60). He was between 30 and 40 years of age at death and was about 70 inches tall. The remains were jumbled across the unit, but several of the skull fragments and both arms were in approximately the correct anatomical position. From the position of the arms, the trooper appeared to have been buried face down. There were cutmarks on the sternum and one of the arm bones. In the thorax was a bullet from a .44-caliber Henry. In the area of the skull was a bullet from a .45-caliber Colt revolver. An iron arrowhead was also found adjacent to the excavation. Scattered through the excavations were eleven buttons, including trouser buttons, blouse buttons, and three white Prosser molded shirt buttons.

The single trooper represented by these two markers may have been wounded or killed by the .44-caliber Henry bullet. When the warriors overran the skirmish line, one may have picked up a soldier's Colt revolver and shot this trooper in the head with it. Others may have slashed his chest and arms in a form of ritual mutilation. The possible identities for the man at these markers, based on age and height, include George Custer and William Teeman, both reportedly found elsewhere on the field (Taunton 1986:21), which leaves eleven other possibilities. None of the possible names matches with name of an individual identified in the historical record as being found either on the South Skirmish Line or in Deep Ravine. And none of the possible candidates are from Company E. Statistically this is not likely, since the historically identified men are primarily from Company E. Either this man is one of the few non–E Company men killed in or near Deep Ravine or the men on the South Skirmish Line represent a greater mixture of companies than noted in the historical record, a more likely scenario.

Excavations at paired Markers 52 and 53 near the upper end of the South Skirmish Line yielded only a skull fragment with a bladed tool cutmark (Snow and Fitzpatrick 1989:261), trouser button, Benet primer from an army cartridge, and lead shot, only enough to say that a man had been buried there at one time.

Marker 42 yielded only a few hand bones (Snow and Fitzpatrick 1989:273), although a finger bone was found at this site in 1984.

That bone still had a silver-plated brass wedding band encircling it, a reminder that widows and orphans were also a result of the battle.

The other excavation in this area that uncovered a bone assemblage was the excavation around Markers 33 and 34, located in the middle of the South Skirmish Line. The markers are adjacent to the trail, and after the 1983 fire Fox (1983) found human bone eroding from this area. Formal excavation in 1984 recovered a bullet from a .50–70-caliber weapon, a bullet fragment, and lead shot, demonstrating at least two weapons firing into this position. A rubber button, such as those found on nonregulation ponchos, was found, as well as a mother-of-pearl shirt button, also nonregulation. These suggest European-style, nonregulation clothing. The bone found included fragments of a skull, teeth, cervical vertebra, wrist and hand bones, and coccyx. In all, they suggest an individual of about 35–45 years. The teeth were worn in such a manner to suggest pipe smoking. Also interesting is the fact that the face bones of the individual indicate racially mixed parentage, part white and part American Indian (Snow and Fitzpatrick 1989:257–58).

There were only a few men with Custer that day who match this description. Lt. Donald McIntosh was part European Canadian and part American Indian, but he was killed in the valley fight and not on the main battlefield. The only racially mixed individual known to have been killed with Custer's command is scout Mitch Boyer. Luckily, there is a photograph of Boyer, and using a video superimposition technique it was possible to overlay the photograph over the bone. The fit is excellent, and these are probably Boyer's remains (Scott et al. 1988).

Controversy has reigned concerning the location of Boyer's body. Pvt. Peter Thompson (Magnussen 1974:257) stated that he found the body on the left side of the river, and Sgt. Daniel Knipe (Hammer 1976:95) noted that Boyer was buried in Deep Ravine. Col. John Gibbon (1877:621) stated that "the body of our poor guide Mitch Boyer was found lying in the midst of the troopers slain, as the Sioux had several times reported they had slain him in battle." And scout White-Man-Runs-Him (Magnussen 1974:259n) stated that Boyer was found on a ridge.

These recollections suggest that either Boyer's body was mistakenly identified by the various sources or their memory at the time of the interviews in the early 1900s had dimmed after so many years. Boyer was found at Markers 33 and 34 just below the crest of a ridge that forms the north side of the primary drainage area of Deep Ravine. If this area was considered a part of Deep Ravine by the burial details, then this has important ramifications in reinterpreting the locations of those killed in or near Deep Ravine. However, it is possible that because of the crushed skull and poor condition of the bodies Boyer's remains were confused with those of other individuals. The identification of Boyer on the South Skirmish Line agrees more with Gibbon's and White-Man-Runs-Him's accounts that Boyer was found among the slain troopers and on a ridge. The importance of the findings, however, is that the archaeological data flatly contradict some common interpretations of the historical accounts. Either the accounts or their interpretations are inaccurate. Since one of the places Boyer was identified is in Deep Ravine, this is interesting in the light of understanding what happened to the men in Deep Ravine.

South of the South Skirmish Line and across Deep Ravine are a few scattered markers that run in a rough line toward Greasy Grass Ridge. Four of these markers in three groups were excavated. Paired Markers 5 and 6, situated on the south edge of Deep Ravine, yielded nothing. In fact, bedrock was encountered only a few inches below the surface. No one appears ever to have been buried here. Marker 252 likewise yielded nothing, but there may be a reason for this. The marker was not set in a brick base. A brick base was located a few yards away on the edge of a shallow ravine. The present marker was probably relocated.

Marker 257, also several hundred yards south of Deep Ravine, did yield a few human bones. The bones of the hand and foot were badly eroded, suggesting that they had lain on the ground surface at some time in the past (Snow and Fitzpatrick 1989:266). Although these bones could be identified only as adult human, this marker location is identified in the Camp notes and on his marker map (Taunton 1986) as the site where Company F's Corp. John Briody's body was found. According to Camp's notes, Briody was found with his leg severed from his body and placed under his head. The archaeologically recovered bones were found in such an orientation that they could be interpreted in this manner, but so few were found that no positive conclusion can be reached. That Marker 257 is the site of John Briody's burial must remain speculation and an intriguing possibility.

LAST STAND HILL

> The horses were killed and scattered all over the hill, and at the point where Custer lay [it] showed to be the last stand. There was not hardly any horses around where he was lying when found. The soldiers lay thick at this point, Custer was lying across two or three soldiers, just a small portion of his back touching the ground. There is no such thing as them arrange to corral their horses, or to make a fortification out of their horses, as there was nothing to show this. Custer had no clothing on whatever, nor none of the soldiers. There was nothing left but a foot of a boot; the leg of this being gone, on Custer. (Kanipe to Camp 1908, in Hammer 1976:91–98)

Last Stand Hill is at the north end Custer Ridge. Perhaps because most of the officers with Custer were on Last Stand Hill, the aftermath of the battle has been better described here than elsewhere on the field. In this one place lay Custer with five officers and perhaps forty men scalped and mutilated (Taunton 1987:26).

The bodies of twenty-seven men have been documented as being on Last Stand Hill. These include fourteen privates, two civilians, a surgeon, a trumpeter, four noncommissioned officers, and five commissioned officers Within the currently fenced area of Last Stand Hill there are fifty-two markers, and five excavations were undertaken that investigated seven of those markers. Two excavations (around Markers 63 and 86 and 88) revealed little material. Marker 63 yielded no human remains and Markers 86 and 88 yielded only the patella of an adult (Snow and Fitzpatrick 1989:271).

Marker 105 identifies it as the site where Lt. Algernon Smith fell. The excavation unit revealed a complete, and nearly articulated, lower left arm and hand as well as other bones of the right hand, back, and foot. The remains represent an adult male of 30–40 years and about 63 inches tall. Lieutenant Smith was taller. The foot bones excavated showed that this individual had fractured his foot sometime before the battle, and that it had had time to heal. There was a cutmark on a vertebra that could have been caused by either a knife or an arrowhead (Snow and Fitzpatrick 1989:261–62). Also found in the excavations were two regulation buttons of the style used on trouser flies and suspenders. A .45–55-caliber cartridge and a .45–405-caliber bullet were also found in the excavations.

Based on the age and height information, there were nine men killed on the main battlefield to which the remains at Marker 105 could belong. None are officers. One trooper on the possible list was documented as actually being found on Last Stand Hill. This is Pvt. Werner Lieman of Company F, who was 33 years old when he died and 65 inches tall. Born in Bremen, Germany, Lieman had blue eyes, brown hair, and a light complexion.

The excavations at Marker 78 also uncovered human bone. There were several skull fragments, a tooth, almost all the bones of the left hand, a few of the right hand, three small bones from a foot, and the shattered lower third of the left ulna and radius. The ulna was shattered by a gunshot; lead fragments were still imbedded in the bone (Snow and Fitzpatrick 1989:272). Four regulation trouser buttons and a .45-caliber Colt bullet were also found. The bones were consistent with those of a single individual, someone between about 18 and 30 years old at the time of death. There was not enough information to determine the individual's height, so there was not enough information to determine possible identities.

The area around paired Markers 67 and 68 was also excavated. It is at the top of Last Stand Hill, near the fence enclosing the area. The remains of two individuals were found in this area; one was a horse and the other a human. The human remains include skull fragments, teeth, ribs, lumbar vertebrae, and a finger bone (Snow and Fitzpatrick 1989:272–73). One of the vertebrae had a collapsed body, a rib may have a gunshot wound, and the skull possibly received a massive blow. The human remains are consistent with those of a male of 35–45 years. These remains are not enough to determine the individual's height or possible identification.

ISOLATED MARKERS

Markers 112 and 113 were excavated southwest of Last Stand Hill. These markers are isolated and like the others excavated revealed bones consistent with only one individual. The bones were a tooth crown, a coccyx (tailbone), one finger bone, and two toe bones (Snow and Fitzpatrick 1989:266). All that can be said of these remains is that they are from a person 35–45 years old. The few artifacts found include the soldier's trouser buttons, a Prosser molded shirt button, and a .44- or .45-caliber ball fired by the warriors.

The Reno Retreat Remains

The summer of 1989 took archaeologists and a group of volunteers back to the Little Bighorn Battlefield National Monument to conduct further investigations. The weather refused to cooperate the first week of work. During a "rain day" a special find was made (Scott and Snow 1991b). Four volunteers decided to take a look at the Reno retreat crossing of the Little Bighorn River. While wandering the riverbank, Monte Kloberdanz spotted a human skull and two other bones eroding from the west bank just across the river from the Hodgson marker. The volunteers reported their find to the archaeologists and acting park superintendent Douglas McChristian. Because the remains appeared to be of a young white male with evidence of trauma of a type that could be combat-induced and were found in an area historically associated with the battle, the local coroner decided to appoint the acting superintendent and archaeologists official investigators.

All that was found at the site were the skull, left humerus, and right clavicle (Scott and Snow 1991b). The bones were found in such a position to suggest that they had fallen out of their original context as a result of erosion of the riverbank because of the high water that spring. The other bones probably washed away in the high water, leaving behind only these remains to be found. The bones were found in such a precarious position that another rain would have washed them away as well.

The humerus and clavicle indicated an adult about 68 inches tall. The skull indicated that he was a white male of 30–40 years. It also indicated that he had been ill at some time in his life with a high fever; some of the back of the skull was remodeled due to this illness. The teeth were in good shape, although a few were lost after death. One molar had a small cavity and one third molar (wisdom tooth) was impacted. The other third molar had been pulled or lost not long before his death, based on the amount of bone regrowth in the old tooth socket. The skull displayed evidence of trauma suffered about the time of death.

The right canine and premolars were broken off at the roots, and there was a horizontal fracture running across the face just below the nose. This fracture was indicative of blunt force trauma. About the time of death he was struck across the mouth by a blunt object, such as a lance or gun barrel, with enough force to fracture the bone and break off the crowns of three teeth. If he was on horseback trying to reach the river, such a blow would have unseated him, and as he fell he may have struck his face on a rock, log, or other such object. No other injuries were evident on the bones.

With the knowledge that the man was 68 inches tall and 30–40 years of age, a list of casualties in that age and height range was constructed. Concentrating on those men with Reno who were killed in the valley fight or the retreat and adding those whose location of death was not known yielded six possible candidates. Of these six, two are considered highly probable because the historical documentation places them in the area of the retreat crossing: Sgt. Edward Botzer and Pvt. William Moodie. Hammer (1976:134) places Botzer as being killed near the river during the retreat. Augustus DeVoto recalled in 1917 (Schoenberger 1990:70) during the recovery of Lieutenant Hodgson's body that "nearby were several dead members of G Troop. One I remember was Sgt. Botzer." This may imply that Botzer was on the east side of the river, since that is where Hodgson's body was found. Moodie was reported to have been buried on the west bank of the river at the retreat crossing (Hardorf 1989).

A facial reconstruction was completed to provide a face from the past, one of the men killed during Reno's retreat. In another case of serendipity common to much of the research at Little Bighorn, a television special, "Custer's Last Trooper," produced by the late Bill Armstrong, featured the finding of the Reno crossing remains. It aired in early 1990 and was viewed by a mother and daughter who thought the facial reconstruction bore a resemblance to a progenitor, Rudolph Batzer. Mr. Batzer had emigrated from Germany during the late 1860s about the same time as Botzer. A comparison of a family photograph of Rudolph to the facial approximation demonstrated an uncanny resemblance, possibly a family association, implying that the skull was a relative of Rudolph Batzer. An attempt was made to extract DNA from the bones, to no avail, so a comparison with Rudolph's descendants' DNA could not be made.

A major breakthrough occurred in the identification process five years later, in early 1995. As a popular part of the Custer Battlefield Historical and Museum Association's journal, the *Greasy Grass* presents portrait photographs of the battle participants. While assembling the 1995 issue, editor Sandy Barnard (1995) was contacted by a Tacoma, Washington, photograph collector who had a portrait attributed to Sergeant Botzer. The portrait showed a uniformed soldier wearing a forage cap and sporting a small goatee, and penciled on the back of the print was Sergeant Botzer's name. The collector was interested in having it included in the *Greasy Grass* and authenticated. Armed with this information, a photo superimposition was attempted with the skull and photograph. A copy of the portrait and a cast of the Reno crossing skull were forwarded to Dr. P. Willey for superimposition. Although it cannot be unequivocally proven, the two images coincided.

Miscellaneous Remains

Over the years other bones have been found on the Monument proper by park staff and custodians and placed in the Monument's museum collection. These bones were given a complete examination in 1985 by Clyde Snow (Snow and Fitzpatrick 1989) as a part of the archaeological project. Subsequent discoveries and repatriated remains were studied by Willey (1995) and Owsley (1994).

In the course of the osteological examination, Snow and Fitzpatrick found that some of the bones listed in the museum accession records as human were, in fact, animal bones. Also, in several cases bones correctly identified as human were incorrectly identified anatomically. When these mistakes were rectified, the collection was reduced to thirty-seven human bones and a single tooth. Examination of the bones and available records shows that the collection can be subdivided into sixteen assemblages, each representing a separate individual. Four of these assemblages were found on the Custer battlefield and five on the Reno-Benteen defense site; of the remaining seven, two were found in another area, and the records of five contain no indication of where they were found.

Near the marker of George Custer on Last Stand Hill, a right hamate bone was found in 1956. It was that of an adult male with no evidence of pathology or trauma noted. Another Last Stand Hill assemblage consisted of four foot bones and a cranial fragment that were described as having been found near the grave marker of 1st Lt. W. W. Cooke. The date of the find is not given in the museum records. The cranial fragment margins displayed the abrupt fracture lines indicative of perimortem blunt force trauma. The foot bones, based on size and morphology, were identified as those of an adult male.

The third assemblage consisted of four hand bones and a left tibia found "near drain on Custer Hill" in 1941 and may be associated with the horse bone grave found that year. The leg bone was missing its proximal end, but whether this loss occurred at the time of death or some years later was not determined. Although the damage precluded an exact measurement, stature was estimated to be approximately 66–67 inches and the age was judged to range between 18 and 35. The four hand bones of this assemblage were noted as having been found in a boot. They were adult in size and morphology and displayed no pathologies or signs of perimortem trauma.

The final Last Stand Hill bone was a single sternal fragment of a ninth right rib. It showed evidence of an old healed fracture. It was found among the marble markers below the granite monument on the hill, although the exact site and date of recovery are unknown.

Another bone assemblage, consisting of a right radius and ulna, was found in 1942 near the grave marker of Mark Kellogg, a civilian newspaper correspondent. Stature was estimated to be 65.75 inches. Kellogg's stature is unknown. Kellogg did break an arm or wrist during a fall a year or two before his death (Warren "Sandy" Barnard, personal communication, 1985), but the extent of the injury and exact location of the fracture site are not known. These bones displayed no evidence of old injury. In all probability the marker for Kellogg (Marker 247) is not where his body was originally found. Today Kellogg's marker is situated on the east side of Last Stand Hill, but Kellogg's body was found by Col. John Gibbon several hundred yards to the west of Last Stand Hill (Moore and Donahue 1991). The skeletal evidence indicates that someone was buried at the site of Kellogg's marker, but it was probably not Kellogg.

In 1993, John Doerner found a much weathered adult left mandibular fragment near Marker 25 near Deep Ravine Trail. Two years later, during remote sensing surveys for the troopers in Deep Ravine, an adult left wrist bone was found near Marker 35. There were marks on the bone that may be cuts but more likely were caused by plant roots etching the bone surface.

Also among the miscellaneous assortment of bones accumulated in the museum collection are a few attributed to the Reno-Benteen area. One item is a single tooth, a right maxillary lateral incisor that was found by a visitor in 1959. It was found in the vicinity of the Benteen counterattack or charge. It lacks any depression or shoveling on the lingual (tongue) surface, which is characteristic of American Indians; therefore, it is probably from one of the troopers. One soldier, Private Tanner, was killed in the charge and left behind until he could be recovered later.

Another assemblage, found by Don Rickey in 1956, consists of three foot bones and a fingertip bone. An unprovenienced wrist bone (left lunate) was found in 1954 by two individuals identified as only Woodward and Shick. A left humerus was found in the gulch below Reno Hill in 1934. The proximal epiphysis is fused, indicating that the individual was over 20 years old. There is a very faint transverse cutmark on the midshaft; this may be a mutilation mark. The individual's stature was between 68.5 and 72.1 inches. The museum catalog card notes that the bone was found not far from where Lieutenant Hodgson was supposed to have been killed. The only individual of that stature known to have been killed on the bluffs is Pvt. William Meyer of Company M. In an interview with Walter Camp, Pvt. William Morris (Hammer 1976:131) noted that Meyer was killed where the bluffs become steep. Other individuals known to have been killed in this vicinity are Pvt. Henry Gordon (66 inches tall), Pvt. Elihu Clear (66.5 inches), and Corp. Henry Cody (aka Scollin; 67 inches). Hodgson's body was not buried where he was killed but moved to the top of the hill for burial. Although it is tempting to identify this bone as belonging to Meyer, there are at least nine other candidates in that height range who were killed at Reno-Benteen. Although Meyer is the only one to meet both the criteria of height and location where the bone was found, we cannot dismiss the others. A single bone is rarely enough to make a positive identification.

A left first metatarsal was found in 1988 in the Reno-Benteen entrenchment area, although a more precise location is not available. It is from an adult and displayed alterations consistent with much weathering and exposure (Willey 1995).

A left parietal fragment, reportedly from north Medicine Tail Coulee, exhibited linear fracturing indicative of perimortem blunt force trauma. It was found in 1957.

Six other assemblages are known, but their discovery location and date are undocumented. One is a fifth metacarpal with a perimortem fracture to the lower third of the shaft. Another is a complete set of five right metacarpals and a single proximal phalanx bone. A set of five wrist bones is also present. Several single bones were also examined, including a normal left adult rib, a normal adult third right metatarsal, and a normal adult third left metatarsal, although these may be the bones found near Tom Custer's marker by Edward Luce in 1941 (Luce to Charles Khulman, April 2, 1941, Charles Khulman Papers, RG12.14-23, University of Nebraska Special Collections, Love Library). Little can be said of these bones because of the lack of association with a specific location and their nondiagnostic nature.

While many of the National Cemetery specimens were being analyzed in 1992, another bone collection, presumed to be from the battlefield, emerged. The collection, consisting of the top of a cranial vault and a tooth, had been in a Pennsylvania man's artifact collection, and after his death they were sent to the Little Bighorn National Monument, arriving with the morning's mail shortly before Christmas (McChristian 1993). Although the origin of these battlefield specimens is questionable, there are some indications that at least the skull vault may be associated with the battle.

Preservation of the skull fragment was in keeping with other Little Bighorn specimens. Penciled words on the vault have been interpreted as indicating that the bones were found in a draw in November 1941. The fragment is consistent with a cavalryman. It was a young adult or possibly an older adolescent, and, probably, on basis of the single measurement possible, a white male. The most convincing indicator of its Little Bighorn affiliation is a gunshot wound. The bullet entered the right side of the vault and exited through the left side. This pattern is typical of right-handed suicide victims, although homicides may display similar wounds, as seen in the National Cemetery Burial 3 skull. Given the uncertainty of the specimen's provenience and the sketchy osteological conclusions, there are a multitude of possible identities. None can be considered any more likely than another.

In 1994 four specimens were returned to the Little Bighorn Battlefield National Monument from the Sioux City Public Museum in Iowa. That museum's registrar, Patricia Martin, came across the specimens while inspecting the museum collection, and she sent the bones to the Monument. A penciled note with the elements reads "Bones from Custers Battle Field June 26-76 Found by F. Todd July 1900."

The date attributed to the battle is interesting. If the June 26 date is correct, then the death must have happened in the Reno-Benteen entrenchment area. Fighting occurred only there that day. Fighting had ended on the Custer field the previous day. It is likely, however, that the date is simply an error. The four bones included were a parietal or frontal fragment, an adult right navicular, and a lunate, as well as a bone from a large nonhuman mammal (Willey 1995). The wrist bones had slight arthritic changes. All of the human remains were consistent with those of troopers, but little else could be concluded.

Also in 1994 another specimen surfaced, but in a different manner. This is a single middle phalanx with arthritic changes (Owsley 1994). This bone, apparently found near Marker 174, was looted from the battlefield in the early 1980s and recently returned to the park at the culmination of a lengthy and successful law enforcement investigation.

One other bone assemblage was recently studied. A purported human finger bone necklace, the fingers allegedly taken from dead soldiers at the Little Bighorn, was found at the Dallas Historical Society, Dallas, Texas. An examination of the bones determined that they were not human but artiodactyl (families that include cattle, sheep, and pigs) (Shaffer 2008). The necklace is clearly a piece meant to defraud and is a reminder of the gullibility of many individuals and museums who often suspend their disbelief and accept an item based on inexpert opinion or downright fraudulent testimony.

Summary of Human Remains Studies

Among the many legacies of the Battle of the Little Bighorn are the skeletal remains of those who died in the fight. In the intervening years, some of those remains became exposed and were collected for reburial in Custer National Cemetery, and others were discovered during formal archaeological investigations. One element of the Little Bighorn archaeological investigations was to ascertain if the marble markers were accurately placed on the field in 1890. The investigations did determine that most markers are indeed correct, but that the paired markers are most likely mark only a single interment. The recovery of human bone at many of the markers indicates that the 1881 reburial team did a good, but not complete, job of recovery of the dead.

Among the research questions raised during the archaeological studies were those related to the study of human remains. These questions were designed to gather data from any available skeletal remains to identify them with individual battle casualties, if possible, through proper and complete skeletal examination. The study was also intended to examine evidence that might add information on the health, status, wound trauma, and general lifestyle of the soldiers killed at the Little Bighorn.

The archaeological and physical anthropological data on the skeletal sample have added a new scope of information on the men of the Seventh Cavalry. In the realm of the sciences, data on the skeletal remains are presented as a series of identifications and interpretations. These interpretations woven together provide clues to the lives represented by the remains. Although individual identifications cannot often be made, the composite data provide a glimpse into life ways of the men who made up the Seventh Cavalry and died on the battlefield. There is now a sizable body of information, gleaned from the skeletal series on ages, stature, diet, and health, which is more fully reported in Scott et al. (1998). The Little Bighorn human skeletal evidence has wider value than just telling the story of the soldiers who fell during the battle. One example of its value to science is that the data were used in a broader study of the effects of nineteenth-century lifestyles on those in military service (Sledzik and Sandberg 2002).

The marker excavations yielded partial remains of twenty-one individuals, a 10 percent sample of those killed during the battle. The National Cemetery exhumations yielded thirteen nearly complete skeletons. In addition to the excavated remains, surface material found by the archaeological crew, visitors, and park staff yielded partial remains of another thirteen individuals. This provides a group of remains representing forty-seven of the soldiers who died at the Little Bighorn (roughly an 18 percent sample).

The human remains examined exhibited substantial evidence of perimortem trauma. The osteological data clearly demonstrate that some of the men were mutilated about the time of death. To what extent the bodies were mutilated cannot be precisely determined because of the lack of tissue, and many were missing some skeletal elements, but a relative impression of the type and extent of the injuries can be suggested based on the osteological analysis.

Many contemporary accounts of the June 27, 1876, burials note that mutilation was prevalent among the dead. The most common type of mutilation mentioned was the crushed skull. The archaeological evidence for incised wounds, those made by knives, arrows, and hatchets, was present in about 21 percent of the remains from Custer battlefield and in only one case from the Reno-Benteen defense site. Wounds related to knives or arrows were seen in 11 percent of the Custer individuals, and hatchet-related injuries were noted in 10 percent of the Custer sample. It must be remembered that not all injuries are likely to have affected the bone; the sample reflects only those injuries that penetrated to the bone. Nevertheless, it appears that a significant percentage of the soldiers killed must have been shot with arrows, cut with knives, or struck with hatchets about the time of death.

Blunt instrument trauma to the skull is the most prevalent perimortem feature in the contemporary accounts, and the archaeological evidence supports this. There are fourteen cases in the Custer battlefield archaeological record where skull fragments are present. All cases exhibit blunt instrument trauma. This group accounts for 41 percent of the Custer battlefield individuals represented archaeologically and all of those cases where skull fragments were present. This direct physical evidence suggests that blunt force trauma to the skull was common.

The incomplete nature of the skeletal remains recovered limits the quantification of the amount of mutilation at the Custer battlefield. Qualitatively, it is obvious from the archaeological evidence that mutilation was common. This is in concert with the historical record. But the cause of mutilation must be placed in a cultural context. Most of our current perspective of mutilation is derived from the Victorian view that mutilation is barbaric. That viewpoint has been perpetuated in much of the literature about American Indian "atrocities." It is, however, more appropriate to view mutilation from the cultural context of the Sioux and Cheyennes rather than the Victorians. One of the most common themes in American Indian explanations of mutilation is one that pervades human nature—a sense of rage and revenge. White Necklace, Wolf Chief's wife, found her niece decapitated after the Sand Creek massacre, and in revenge she decapitated a soldier at the Little Bighorn with her belt ax (Powell 1969). And though revenge may have been the most obvious motivation for mutilation, there are also deeper cultural meanings ascribed to the practice. Brig. Gen. Henry B. Carrington (1973) interviewed a member of Red Cloud's band about the reason for the mutilation of the dead at the 1866 Fetterman fight near Fort Phil Kearney, Wyoming. Carrington reported that the key to understanding the mutilation was an understanding of American Indians' own view of life after death:

> Their idea of the spirit land is that it is a physical paradise; but we enter upon its mysteries just in the condition we hold when we die. In the Indian paradise every physical taste or longing is promptly met. . . . In the light of this idea, those tortured bodies had a new significance. With the muscles of the arms cut out, the victim could not pull a bowstring or trigger; with other muscles gone, he could not put foot in a stirrup or stoop to drink; so that, while every sense was in agony for relief from hunger or thirst, there could be no relief at all.

In this context, mutilation, in the view of the Sioux and Cheyenne participants, was a part of their culture. It must be viewed as a normal cultural expression of victory over a vanquished foe. That expression has two levels. One is the overt and obvious level of rage and revenge. The second is symbolic or religious—a level at which mutilation is a means to ensure that an enemy cannot enjoy the afterlife in the fullness that the victor might anticipate. Thus the mutilated dead at the Little Bighorn become symbols of victory to the culture that defeated them.

The men with Custer may have died in 1876, but their bones tell a detailed story of their lives and deaths. Physical anthropologists have not only determined their age, stature, and probable cause of death but discovered new information about their lifestyle that cannot be garnered from the historical record alone. Perhaps most revealing is the harsh and rugged life led by these relatively young men as seen in the extent to which their lifestyle as cavalrymen on the frontier restructured and remodeled their bones. Clearly reflected there is evidence of horseback riding and tobacco use. Equally important is correlation of the historical records with physical anthropological data, which has resulted in the probable identification of Miles O'Hara, Edward Botzer, Vincent Charley, and possibly two others. Facial approximations of other skulls have added potential likenesses of five, as yet unidentified, battle participants to the gallery of those who served in the Seventh Cavalry.

The tools of modern physical anthropology, though not solving every possible question of interest about the men, add to a growing historical and anthropological database. Of real significance is the identification of one set of remains as an American Indian female, possibly a Crow. This elderly woman's remains were discovered in 1928 and, without benefit of any analysis at that time, were buried in the National Cemetery as an unknown soldier. Such an error underscores the value of thorough and complete scientific investigation of human remains found on the field of battle. Thus it becomes apparent that researchers should not assume that human remains found on or near the battlefield are those of a soldier. Other peoples have lived on and utilized the site for thousands of years. Our single-event focus on the Little Bighorn site requires expansion to appreciate the whole history of the place.

CHAPTER 7

Accomplishments of
the Archaeological
Investigations

A Summary

Artifacts found on the field of battle and removed without context
are just relics, curiosities that arouse romantic imagination. But
when the recovery of those artifacts is accomplished in a systematic manner and the provenience and context properly recorded,
the data become a valuable new source of information on the battle.
Recovered battlefield artifacts, as the physical evidence of the event,
are useful for several purposes. At one level they are the tangible
evidence of the event and can be used in a museum setting to interpret the event. The data contained in the artifact and in its context
in the ground are also a new and independent source of evidence
for detailed analysis of specific battle elements, such as combatants'
attire, armament, deployment, and movements. As this book demonstrates, appropriate collection and analysis of the archaeological
record allow for far more than mere reconstruction of battle events.
Using the growing array of archaeological theory and techniques,
we can derive a greater understanding of American Indian and U.S.
Army strategy and tactics from the artifacts and the context in which
they are found.

The archaeology of the Battle of the Little Bighorn has yielded
thousands of artifacts, reams of notes and other records, and a pile
of reports, monographs, and books. Those who participated in
these projects, whether as archaeologist or volunteer, know that not
everything has been found, nor has everything there is to know been

learned. But, in more than twenty-five years of continuing archaeological investigation, many items recovered and interpreted have demonstrated that the historical record is correct on many points, that American Indian oral history and oral tradition likewise explain some details better than the army accounts, and that neither oral tradition nor the documentary records have mentioned everything worth mentioning. The Little Bighorn archaeological record is not better than the other sources; rather, it should be viewed as another set of information to be compared and correlated with the others. Archaeological data are physical evidence of the battle and as such are visible reminders of those past events that have come to play such a role in our lives. The artifacts and the information they convey are a very real part of the interpretation of the Battle of the Little Bighorn.

The artifacts recovered during the archaeological investigations do not just sit on shelves in the park vault. A variety of researchers study some aspect of the data set nearly every year. And some of artifacts, including some very poignant ones, are on display in the museum, aiding in bringing the battle story to life for the visitor.

Recommendations for further archaeological investigation of the Little Bighorn battlefield were made by Scott (2010b) in the park archaeological overview and assessment to follow up on a variety of issues raised during earlier archaeological investigations. The project recommendations are based on securing a comprehensive understanding of the archaeological record associated with the Battle of the Little Bighorn; thus, they are not limited to park-owned and -managed lands exclusively. One recommended goal is to complete a systematic and comprehensive inventory of areas not previously surveyed around the park, if landowner permission can be obtained. Some recommended inventory areas are on privately owned land, some on Crow tribal lands, and some on property owned by the Custer Battlefield Land Preservation Fund. Other projects are recommended within and around the park to gain a fuller understanding of the battle-era use of the landscape and terrain and to build upon the efforts of Luce, Rickey, and other earlier researchers who laid such an important foundation for the finding, study, and analysis of the physical remains of the battle and its aftermath.

The recommendations were made in order to be useful to the park in determining the nature and extent of individual battle areas and features as contributing or noncontributing resources to the significance of the Little Bighorn battlefield. Knowledge of the features and areas of significance is critical to making informed management decisions when even small-scale construction or development activities must be undertaken to provide visitor services, such as new trails, enhancement of the viewshed through vegetative manipulation, and other activities.

One recommendation suggests actions to be taken for bones that are likely to continue to be found as isolates or overlooked burials in the coming years. Natural erosion as well as changing land uses are likely to cause human remains to become exposed. Custer's men were hastily buried after the battle in shallow graves marked with crude markers made from tepee poles from the abandoned Indian encampments. Natural decomposition processes, soil erosion, animal activity, and human disturbance caused some of the remains to become scattered. In 1877, Custer, ten officers, and two civilians were transferred to eastern cemeteries, and in 1881 the remaining Seventh Cavalry dead, or at least some bones from most of the army dead, were placed in a mass grave on Last Stand Hill. In 1890 white marble markers replaced the original Seventh Cavalry burial stakes, leaving a unique record of where the soldiers fell on the field that provides a visual understanding of the battle absent from most battlefields. The need to care for the fallen men also led to the designation of the site as a national cemetery, and subsequent reinterments from abandoned frontier forts and more recent burials from later U.S. wars fill the cemetery. Human remains that are discovered because of erosion or land-altering work should be carefully examined by trained physical anthropologists to ascertain if they are soldier or American Indian. Then appropriate disposition of those remains can be made in consultation with the appropriate parties as required by law and regulation.

Lakotas and Cheyennes laid their casualties to rest in some of the camp's abandoned tepees as well as on burial scaffolds, or they were interred along hillsides or sandstone outcroppings in Little Bighorn Valley. Some families of these dead later erected stone cairns at some of the casualty sites to preserve the location where their loved ones died or were mortally wounded. Because of the important cultural associations of the battle beginning immediately after it occurred, the battlefield has also been the site of cultural disputes, especially by

American Indians demanding more recognition. Beginning in 1999, chief park historian John Doerner began erecting red granite markers for Cheyenne and Lakota warrior casualties from the battle on the basis of oral traditions related to the various known stone cairns denoting warrior causality locations. After a long debate, planning, and funding process, the Indian Memorial was dedicated in 2003 (figure 54). These two historically significant changes are important and powerful additions to the park's cultural landscape and provide an interpretive balance as well as visual representations to differing cultural perspectives of memorialization and commemoration that the site lacked for more than 120 years. Little Bighorn Battlefield National Monument now acknowledges the Cheyenne and Lakota

Figure 54. The Indian Memorial completed in 2003 commemorates all tribes' participation in the Battle of the Little Bighorn. Midwest Archeological Center, National Park Service.

sacrifice and loss that occurred during the battle and provides a new interpretive balance to the story for park visitors. The rock cairns are an extremely fragile expression of American Indian memorialization and commemoration of the battle and their sacrifice to protect their way of life. As such, they are archaeological resources in and of their own right. Additional ones may be discovered and new ones occasionally constructed. These should be recorded and afforded appropriate protection and respect.

Many Little Bighorn visitors and battle enthusiasts are fascinated with the archaeological work and finds. One outcome of additional inventory and study is the potential for working with related sites in nearby areas that would continue to allow development of a more complete understanding of the prehistory and history of land use in the area through time as well as the battle story itself. Volunteers have been a valued, important, and economically advantageous aspect of most of the archaeological projects undertaken to date. Interested volunteers not only provide real and valued assistance to a project, they also function as unofficial goodwill ambassadors for the site and its long-term preservation and study. However, their efforts must continue to be directed and supervised by qualified professional archaeologists to ensure that all professional standards are met or exceeded in any work in which volunteers are used.

The visiting public's interest in archaeology and history can be addressed in a variety of means. Interpretation of any in-progress archaeological projects can be included in park tours or announcements at the visitor contact areas. The artifacts resulting from archaeological investigations may very well aid in presenting a more complete picture of the history to the visitor by presenting the physical evidence to them. In turn, data generated by archaeological work can be used by park interpreters to enhance the site interpretation through a variety of methods—exhibits, personal presentations, brochures, publications.

The archaeological evidence of the Battle of the Little Bighorn has contributed much to an understanding of the particulars of the fight and added to the historical significance of the battle and its aftermath. Clearly the remaining archaeological deposits, which are substantial, are likely to yield additional significant information about the battle and individual participants that will further refine our understanding of the events of June 25–26, 1876.

Beyond these particularistic results is the significance of the archaeological study of the battlefield within the context of anthropological theory. At one level, the result of the archaeological studies at the Little Bighorn have shown that individual movements, unit movements, and unit composition in the most chaotic of human endeavors, a pitched battle, can be revealed. The opposition's deployment can be discerned and the flow of the battle followed. Details lost to history can be discovered and interpreted in terms of the cultural conditioning and training received by opposing forces. The Little Bighorn archaeological investigations generated a model of battlefield behavior that was based on empirical evidence and has subsequently been tested in other situations. That model (Fox and Scott 1991) was predicated upon an axiom basic to archaeological investigation: human behavior is patterned. Behavioral patterns are expressed through individual behaviors constrained by the norms, values, sanctions, and statuses governing the group within which the individual operates.

War tactics, which represent patterned behavior, include establishment of positions and the deployment and movement of combatants. The residues of tactics in warfare—artifacts, features, and their contextual relationships—have been shown to be patterned and reflect details of battlefield behavior. The Little Bighorn Battlefield National Monument archaeological investigations are the first battlefield studies to go beyond the particularistic and place the results of a hostile cultural conflict in the context of a theoretical model of behavior. The Battle of the Little Bighorn archaeological work has added significantly to the theory of the anthropology of war and become a signal event in the development of new methods to study battlefields and fields of conflict. In turn, the work has developed and influenced new theoretical constructs that are now at the heart of battlefield archaeology and conflict archaeology studies worldwide. This may be the most important legacy of the Battle of the Little Bighorn's archaeological studies.

References

Allen, William A.

1903 *Adventures with Indians and Game*. A. W. Bowen, Chicago.

Alt, D. and D. W. Hyndman

1986 *Roadside Geology of Montana*. Mountain Press Publishing, Missoula, Mont.

Anders, Frank L.

1983 *Custer Trail: A Narrative of the Line of March of Troops Serving in the Department of Dakota in the Campaign against Hostile Sioux,* edited by John M. Carroll. Arthur H. Clark, Glendale, Calif.

Applied Ground Imaging

1996 Little Bighorn Battlefield, Montana, Non-Intrusive Characterization Survey Field Project, Ground Penetrating Radar Survey. Ms. report on file, Midwest Archeological Center, National Park Service, Lincoln, Neb.

Athnason, Michael

2006 Modeling Bullet Trajectory on Historic Battlefields Using Exterior Ballistic Simulation and Target-Oriented Visibility. *Archaeological Computing Newsletter* 65:1–7.

Barnard, Warren E. "Sandy"

1985 Volunteers Crucial in Custer Battle Dig. *CRM Bulletin* 8(5):2–3.

1995 Edward Botzer: Was He Custer's 'Last Trooper?' *Greasy Grass* 11:2–4.

1998   *Digging into Custer's Last Stand.* AST Press, Terre Haute, Ind.

Beckes, M. R., and J. D. Keyser
1983   *The Prehistory of the Custer National Forest: An Overview.* U.S. Department of Agriculture, Custer National Forest, Billings, Mont.

Bennett, Connie
1977   Preconstruction Archeological Investigations at Custer Battlefield National Monument. Memo report on file, National Park Service, Midwest Archeological Center, National Park Service, Lincoln, Neb.

Benson, Christopher
2005   A GIS for the Little Bighorn Battlefield National Monument. Professional Papers 338, http://proceedings. esri.com/library/userconf/proc00/professional/papers/ PAP338/p338 .htm.

Binkowski, Don
1995   *Col. P. W. Norris: Yellowstone's Greatest Superintendent— America's Early Environmental Champion (1877–1882).* C & D of Warren, Warren, Mich.

Bozell, John R.
1985   Non-Human Vertebrate Faunal Remains Recovered during 1984 Surface Collections at the Custer Battlefield National Monument, Montana. Ms. on file, Midwest Archeological Center, National Park Service, Lincoln, Neb.
1989   Non-Human Vertebrate Faunal Remains from Custer Battlefield National Monument. In *Archaeological Perspectives on the Battle of the Little Bighorn,* by Douglas D. Scott, Richard A. Fox, Jr., Melissa A. Connor, and Dick Harmon, pp. 283–98. University of Oklahoma Press, Norman.

Bray, Robert
1958   A Report of Archeological Investigations at the Reno-Benteen Site Custer Battlefield National Monument June 2–July 1, 1958. Ms. on file, Midwest Archeological Center, National Park Service, Lincoln, Neb.
1967   An Archeological Survey and Excavations at Wilson's Creek Battlefield National Park, Missouri. Ms. on file, Midwest Archeological Center, National Park Service, Lincoln, Neb.
1996   Archaeological Investigations at the Renon-Benteen

Defense Site, Little Bighorn Battlefield, Montana. *Missouri Archaeologist* 57:58–95.

Brome, Jeff

2000   On Locating the Kidder Massacre Site of 1867. *Denver Westerners Roundup* 56(4):3–18.

2002   Custer, Kidder and Tragedy at Beaver Creek. *Wild West* 15(1):38–48.

2003   Indian Massacres in Elbert County, Colorado: New Information on the 1864 Hungate and 1868 Dietemann Murders. *Denver Westerners Roundup* 60(1):3–30.

2006   Custer's Summer Indian Campaign of 1867: New Information on the U.S. Seventh Cavalry Desertions at Riverside Station. *Little Big Horn Associates Research Review* 20(2):17–30.

2007a Custer's First Fight with Plains Indians. *Wild West* 20(1):28–35.

2007b Custer's Summer Indian Campaign of 1867. *Denver Westerners Roundup* 65(4):3–33.

2009   *Custer into the West with the Journal and Maps of Lieutenant Henry Jackson.* Upton and Sons, El Segundo, Calif.

Brown, Barron

1973   *Comanche: The Sole Survivor of all the Forces in Custer's Last Stand, the Battle of Little Big Horn.* Sol Lewis, New York.

Brown, M. H.

1961   *The Plainsmen of the Yellowstone: A History of the Yellowstone Basin.* University of Nebraska Press, Lincoln.

Brust, James

1995   Lt. Oscar Long's Early Map Details Terrain, Battle Positions. *Greasy Grass* 11:5–13.

Bryson, R. A., D. A. Barerreis, and W. M. Wendland

1970   The Character of Late-Glacial and Post-Glacial Climatic Changes. In *Pleistocene and Recent Environments of the Central Plains,* edited by W. Dort and J. K. Jones, 53–74. Kansas University Press, Lawrence.

Carrington, Henry

1973   *The Indian Question.* Sol Lewis, New York.

Carroll, John M. (editor)

1987   *Custer's Chief of Scouts: The Reminiscenses of Charles A. Varnum.* University of Nebraska Press, Lincoln.

1993   *They Rode with Custer: A Biographical Directory of the Men that Rode with General George A. Custer.* Carroll and Company, Mattituck, N.Y.

Carstensen, Vernon
    1968   *The Public Lands: Studies in the History of the Public Domain.*
            University of Wisconsin, Madison.
Cecil, Jerry
    1995   Researching the Tale of Lt. Crittenden's Pocket Watch.
            Greasy Grass 11:34–38.
Chittenden, Hiram Martin
    1900   *The Yellowstone National Park: Historical and Descriptive.*
            3rd. ed. Robert Clarke Company, Cincinnati, Ohio.
Chorne, Laudie
    1997   *Following the Custer Trail of 1876.* Printing Plus, Bismarck,
            N.Dak.
Coleman Research
    1996   Little Bighorn Measurements II, Processing Results, Final
            Report. Coleman Research Corp. Ms. on file, Midwest
            Archeological Center, National Park Service, Lincoln, Neb.
Connor, Melissa
    1986   Exhumation of Grave 402, Block B, Custer Battlefield
            National Cemetery. Rocky Mountain Region Archeological
            Project Report, April 8, 1986. On file, Midwest
            Archeological Center, National Park Service, Lincoln, Neb.
    1991   The Application of Comparative Bone Histology to
            Fragmented Archeological Bone from the Reno-Benteen
            Dump, Custer Battlefield National Monument. Appendix
            B of Archeological Investigations at the Reno-Benteen
            Equipment Disposal Site, in Papers on Little Bighorn
            Battlefield Archeology: The Equipment Dump, Marker
            7, and the Reno Crossing, edited by Douglas D. Scott,
            pp. 148–66. *Reprints in Anthropology* 42, J and L Reprint,
            Lincoln, Neb.
    1994   Exhumation of Human Remains on the Pitsch Property
            near Little Bighorn Battlefield National Monument. Ms.
            on file, Midwest Archeological Center, National Park
            Service, Lincoln, Neb.
Connor, Melissa, and Douglas D. Scott
    1998   Metal Detector Use in Archaeology: An Introduction.
            Historical Archaeology 32(4):73–82.
Cross, Walt
    2006   *Custer's Lost Officer: The Search for Lieutenant Henry Moore
            Harrington, 7th US Cavalry.* Cross Publications, Stillwater,
            Okla.

2011   *From Little Bighorn to the Potomac: The Story of Army*
          Surgeon Dr. Robert Wilson Shufeldt. Cross Publications,
          Stillwater, Okla.

Dary, David
    1976   *Comanche.* University of Kansas Museum of Natural
            History Public Education Series 5, Lawrence, Kans.

Davis, C. M.
    1976   A Preliminary Archaeological Reconnaissance Survey,
            Bureau of Land Management Lands, Southeastern
            Montana. University of Montana for Bureau of Land
            Management, Miles City.

Davis, L. B., S. A. Aaberg, and J. W. Fisher, Jr.
    1980   *Cultural Resources in the Limestone Hills Montana*
            Army National Guard Training Site, Broadwater County,
            Montana. Montana State University for Bureau of Land
            Management, Montana State Office, Billings.

Deaver, Kenneth, and Steven Aaberg
    1977   *Archaeological Survey of the Kansas-Nebraska Pipeline Project*
            Area: Phillips County, Montana. Professional Analysts for the
            Bureau of Land Management, Lewistown District, Mont.

Deaver, Kenneth, and Sherry Deaver
    1988   *Prehistoric Cultural Resource Overview of Southeast Montana.*
            Ethnoscience for Bureau of Land Management, Miles City,
            Mont.

De Vore, Steven L.
    2002a   Search for the Horse Burial Pit: Conductivity and
            Magnetic Gradient Investigations at Last Stand Hill,
            Little Bighorn Battlefield National Monument, Montana.
            Midwest Archeological Center, National Park Service,
            Lincoln, Neb.
    2002b   Search for the Horse Burial Pit: Conductivity and
            Magnetic Gradient Investigations at Last Stand Hill,
            Little Bighorn Battlefield National Monument, Montana.
            Appendix B in Archeological Investigations of the "Horse
            Cemetery" Site, Little Bighorn Battlefield National
            Monument, by Douglas D. Scott. Midwest Archeological
            Center, National Park Service, Lincoln, Neb.
    2002c   Trip Report: Inadvertent Discovery of Remains related to
            Fort Phil Kearney Reinterments. Memorandum on file,
            Midwest Archeological Center, National Park Service,
            Lincoln, Neb.

2005   Geophysical Investigations of the Reno-Benteen Defensive
        Site, Little Bighorn Battlefield National Monument,
        Bighorn County, Montana. Report on file, Midwest
        Archeological Center, National Park Service, Lincoln, Neb.

Doerner, John A.
2002   The Enduring Monument: The Enigma of Custer Hill.
        Paper, 6th Annual Denver Custer/Indian Wars Symposium,
        February 23, Denver.

Donahue, Michael
2008   *Drawing Battle Lines: The Map Testimony of Custer's Last
        Fight.* Upton and Sons, El Segundo, Calif.

Doran, R. E.
1987   The Man Who Got to the Rosebud. Papers of the
        Custer Battlefield Historical and Museum Association
        Symposium, June 26, 19–33, Custer Battlefield Historical
        and Museum Association, Crow Agency, Mont.

Duke, Phillip G.
1991   *Points in Time: Structure and Event in a Late Northern
        Plains Hunting Society.* University Press of Colorado,
        Niwot, Colo.

du Mont, John
1974   *Custer Battle Guns.* Old Army Press, Fort Collins, Colo.

Dustin, Fred
1953   Some Aftermath of the Little Bighorn Fight in 1876: The
        Burial of the Dead. In *The Custer Myth, a Source Book of
        Custeriana,* by W. A. Graham, pp. 362–72. Bonanza Books,
        New York.

Ewers, John C.
1958   *The Blackfeet: Raiders on the Northwestern Plains.* University
        of Oklahoma Press, Norman.
1980   *The Horse in Blackfoot Indian Culture.* Reprinted,
        Smithsonian Institution, Washington, D.C. Originally
        published 1955, Bureau of American Ethnology Bulletin
        159, Smithsonian Institution.

Forbis, Richard G.
1962   The Old Women's Buffalo Jump, Alberta. *Contributions
        to Anthropology, 1960,* 1:55–123. National Museums of
        Canada, Bulletin 180, Ottawa, Ontario.

Fox, Richard A., Jr.
1983   1983 Archeological Investigations at Custer Battlefield
        National Monument. Ms. on file, Midwest Archeological
        Center, National Park Service, Lincoln, Neb.

1984 Suggestions for Archaeological Investigations at Custer
       Battlefield National Monument. Ms. on file, Little Bighorn
       Battlefield National Monument, Crow Agency, Mont.

1988 Discerning History through Archaeology: The Custer
       Battle. Ph.D. Dissertation, Department of Archaeology,
       University of Calgary, Alberta.

1993 *Archaeology, History, and Custer's Last Battle: The Little
       Bighorn Reexamined.* University of Oklahoma Press,
       Norman.

1996a West River History: The Indian Village on Little Bighorn
       River, June 25–26, 1876. In *Legacy: New Perspectives on the
       Battle of the Little Bighorn,* edited by Charles E. Rankin,
       pp. 139–66, Montana Historical Society Press, Helena.

1996b The Value of Oral History: White Eagles Account. 9th
       Annual Symposium, Custer Battlefield Historical and
       Museum Association, Hardin, Mont.

1996c Significance of the Investigations: Archaeological
       Investigations at the Reno-Benteen Defense Site, Little
       Bighorn Battlefield, Montana. *Missouri Archaeologist*
       57:87–88.

2005 Native and "Newcomer": Battle of the Little Bighorn.
       In *Unlocking the Past: Celebrating Historical Archaeology
       in North America,* edited by Lu Ann De Cunzo and
       John H. Jameson, Jr., pp. 166–73. Society for Historical
       Archaeology and University Press of Florida, Gainesville.

n.d.   The Custer Trail Project (1992–1994, 1999): A Synthesis.
       Draft Ms. in possession of author.

Fox, Richard A., Jr., and Douglas D. Scott
1991 The Post-Civil War Battlefield Pattern. *Historical
       Archaeology* 25(2):92–103.

Frison, George
1991 *Prehistoric Hunters of the High Plains.* 2nd ed. Academic
       Press, San Diego.

Frison, G. C., D. Schwab, L. A. Hannus, P. Winham, D. Walter, and
R. C. Mainfort
1996 Archaeology of the Northwestern Plains. In *Archaeological
       and Bioarchaeological Resources of the Northern Plains,* edited
       by G. C. Frison and C. Mainfort. Tri-Service Cultural
       Research Center, USACERL Special Report 97/2.

Gatliff, Betty Pat
1984 Facial Sculpture on the Skull for Identification. *American
       Journal of Forensic Medicine and Pathology* 5(4):327–32.

Gibbon, John
1877 Last Summer's Expedition Against the Sioux. *American Catholic Quarterly Review* 2(1):271–304.
Glenner, Richard A., P. Willey, and Douglas D. Scott
1994 Back to the Little Bighorn: Remains of a 7th Cavalry Trooper, Recovered at the Little Bighorn Battlefield in 1903, Provide a Glimpse of Nineteenth Century Dental Practices. *Journal of the American Dentistry Association* 125:835–43.
Graham, W. H.
1953 *The Custer Myth: A Source Book.* Bonanza Books, New York.
Gray, John
1963 Last Rites for Lonesome Charley Reynolds. *Montana The Magazine of Western History* 13(4):40–51.
1975 Nightmares into Day Dreams. *By Valor and Arms* 1(4): 30–39.
1976 *Centennial Campaign: The Sioux War of 1876.* Old Army Press, Fort Collins, Colo.
1991 *Custer's Last Campaign: Mitch Boyer and the Little Bighorn Reconstructed.* University of Nebraska Press, Lincoln.
Greene, Jerome A.
1986 *Evidence and the Custer Enigma: A Reconstruction of Indian-Military History.* Outbooks, Reno, Nev. Reprint of 1976 ed.
2008 *Stricken Field: The Little Bighorn since 1876.* University of Oklahoma Press, Norman.
Gregg, Michael L.
1985 *An Overview of the Prehistory of Western and Central North Dakota.* Cultural Resources Series 1. Bureau of Land Management, Montana State Office, Billings.
Hammer, Kenneth
1976 *Custer in '76: Walter Camp's Notes on the Custer Fight.* Brigham Young University Press, Provo, Utah.
1995 *Men with Custer: Biographies of the 7th Cavalry.* Custer Battlefield Historical and Museum Association, Hardin, Mont.
Hardorff, Richard (Dutch) G.
1984 Burials, Exhumations and Reinterments: A View from Custer Hill. In *Custer and His Times,* Book 2. Little Bighorn Associates, New York.
1985 *Markers, Artifacts, and Indian Testimony: Preliminary Findings on the Custer Battle.* Don Horn Publications, Short Hills, N.J.

1989 *The Custer Battle Casualties.* Upton and Sons, El Segundo, Calif.

1997 *Camp, Custer, and the Little Bighorn: A Collection of Walter Mason Camp's Research Papers on General Custer's Last Fight.* Upton and Sons, El Segundo, Calif.

Harris, C. E.
1980 Sherlock Holmes Would Be Impressed. *American Rifleman* 128(5):36–39, 82.

Hatcher, Julian, Frank J. Jury, and Jac Weller
1977 *Firearms Investigation, Identification and Evidence.* Stackpole Books, Harrisburg, Pa.

Haynes, C. Vance, Jr.
1989 Archaeological Geology of Deep Ravine, Custer Battlefield National Monument. In *Archeological Perspectives on the Battle of the Little Big Horn.* by Douglas D. Scott, Richard A. Fox, Jr., Melissa A. Connor, and Dick Harmon, pp. 224–42, University of Oklahoma Press, Norman.

1990 Geoarchaeological Investigations at Custer Battlefield National Monument, 1989. Ms. on file Midwest Archeological Center, National Park Service, Lincoln, Neb.

1991 Geoarcheological Investigations at Custer Battlefield National Monument. Appendix C. of Archeological Investigations at the Reno-Benteen Equipment Disposal Site, in Papers on Little Bighorn Battlefield Archeology: The Equipment Dump, Marker 7, and the Reno Crossing, edited by Douglas D. Scott, pp. 167–84. *Reprints in Anthropology* 42, J and L Reprint, Lincoln, Neb.

Hedren, Paul L.
1973 Carbine Extraction Failure at the Little Big Horn: A New Examination. *Military Collector and Historian* 25(2):66–68.

2011 *Great Sioux War Orders of Battle: How the United States Army Waged War on the Northern Plains, 1876–1877.* Arthur H. Clark, Norman, Okla.

Heinz, Ralph
1989 Tack Rivets. In *Archaeological Perspectives on the Battle of the Little Bighorn,* by Douglas D. Scott, Richard A. Fox, Jr., Melissa Connor, and Dick Harmon, pp. 205–206. University of Oklahoma Press, Norman.

1990 Cavalry Equipment from the Reno/Benteen Dump Site (1989). Ms. on file Midwest Archeological Center, National Park Service, Lincoln, Neb.

Heski, Thomas M.
  1997 "Digging" and "Picking" to the Powder: The Yellowstone
        Expedition's Route from O'Fallon Creek to Powder River,
        June 7, 1876. *Research Review: The Journal of the Little Big
        Horn Associates* 11(1):11–17, 31.
  2001 Camp Powell: The Powder River Supply Depot. *Research
        Review: The Journal of the Little Big Horn Associates*
        17(1):13–24.
Hommon, H. B.
  1940 Report of Inspections at Custer's Battlefield National
        Monument, Montana. File 660-033, Sanitation, RG 79,
        Box 167, Records of National Park Service Region II
        Central Classified Files 1936–1952, National Archives and
        Records Administration, Federal Records Center, Kansas
        City, Mo.
Horsted, Paul, Ernest Grafe, and Jon Nelson
  2009 *Crossing the Plains with Custer.* Golden Valley Press, Custer,
        S.Dak.
Husted, Wilfred M.
  1969 *Bighorn Canyon Archaeology.* River Basin Surveys,
        Publications in Salvage Archaeology 12, Smithsonian
        Institution, Washington, D.C.
Hutchins, James
  1976 *Boots and Saddles at the Little Bighorn: Weapons, Dress,
        Equipment, Horses, and Flags of General Custer's Seventh U.S.
        Cavalry in 1876.* Old Army Press, Fort Collins, Colo.
Hyson, John M., and Joseph W. A. Whitehorne
  1993 Dental Forensics: The Fate of Lieutenant Harrington
        at the Little Big Horn. *Bulletin of the History of Dentistry*
        41(3):103–107.
Johnson, Randy, and Nancy Allan
  1999 *A Dispatch to Custer: The Tragedy of Lieutenant Kidder.*
        Mountain Press Publishing, Missoula, Mont.
Jones, Bruce A.
  2002 *Historical Archeology at the Village on Pawnee Fork, Ness
        County, Kansas.* Technical Report 86, Midwest Archeo-
        logical Center, National Park Service, Lincoln, Neb.
Josten, N. E., and G. S. Carpenter
  1995 *Results from Rapid Geophysical Surveyor Investigation of
        Archaeological Sites at the Little Bighorn Battlefield National
        Monument.* Idaho National Engineering Laboratory, Idaho
        Falls.

Kehoe, Alice B.
  1973   *The Gull Lake Site: A Prehistoric Bison Drive Site in
         Southwestern Saskatchewan.* Milwaukee Public Museum,
         Publications in Anthropology and History 1. Milwaukee,
         Wisc.
King, W. Kent
  1981   *Tombstones for Bluecoats: New Insights into the Custer
         Mythology.* Published by the author, Marion Station, Calif.
Kuhlman, Charles
  1951   *Legend into History: The Custer Mystery; an Analytical Study of
         the Battle of Little Bighorn.* Stackpole Books, Harrisburg, Pa.
Lahren, Lawrence A.
  1976   *The Myers-Hindman Site: An Exploratory Study of Human
         Occupation Patterns in the Upper Yellowstone Valley from 7000
         B.C. to A.D. 1200.* Anthropologos Researches International,
         Livingston, Mont.
Lawrence, Elizabeth Atwood
  1989   *His Very Silence Speaks: Comanche—The Horse Who Survived
         Custer's Last Stand.* Wayne State University Press, Detroit,
         Mich.
Lee, Ronald F.
  1970   The Antiquities Act of 1906. Department of the Interior,
         Washington, D.C.
Lees, William B., Douglas D. Scott, and C. Vance Haynes
  2001   History Underfoot: The Search for Physical Evidence of
         the 1868 Attack on Black Kettle's Village. *Chronicles of
         Oklahoma* 79(2):158–81.
Lewis, Berkeley R.
  1972   *Small Arms Ammunition at the International Exposition
         Philadelphia, 1876.* Smithsonian Studies in History and
         Technology 11. Smithsonian Institution, Washington, D.C.
Libby, O. G. (editor)
  1920   The Arikara Narrative of the Campaign Against the Hostile
         Dakotas, June, 1876. *North Dakota Historical Society
         Collections* 6.
Liddic, Bruce R., and Paul Harbaugh
  1995   *Camp on Custer: Transcribing the Custer Myth.* Arthur H.
         Clark, Spokane, Wash.
Loendorf, Lawrence L.
  1969   *The Results of the Archaeological Survey in the Pryor
         Mountain–Bighorn Canyon Recreation Area—1968 Field
         Season.* Report for the United States Department of

Interior (BLM), National Park Service and the University of Montana, Missoula.

1973   *Prehistoric Settlement Patterns in the Pryor Mountains, Montana.* Ph.D. dissertation. University of Missouri. UMI Dissertation Services, Ann Arbor, Mich.

Logan, Michael H., and Douglas A. Schmittou

2007   Inverted Flags in Plains Indian Art: A Hidden Transcript. *Plains Anthropologist* 52(202):209–27.

2008   The Changing Symbolism of Flags in Plains Indian Culture. *Whispering Wind, American Indian: Past and Present* 37(4):4–12.

Luce, Edward S.

1939   *Keogh, Comanche, and Custer.* John S. Swift, St. Louis, Mo.

1941a Memorandum to Superintendent, Yellowstone National Park, April 9, 1941. Accession 381, Administrative correspondence, on file, Little Bighorn Battlefield National Monument, Crow Agency, Mont.

1941b Discovery of Human Bones on Custer Battlefield Area. Memorandum to Quartermaster General, April 18, 1941. Accession 381, Administrative correspondence, on file, Little Bighorn Battlefield National Monument, Crow Agency, Mont.

1941c Memorandum to Superintendent Yellowstone National Park, May 6, 1941. Accession 381, Administrative correspondence, on file, Little Bighorn Battlefield National Monument, Crow Agency, Mont.

1941d Letter to Colonel Elwood Nye, May 27, 1941. Elwood Nye scrapbook, 1941–1961, Accession 253, on file, Little Bighorn Battlefield National Monument, Crow Agency, Mont.

MacNeish, Richard S.

1958   An Introduction to the Archaeology of Southeastern Manitoba. National Museums of Canada, Bulletin 157. Ottawa, Canada.

Magnussen, Daniel O.

1974   *Peter Thompson's Narrative of the Little Bighorn Campaign 1876: A Critical Analysis of an Eyewitness Account of the Custer Debacle.* Arthur Clark, Glendale, Calif.

Mahan, D. H.

1861   *An Elementary Treatise on Advance Guard, Outpost, and Detachment of Service of Troops.* John Wiley, New York.

Malone, M. P., R. B. Roeder, and W. L. Lang
    1991   *Montana: A History of Two Centuries.* University of
        Washington Press, Seattle, Wash.
Mangum, Neil C.
    1987a *Battle of the Rosebud: Prelude to the Little Bighorn.* Upton
        and Sons, El Segundo, Calif.
    1987b Popular Reaction to Custer: The Public's Perception. *1st
        Annual Symposium Custer Battlefield Historical and Museum
        Association,* pp. 54–61. Custer Battlefield Historical and
        Museum Association, Hardin, Mont.
Marquis, Thomas B.
    1931   *Wooden Leg: A Warrior Who Fought Custer.* University of
        Nebraska Press, Lincoln.
    1976   *Keep the Last Bullet for Yourself: The True Story of Custer's Last
        Stand.* Reference Publications, Algonac, Mich.
McChristian, Douglas
    1993   Historian's Corner. *Battlefield Dispatch* 12(1):10.
    1995   *The U.S. Army in the West, 1870–1880.* University of
        Oklahoma Press, Norman.
    1996   Burying the Hatchet: The Semi-Centennial of the Battle
        of the Little Bighorn. *Montana The Magazine of Western
        History.* 46(2):50–65.
    2009   *Fort Laramie: Bastion of the Plains.* University of Oklahoma
        Press, Norman.
McDermott, John D.
    2003   *Circle of Fire: The Indian War of 1865.* Stackpole Books,
        Mechanicsburg, Penn.
Mengel, Robert M.
    1969   Comanche: Silent Horse on a Silent Field. University of Kan-
        sas Museum of Natural History Annual 1968, Lawrence.
Michno, Gregory
    1993   Crazy Horse, Custer, and the Sweep to the North.
        Montana The Magazine of Western History 43(3):42–53.
    1994   *The Mystery of E Troop: Custer's Gray Horse Company at the
        Little Bighorn.* Mountain Press, Missoula, Mont.
Moore, Donald
    2011   *Where the Custer Fight Began: Undermanned and
        Overwhelmed, the Reno Valley Fight.* Upton and Sons, El
        Segundo, Calif.
Moore, Michael, and Michael Donahue
    1991   Gibbon's Route to Custer Hill. *Greasy Grass* 7:22–31.

National Park Service
    1997   National Park Service, Cultural Resource Management
            Guideline, Release No. 5. National Park Service,
            Washington, D.C.
Nickel, Robert K.
    2002   A Ground-Penetrating Radar Search for a Horse Burial
            Pit Associated with the 1876 Battle of the Little Bighorn,
            Appendix A in Archeological Investigations of the "Horse
            Cemetery" Site, Little Bighorn Battlefield National
            Monument, by Douglas D. Scott. Midwest Archeological
            Center, National Park Service, Lincoln, Neb.
Nichols, Ronald H. (editor)
    1992   *Reno Court of Inquiry.* Custer Battlefield Museum and
            Historical Association, Hardin, Mont.
Norris, Frank
    1981   Report concerning the Restaking of the 1958 Arch-
            aeological Survey Point Finds. Ms. on file, A-86, Little
            Bighorn Battlefield National Monument, Crow Agency,
            Mont.
Norris, Philetus W.
    1884   *The Calumet of the Coteau, and Other Poetical Legends of the
            Border.* J. B. Lippincott, Philadelphia.
Nye, Elwood
    1946   Letter to Superintendent Edward Luce, 1946. Accession
            381, Administrative correspondence, on file, Little Bighorn
            Battlefield National Monument, Crow Agency, Mont.
Orser, Charles E., Jr.
    2004   *Historical Archaeology.* Pearson Prentice Hall, Upper Saddle
            River, N.J.
Owsley, Douglas W.
    1994   A Report on Bone Specimens 94MAR5(3M) and
            94MAR5(4M6). Ms. on file, Little Bighorn Battlefield
            National Monument, Crow Agency, Mont.
Palmer, Robert G.
    1975   White Handled Revolvers. *By Valor at Arms* 2(1):28–33.
Payne, G. F.
    1973   *Vegetative Rangeland Types in Montana.* Montana
            Agricultural Experiment Station Bulletin 671, Bozeman,
            Mont.
Phillips, Patrick
    1989   Tin Cans. In *Archaeological Perspectives on the Battle of
            the Little Bighorn,* by Douglas D. Scott, Richard A. Fox,

Jr., Melissa Connor, and Dick Harmon, pp. 215–21.
University of Oklahoma Press, Norman.

1987 Cannibalism, Combat and Post Battle Mutilation:
      Observed Similarities between Cannibalism Criteria and
      Human Remains from Custer Battlefield. M.A. thesis,
      Department of Anthropology, University of Nebraska,
      Lincoln.

Pieters, Nancy, and Sandy Barnard
1986 Reburial Service at Custer Battlefield. *Courier, NPS
      Newsletter* 31(10):21–22.

Pitsch, Jason, with Keith Werts
2009 The Burial Site of Limber Bones. *Greasy Grass* 25:40–42.

Polka, George E.
1994 *Fort Custer: 1877–1898 Then and Now.* George E. Polka,
      Billings, Mont.

Powell, Peter J.
1969 *Sweet Medicine.* University of Oklahoma Press, Norman.

Rea, Bob
1998 The Washita Trail: The Seventh U.S. Cavlary's Route of
      March to and from the Battle of the Washita. *Chronicles of
      Oklahoma* 76(3):244–61.

Reedstrom, Ernest L.
1977 *Bugles, Banners, and War Bonnets.* Bonanza Books, New York.

Reeves, Brian O. K.
1990 Communal Bison Hunters of the Northern Plains. In
      Hunters of the Recent Past, edited by L. B. Davis and
      B. O. K. Reeves. Unwin Hyman, London.

Rickey, Don, Jr.
1956 Research Project to Locate Positions Held by Hostile
      Indians, June 25–26, 1876, around the Reno-Benteen
      Defense Perimeter. Ms. on file, Harpers Ferry Center
      Archives, National Park, Harpers Ferry, W.Va.

1967 *History of the Custer Battlefield.* Custer Battlefield Historical
      and Museum Association. Billings, Mont.

1996 Preface to Archaeological Investigations at the Renon-
      Benteen Defense Site, Little Bighorn Battlefield, Montana.
      Missouri Archaeologist 57:58–59.

Rickey, Don, Jr., and J. W. Vaughn
n.d. Metal Detection Survey at Reno-Benteen Battlefield,
      June 26–July 3, 1956, with handwritten addendum dated
      1958. Ms. on file, White Swan Library, Little Bighorn
      Battlefield National Monument, Crow Agency, Mont.

Roll, Tom, and Kenneth Deaver
    1980   *The Bootlegger Trail Site: A Late Prehistoric Spring Bison Kill.*
            Report for Interagency Archaeological Services, Denver,
            Colo.
Ruebelmann, G. N.
    1983   An Overview of the Archaeology and Prehistory of
            the Lewistown Bureau of Land Management District,
            Montana. *Archaeology in Montana* 24:3–165.
Schoenberger, Dale T.
    1990   A Trooper with Custer: Augustus DeVoto's Account of the
            Little Big Horn. *Montana The Magazine of Western History*
            40(1):68–71.
Scott, Douglas D.
    1984a   Archeological Research Design and Work Plan for Custer
            Battlefield National Monument, April 12, 1984. On file,
            Midwest Archeological Center, National Park Service,
            Lincoln, Neb.
    1984b   Review of Custer Battlefield Archeological Project. Mem-
            orandum to Regional Archeologist Anderson, July 2, 1984.
            On file, Midwest Archeological Center, National Park
            Service, Lincoln, Neb.
    1987a   Prehistoric Resources of Custer Battlefield. Rocky
            Mountain Region Archeological Project Report, April 1,
            1987. On file, Midwest Archeological Center, National
            Park Service, Lincoln, Neb.
    1987b   Surviving the Second Battle of the Little Bighorn: Effective
            Means of Dealing with a Media Blitz. In *Captivating the
            Public through the Media while Digging the Past.* Technical
            Series 1, Baltimore Center for Urban Archaeology, Md.
    1987c   The Recovery and Replacement of a Cremated Burial at
            Custer Battlefield National Monument. Rocky Mountain
            Region Archeological Project Report, February 27, 1987.
            On file, Midwest Archeological Center, National Park
            Service, Lincoln, Neb.
    1987d   Identification of Additional Markers with Human Bone
            Association. Memorandum to Superintendent, Custer
            Battlefield National Monument, December 21, 1987. On
            file, Midwest Archeological Center, National Park Service,
            Lincoln, Neb.
    1989a   Testing and Evaluation of Two Prehistoric Sites at Custer
            Battlefield National Monument. Rocky Mountain Region
            Archeological Project Report, September 1989. On file,

Midwest Archeological Center, National Park Service, Lincoln, Neb.

1989b Firearms Identification for the Archeologist. In *From Chaco to Chaco,* Archeological Society of New Mexico 15, edited by Meliha S. Duran and David T. Kirkpatrick, pp. 141–51.

1990 Interpreting Archaeology at Custer's Last Stand. In *What's Past Is Prologue: Our Legacy Our Future,* edited by David L. Kulhavy and Michael H. Legg, pp. 159–63. National Interpreters Workshop, Center for Applied Studies, School of Forestry, Stephen F. Austin State University, Nacogodoches, La.

1991a Papers on Little Bighorn Battlefield Archeology: The Equipment Dump, Marker 7, and the Reno Crossing. *Reprints in Anthropology* 42, J and L Reprint, Lincoln, Neb.

1991b Archeological Investigations at the Reno-Benteen Equipment Disposal Site. In Papers on Little Bighorn Battlefield Archeology: The Equipment Dump, Marker 7, and the Reno Crossing, edited by Douglas D. Scott, pp. 1–184. *Reprints in Anthropology* 42, J and L Reprint, Lincoln, Neb.

1991c Trip Report on Reburial of Soldier Remains at Custer Battlefield National Monument. Memorandum to Chief, Midwest Archeological Center, June 22, 1991. On file, Midwest Archeological Center, National Park Service, Lincoln, Neb.

1992a Exhumation of Little Bighorn Battle-Related Human Remains from the Custer Battlefield National Cemetery. Rocky Mountain Region Archeological Project Report, May 20, 1992. On file, Midwest Archeological Center, National Park Service, Lincoln, Neb.

1992b So as to Render Unserviceable to the Enemy: Archaeology at the Reno-Benteen Equipment Disposal Site. *5th Annual Symposium,* pp. 84–96. Custer Battlefield Historical and Museum Association, Hardin, Mont.

1992c Deep Ravine Overlook Site Little Bighorn National Battlefield, Montana. Rocky Mountain Region Archeological Project Report, July 14, 1992. On file, Midwest Archeological Center, National Park Service, Lincoln, Neb.

1992d Trip Report to Little Bighorn Battlefield National

Monument (LIBI). Memorandum to Chief, Midwest Archeological Center, dated June 30, 1992. On file, National Park Service, Midwest Archeological Center, Lincoln, NE.

1992e Trip Report for National Archives Research. Memorandum to Chief, Midwest Archeological Center, September 10, 1992. On file, Midwest Archeological Center, National Park Service, Lincoln, Neb.

1993a Archeological Mapping of the Pitsch Property: The Valley Fight Segment of the Battle of the Little Bighorn, Montana. Rocky Mountain Region Archeological Project Report, August 31, 1993. On file, Midwest Archeological Center, National Park Service, Lincoln, Neb.

1993b Exhumations in Custer National Cemetery, Little Bighorn Battlefield National Monument, Montana. Ms. on file, Midwest Archeological Center, National Park Service, Lincoln, Neb.

1993c Trip Report on the Reno-Benteen Walkway Fill Project, Little Bighorn National Battlefield. Memorandum to Chief, Midwest Archeological Center, September 20, 1993. On file, Midwest Archeological Center, National Park Service, Lincoln, Neb.

1994 Assessment of Little Bighorn Grassfire on Cultural Resources. Memorandum to Assistant Regional Director, Anthropology/Archeology, August 10, 1994. Copy on file, Midwest Archeological Center, National Park Service, Lincoln, Neb.

1995 Little Bighorn Battlefield National Monument Remote Sensing Exercise and Percolation Test Sites Inventory. Memorandum to Acting Assistant Regional Director, Anthropology/Archeology, March 24, 1995. Copy on file, Midwest Archeological Center, National Park Service, Lincoln, Neb.

1996a Archaeological Perspectives on the Battle of the Little Bighorn: A Retrospective. In *Legacy, New Perspectives on the Battle of the Little Bighorn,* edited by Charles E. Rankin, pp. 167–88. Montana Historical Society Press, Helena.

1996b A Look at Cedar Coulee and Sharpshooter Ridge: Archeological Inventory of the Faron Iron Property near Little Bighorn Battlefield National Monument. Ms. on file, Midwest Archeological Center, National Park Service, Lincoln, Neb.

1996c Trip Report on Riflepit Restoration at Reno-Benteen
       Defense Site, Little Bighorn Battlefield National
       Monument. On file, Midwest Archeological Center,
       National Park Service, Lincoln, Neb.
1998a Archeological Inventory of the Indian Memorial Site,
       Little Bighorn Battlefield National Monument. Ms. on
       file, Midwest Archeological Center, National Park Service,
       Lincoln, Neb.
1998b Archeological Inventory of the Western Portion of the
       Irons Property and the Stops Property, Bighorn County,
       Montana. Ms. on file, Midwest Archeological Center,
       National Park Service, Lincoln, Neb.
1999a Archaeologists: Battlefield Detectives. In *Little Bighorn
       Remembered: The Untold Story of Custer's Last Stand,* edited
       by Herman J. Viola, pp. 165–77, Times Books, New York.
1999b Archeological Inventory of the Site of a Water Gauging
       Station on the Little Bighorn River, Montana. Ms. on file,
       Midwest Archeological Center, National Park Service,
       Lincoln, Neb.
2000a Outside the Boundaries: The 1999 Archeological Inventory
       of Properties near the Little Bighorn Battlefield National
       Monument, 24BH2175. On file, Midwest Archeological
       Center, National Park Service, Lincoln, Neb.
2000b Archeological Investigations of Custer's June 23, 1876
       Campsite, Rosebud County, Montana. Ms. on file,
       Midwest Archeological Center, Lincoln, Neb.
2001   Washita Present Comments. In *Washita Symposium:
       Past, Present, and Future,* pp. 59–63. Washita Battlefield,
       Cheyenne, Okla.
2002a Cartridges, Bones, and Bullets: A Look Back at
       Archaeology of the Little Bighorn. *Greasy Grass* 18:24–30.
2002b Cartridges, Bullets, and Bones: The Value of Archaeology
       of the Little Bighorn Battle. *Battlefields Review,* no.
       19:26–31.
2002c Archeological Investigations of the "Horse Cemetery"
       Site, Little Bighorn Battlefield National Monument. On
       file, Midwest Archeological Center, National Park Service,
       Lincoln, Neb.
2004a Men with Custer: The Dead Tell Their Tale. In *G. A. Custer:
       His Life and Times,* by Glenwood J. Swanson, pp. 266–87.
       Swanson Productions, Agua Dulce, Calif.
2004b The Little Bighorn Battlefield. In *Encyclopedia of the Great*

Plains, edited by David J. Wishart, pp. 830–31. University of Nebraska Press, Lincoln.

2005a Archeological Inventory of the Little Bighorn Battlefield National Monument Visitors Center. Ms on file, Midwest Archeological Center, National Park Service, Lincoln, Neb.

2005b Preliminary Artefact Finds. In *Battlefields Annual Review,* edited by Jon Cooksey, p. 12. Pen and Sword Military Books, Barnesly, South Yorkshire, U.K.

2005c Interpreting Archeology at the Little Bighorn Battlefield National Monument. In *Preserving Western History,* edited by Andrew Gulliford, pp. 20–31. University of New Mexico Press, Albuquerque.

2006 *Archeological Mitigation of the Federal Lands Highway Program Plan to Rehabilitate Tour Road, Route 10, Little Bighorn Battlefield National Monument, Montana.* Midwest Archeological Center Technical Report 94, National Park Service, Lincoln, Neb.

2009 Battlefield Archaeology: Some New Insights into Custer's Last Stand. In *Schlachtfeldarchäologie,* edited by Harald Meller, pp. 253–57. Tagungen des Landesmuseums für Vorgeschichte, Halle, Germany.

2010a Investigating the Oxbows and Testing Metal Detector Efficiency at Little Bighorn Battlefield National Monument, Montana. Report on file, Little Bighorn Battlefield National Monument, National Park Service, Crow Agency, Mont.

2010b *Uncovering History: The Legacy of Archeological Investigations at the Little Bighorn Battlefield National Monument, Montana.* Technical Report 124, Midwest Archeological Center, National Park Service, Lincoln, Neb.

Scott, Douglas D., and Peter Bleed

1997 *A Good Walk around the Boundary: Archeological Inventory of the Dyck and Other Properties adjacent to Little Bighorn Battlefield National Monument.* Special Publication of the Nebraska Association of Professional Archeologists and the Nebraska State Historical Society, Lincoln, Neb.

Scott, Douglas D., Peter Bleed, and Stephen Damm

2010 Custer, Cody, and a Grand Duke: The Russian Royal Buffalo Hunt in Nebraska, 1872, a Preliminary View from Archaeology. *Denver Westerners Roundup* 56(4):3–11.

Scott, Douglas D., Peter Bleed, Andrew E. Masich, and Jason Pitsch

1997 An Inscribed Native American Battle Image from the

Little Bighorn Battlefield. *Plains Anthropologist* 42(161): 287–302.

Scott, Douglas, and Melissa Connor
1986   Post-mortem at the Little Bighorn. *Natural History* 95(6): 46–55.
1988   Reburial at the Little Bighorn. *CRM Bulletin* 11(5–6):6–8.

Scott, Douglas, Melissa Connor, and Clyde Snow
1988   Nameless Faces of the Little Bighorn. *Greasy Grass* 4:2–5.

Scott, Douglas, and Richard Fox, Jr.
1987   *Archeological Insights into the Custer Battle: A Preliminary Assessment.* University of Oklahoma Press, Norman.

Scott, Douglas D., Richard A. Fox, Jr., Melissa A. Connor, and Dick Harmon
1989   *Archaeological Perspectives on the Battle of the Little Bighorn.* University of Oklahoma Press, Norman.

Scott, Douglas, and Lucien Haag
2009   "Listen to the Minié Balls": Identifying Firearms in Battlefield Archaeology. In *Fields of Conflict: Battlefield Archaeology from Imperial Rome to Korea,* edited by Douglas Scott, Lawrence Babits, and Charles Haecker, pp. 102–20. Potomac Books, Washington, D.C.

Scott, Douglas, and Dick Harmon
1988a A Sharps Rifle from the Battle of the Little Bighorn. *Man at Arms* 10(1):12–15.
1988b A Sharps Rifle from the Battle of the Little Bighorn. In *Guns at the Little Bighorn,* pp. 12–15. Andrew Mowbray, Lincoln, R.I.
2004   Firearms and Fields of Fire. In *G. A. Custer: His Life and Times,* by Glenwood J. Swanson, pp. 288–324. Swanson Productions, Agua Dulce, Calif.

Scott, Douglas, and Douglas Owsley
1991   Oh, What Tales Bones Could Tell—and Often Do! *Greasy Grass* 7:33–39.

Scott, Douglas D., and Clyde Collins Snow
1991a Archeology and Forensic Anthropology of the Human Remains from the Reno Retreat Crossing. In Papers on Little Bighorn Battlefield Archeology: The Equipment Dump, Marker 7, and the Reno Crossing, edited by Douglas Scott, pp. 207–36. *Reprints in Anthropology* 42. J and L Reprint, Lincoln, Neb.
1991b Mitigative Excavations at Marker 7. In Papers on Little Bighorn Battlefield Archeology: The Equipment Dump,

Marker 7, and the Reno Crossing, edited by Douglas Scott, pp. 185–206. *Reprints in Anthropology* 42. J and L Reprint, Lincoln, Neb.

Scott, Douglas D., Thomas D. Thiessen, Jeffrey J. Richner, and Scott Stadler

2006   *An Archeological Inventory and Overview of Pipestone National Monument, Minnesota.* Midwest Archeological Center Occasional Studies in Anthropology 34. Midwest Archeological Center, National Park Service, Lincoln, Neb.

Scott, Douglas, and P. Willey

1995   The Custer Battlefield National Cemetery Human Remains Identification Project. *8th Annual Symposium, Custer Battlefield Historical and Museum Association,* pp. 12–29.

1996   Custer's Men Took Names to Their Graves. *Greasy Grass* 12:20–28.

1997   Little Bighorn: Human Remains from the Custer National Cemetery. In *In Remembrance: Archaeology and Death,* edited by David A. Poirier and Nicholas F. Bellantoni, pp. 155–71. Bergin and Garvey, Westport, Conn.

Scott, Douglas D., P. Willey, and Melissa Connor

1998   *They Died with Custer: Soldiers' Bones from the Battle of the Little Bighorn.* University of Oklahoma Press, Norman.

Scott, Hugh Lenox

1928   *Some Memories of a Soldier.* Century, New York.

Scott, Linda C.

1987   *Pollen Analysis of Stratigraphic Deposits at the Mill Iron Site, Southeastern Montana.* Report by Palynological Associates for Bureau of Land Management, Montana State Office, Miles City.

Shaffer, Brian

2008   Finger Bones Cut from the Men at Little Bighorn. Paper presented at the 73rd Annual Meeting of the Society for American Archaeology, Vancouver, B.C.

Shufeldt, R. W.

1910   Personal Adventures of a Human Skull Collector. *Medical Council* 15(4):123–27.

Shumate, M.

1965   Ancient Surface Finds from the Missouri Valley near Cascade, Montana. *Archaeology in Montana* 6(2):17–19.

Sills, Joe, Jr.
  1994   Weir Point Perspective. *7th Annual Symposium Custer
         Battlefield Historical and Museum Association,* pp. 45–51,
         Hardin, Mont.
Sledzik, Paul S., and Lars G. Sandberg
  2002   The Effects of Nineteenth-Century Military Service on
         Health. In *The Backbone of History: Health and Nutrition in
         the Western Hemisphere,* edited by Richard H. Steckel and
         Jerome C. Rose, pp. 185–207. Cambridge University Press,
         Cambridge.
Snow, Clyde Collins, and John Fitzpatrick
  1989   Human Osteological Remains from the Battle of the
         Little Bighorn. In *Archaeological Perspectives on the Battle
         of the Little Bighorn,* by Douglas D. Scott, Richard A. Fox,
         Jr., Melissa A. Connor, and Dick Harmon, pp. 243–97.
         University of Oklahoma Press, Norman.
Stands in Timber, John, and Margot Liberty
  1972   *Cheyenne Memories.* 2nd ed. University of Nebraska Press,
         Lincoln, Neb.
Stewart, Edgar I.
  1955   *Custer's Luck.* University of Oklahoma Press, Norman.
Swanson, Glenwood J. (Glen)
  2004   *G. A. Custer, His Life and Times.* Swanson Productions,
         Agua Dulce, Calif.
  2011   Locating the Skirmish Line. In *Where the Custer Fight
         Began: Undermanned and Overwhelmed, the Reno Valley
         Fight,* by Donald W. Moore, pp. 119–32. Upton and
         Sons, El Segundo, Calif.
Tabrum, Alan R.
  1978   *Report on the Plesiosaur Collected at Custer Battlefield
         National Monument.* Department of Geology, University
         of Montana, Missoula.
Taunton, Francis B.
  1986   *Custer's Field "A Scene of Sickening Horror."* Johnson-
         Taunton Military Press, London.
  1987   The Enigma of Weir Point. In *No Pride in the Little Big
         Horn,* 17–41. Special Publication 7. English Westerners'
         Society, London.
Utley, Robert
  1972   *The Reno Court of Inquiry: The Chicago Times Account.* Old
         Army Press, Fort Collins, Colo.

1986   On Digging Up Custer Battlefield. *Montana The Magazine of Western History* 36(1):80–82.

1988   *Cavalier in Buckskin: George Armstrong Custer and the Western Military Frontier.* University of Oklahoma Press, Norman.

2004   *Custer and Me: A Historian's Memoir.* University of Oklahoma Press, Norman.

Vaughn, J. W.

1956   *With Crook on the Rosebud.* Stackpole, Harrisburg, Pa.

1966   *Indian Fights: New Facts on Seven Encounters.* University of Oklahoma Press, Norman.

Vihlene, Shannon M.

2008   Custer's Last Drag: An Examination of Tobacco Use among the Seventh Cavalry during the Nineteenth Century. M.A. thesis, Department of Anthropology, University of Montana, Missoula.

Waldbauer, Richard, and Sherry Hutt

2006   The Antiquities Act and Its Centennial. *CRM* 3(1):36–48.

Walker-Kuntz, Patrick J., and Sunday Walker-Kuntz

1999   *Battlefield–East Highway 212 Cultural Resource Inventory in Big Horn County, Montana.* Ethnoscience Inc., Billings, Mont.

War Department

1879   Ordnance Notes, no. 115. Washington, D.C.

Weibert, Don

1989   *Custer, Cases, and Cartridges. The Weibert Collection Analyzed.* Privately published by the author, Billings, Mont.

Weibert, Henry, and Don Weibert

1985   *Sixty-Six Years in Custer's Shadow.* Falcon Press, Billings, Mont.

Wells, Wayne

1989   The Fight on Calhoun Hill. *2nd Annual Symposium Custer Battlefield Historical and Museum Association,* pp. 22–34. Hardin, Mont.

Wheeler, H. W.

1923   *Buffalo Days: Forty Years in the Old West: The Personal Narrative of a Cattleman, Indian Fighter and Army Officer.* Bobbs-Merrill, Indianapolis.

Willey, P.

1989   Unpublished notes on Reno Crossing skeletal remains. On file, Midwest Archeological Center, National Park Service, Lincoln, Neb.

1993   Osteological Analysis of Human Remains from the Custer
       Battlefield National Cemetery. California State University,
       Chico.
1994   *Human Osteology of the Pitsch Burials.* Midwest
       Archeological Center, National Park Service, Lincoln, Neb.
1995   Osteological Analysis of Scattered Human Bones from the
       Little Bighorn Battlefield National Monument. Ms. on
       file, Little Bighorn Battlefield National Monument, Crow
       Agency, Mont.
1996a *Osteological Analysis of Human Skeletons Excavated from the
       Custer Battlefield National Cemetery.* Midwest Archeological
       Center, National Park Service, Lincoln, Neb.
1996b *Human Skull and Mandible (LIBI 1996 HR-1 and HR-2)
       Attributed to and Non-human Bones (LIBI HR-3 through
       HR-6) Found on the Little Bighorn Battlefield, Montana.*
       Department of Anthropology, Chico State University,
       Chico.
1997   *Osteological Analysis of Human Skeletons Excavated from the
       Custer National Cemetery.* Technical Report 50, Midwest
       Archeological Center, National Park Service, Lincoln, Neb.
Willey, P., Amanda Blanchard, Thomas D. Holland, and Douglas D.
Scott
2004   A Case of Mistaken Identity. *Greasy Grass* 20:16–21.
Willey, P., Richard A. Glenner, and Douglas D. Scott
1996   Oral Health of Seventh Cavalry Troopers: Dentitions from
       the Custer National Cemetery. *Journal of the History of
       Dentistry* 44(1):3–14.
Willey, P., and Douglas D. Scott
1996   "The Bullets Buzzed Like Bees": Gunshot Wounds
       in Skeletons from the Battle of the Little Bighorn.
       International Journal of Osteoarchaeology 6(1):15–27.
1997   Abstract: Who's Buried in Custer's Grave? *Proceedings of the
       American Academy of Forensic Sciences* 3.
1999   Clinkers on the Little Bighorn Battlefield: In situ
       Investigations of Scattered Recent Cremains. In *Forensic
       Osteological Analysis: A Book of Case Studies,* edited by
       Scott I. Fairgrieve, pp. 129–40, Charles C. Thomas,
       Springfield, Ill.

Index